What Manner of Man?

What Manner of Man?

An open-ended text book on the Synoptic Gospels

M.A. Chignell

Head of Religious Education
Bolton School Girls' Division

Edward Arnold

First published 1979
by Edward Arnold (Publishers) Ltd.
41 Bedford Square, London WC1X 3DQ

Reprinted 1981, 1983

British Library Cataloguing in Publication Data
Chignell, M.A.
    What manner of man?
    1. Bible. New Testament. Gospels—Commentaries
    I. Title
    226'.07   BS2555.3

    ISBN 0–7131–0375–2

To all my 'O' level students with love and gratitude.

Acknowledgments:

My warmest thanks to my friends, Barbara Windle for her constant and
patient revision of the text, Doreen Sides for so generously giving up her
time to decipher and type the manuscript, Valerie Fisher and Naomi Rich
for their invaluable help and Kathleen Healey for her continual
encouragement.

M.A.C. August 1978

Produced by computer-controlled phototypesetting by
Unwin Brothers Limited
The Gresham Press, Old Woking, Surrey
A member of the Staples Printing Group
and printed in Great Britain by
Spottiswoode Ballantyne Limited,
Colchester and London

Contents

Foreword: To the Student

What could be more boring than to go over the same set text for year after successive year? Nothing—or so one would normally expect. Yet having studied the gospels with 'O' level G.C.E. students for the past sixteen years, I have found quite the reverse happening. In some way the story of Jesus, his personality, teaching and actions, seem to become more alive each time rather than less. What makes a school discussion group so stimulating of course is the variety of opinions expressed and the interchange of ideas; and these discussions, often highly controversial, have illuminated rather than diminished the realism and meaning of Jesus' life and work. It is because I have found re-reading the gospels with my students so rewarding an experience that I have written this book for other schools who are undertaking a similar study.

There are various obstacles which have to be cleared away before we can begin this work together. In the first place we have to appreciate that the material we are looking at was written nearly 2000 years ago. The age of the manuscript however does not mean it is necessarily irrelevant to modern life. The fact that a particular culture is different from our own need not prevent us from understanding its people's way of thinking. Men and women have experienced the same kinds of feelings in whatever age they lived. They have loved, suffered, been happy and died whether they were born at the beginning of the Christian era or now. But there are significant differences and we have to use our imaginations and our intelligence to understand how they viewed their environment and their world.

A second difficulty lies in the way the New Testament documents have been regarded for hundreds of years. They were thought of as sacred literature and therefore not in the category of writings which could be critically examined and discussed. Christians believed so devoutly in Jesus as the Son of God that they accepted the accounts about his life and teaching, his death and resurrection as 'untouchable'. However strange and incomprehensible the events recorded, they were not to be doubted because the Bible was the Word of God for his people and the New Testament records were the basis of faith of the Christian religion. It is only in the last century or so that scholars have been free to look at the text, understand the possible sources for the gospel material, translate the Greek into modern English and examine the situation as objectively as possible.

This book will not assume that every student who reads it is a convinced Christian. Indeed, whilst the commentary on the text always takes accepted scholarship into account, the purpose of the discussion is to put before the reader a number of possible interpretations. Part I takes a long and somewhat leisurely look at Mark's gospel as an introduction to biblical criticism. Part II based on sections from Luke's and Matthew's gospels is much more tightly structured in the hope that by the time it is reached the work will proceed more quickly. At the end of the book are very brief notes on the Matthean and Lucan passages not included in the Contents page. By this process I hope that the particular flavour of each of the gospels will be clear. However it is Jesus the man, who is central to the study and those who read the gospels and this book must make up their own minds as to how they think of him.

Introduction: Essential background information

A   The Jews—a people with an historic past

Some knowledge of the Old Testament is, of course, helpful because Jesus was a Jew and he knew the ancient scriptures of his people. We will discuss various Old Testament passages as they crop up in the text. You will know that the Jews were a unique and extraordinary race in the sense that they were profoundly convinced that they had a special relationship with the one true living God, who was not only the Lord of Creation but also the Lord of History and of Time. Out of all the peoples of the world he had called the Israelites (or Hebrews) to be his special possession. This call was not for privilege or power or greatness in a material sense because the Israelites were a small and insignificant nation who had only two brief periods of peace and stability in their history when they could call their land their own. The special position of this people with their God was that they should mediate knowledge of him to the rest of the world. They were to be a kingdom of priests. (See Exodus 19:5, 6, when the Covenant was made between God and his people at Sinai through Moses, the prophet and law-giver, and the greatest of all Old Testament personalities.)

In Jesus' day the Hebrews, or Jews as they are called in the New Testament and to this day, had been in Palestine for over a thousand years. They had managed to conquer Canaan (the ancient name for Palestine) under Joshua—who succeeded Moses—and eventually established themselves there with David as their king. His son, Solomon, did not live up to his reputation for wisdom and overtaxed his people so that when he died the northern tribes would not accept his son and split into a separate state. This meant that eventually both the northern and southern kingdoms were conquered, because they were so small, by their more powerful neighbours. The Assyrians, who took over the northern kingdom, re-populated it with other peoples and so the *Samaritans* came into being. They were despised by the Jews as being of mixed blood, but they regarded themselves as worshippers of the one true God and used the first five books of the Old Testament as their sacred scriptures. The southern kingdom remained independent for a further couple of hundred years and then it fell to the Babylonians who creamed off the Jewish leadership and took them into captivity in Babylon. Eventually, after several centuries, the exiles returned to the Promised Land. But the Jews did not regain any independence until a century or so before Jesus when they sought to overthrow their Syrian overlords. In the end, the huge Roman state took over the empire of Alexander the Great, which included Syria and Palestine. The Jewish state became a division of the Roman province of Syria and Herod the Idumean became Herod the Great, king of the Jews from 37–4BC.

As is so often the case when a people are subject to another nation, there are some who believe in co-operation with the occupying power and some who believe in a kind of passive resistance, whilst the extreme nationalists are all out for rebellion. This was so in Palestine. The majority of people, however, hated the dominance of Rome and having to pay imperial taxes. They longed for a deliverer to free them from oppression—would God intervene and rescue his people as he had done in the past, especially from Egypt? Those who read the scriptures said such a deliverer was prophesied, but opinions were divided as to the kind of person he would be. Perhaps a warrior king, like David? Perhaps a greater figure even than Moses, possessing more supernatural power? Perhaps even God's Son? We shall discuss all these ideas about the Messiah as they occur in the text but, to appreciate the people's reactions to Jesus, to see why they welcomed him with joy and then later rejected him, we must understand how he failed to fit in with their hopes and dreams of a national liberator.

In contrast to the wishes of the ordinary people, their aristocratic leaders, the *Sadducees*, who were the priestly class, believed in some kind of co-operation with Roman governors, since the High Priest held office under Roman patronage. Furthermore, the House of Herod, which had begun with Herod the Great in 37BC, took advantage of the peace brought about by the might of Rome to establish itself for a short time as the secular (as opposed to the religious) rulers of Palestine. The *Herodians* were those Jews who were devoted to the House of Herod and formed themselves into a political party and were very worldly in their outlook.

The most influential group of people in Jesus' day were the *Pharisees*. Their name may mean 'separated'. Even if this is not true, it certainly described their way of life. They were extremely devoted to the Law—the first five books of the Old Testament, known in Hebrew as the Torah. They believed that the way of holiness was the way of segregation, so they kept themselves apart from ordinary Jews and were scrupulous in their observance of the ritual and ethical regulations of the Torah. From their number came the *Scribes*, or Lawyers, who wrote out the sacred texts, discussed their finer points and endeavoured to interpret their meaning for countless generations. Because it was difficult to find a means of relating every ancient law to contemporary conditions, there grew up an Oral Tradition of the Elders—the result of debate and discussion down the centuries of learned Rabbis. By the time of Jesus, this Oral Tradition had assumed almost as much importance as the actual Written Law: A situation of which Jesus was very critical, as we shall see.

As well as the Sadducees, the Herodians, the Pharisees and their Scribes, there were the *Zealots*, who formed an extreme nationalist group. They were determined to do something about getting the Romans out of their country and they believed in open revolt. We shall meet all these types of people in the Gospel and it would be helpful if you made your own dossier about each group as you go along in order to collect together all the evidence you can.

B The New Testament world picture

It is also important to realise that Jesus and his contemporaries had a completely different world outlook from our own. Let us take several examples:

1 They thought the earth was flat and that the sky came over it like an inverted tin dish. God dwelt in heaven, above the waters, which came down on earth when the sluice gates in the sky were opened. Though this world view may seem surprising at first reading, it is simply based on an intelligent observation of things as they appeared to be at that time. We need not imagine ourselves to be superior merely because we know otherwise.

2 The Jews believed that beneath the earth there was probably an underworld or Sheol; for some it was the place of departed spirits. The Pharisees believed very strongly in angels and demons, although the Sadducees did not. The Pharisees also believed there was a life-after-death—or at least that there would be a resurrection day for God's faithful people. The Sadducees believed only that existence was continued in the blood of one's descendants.

3 Many illnesses were attributed to demon possession and others were thought of as a punishment for sin.

4 Finally, Jesus' contemporaries were not aware of what we call 'the laws of Nature' such as gravity and therefore it was not inconceivable to them that Jesus might walk on water or ascend into heaven.

C The Early Christians—a community whose hope was focused on the future

The gospels themselves are a different kind of literature from any modern form coming off today's presses. They are not biography, simply giving factual information about Jesus of Nazareth. They arose out of a definite need and we must understand how they were written to meet that need. Jesus had died but had risen again; so his disciples believed and experienced. Afterwards they went out into the Roman world to spread the good news of the life-giving energy and power which they felt to be in him and which could be given to others who came to believe in his person. At first it did not seem necessary to write anything down. In that world there were comparatively few books—all had to be written or copied—and ordinary people often could not read and write. In any case, the first disciples of Jesus believed that he would soon return in glory and wind up the whole historical process. They expected the end of the world to happen in their life-time so they had a great sense of urgency to tell all men about Jesus, their Lord and Saviour, who would, they believed, enable men to inherit eternal life. They distilled what they considered to be essential from his life and teaching and relied upon eye witness accounts. The number of important facts about Jesus came to be known as the Proclamation of the Gospel or Good News. When men and women actually became professed believers in him, they were then taught the way they should now live their lives on the basis of the actual teaching of Jesus himself. This came to be known as the Teaching. (The Greek word for Proclamation is Kerygma and that for Teaching is Didache, so these two words are used by scholars to signify the two aspects of the oral tradition created by Jesus' first disciples.) Of course, Jesus' immediate family and friends would know a great deal more and talk about many more details than have come down to us in the gospels.

As the first generation Christians began to die, it was gradually realised that what was of value for preaching and teaching purposes must be preserved and written down. Thus we get the first written sources—which we will discuss in detail later—which led eventually to the four gospels as we now have them in the New Testament, together with letters and other writings from the first century AD or thereabouts. It follows that the three gospels we are going to study were written by men of faith in order to spread that faith to the four corners of the earth. Further, they wished to confirm and strengthen those who had already become believers, especially in those times of persecution, martyrdom and trial, which very soon came upon the tiny Christian community. You may well ask how far can we rely upon the evidence of such outright propaganda and I can only answer that we have got to accept that there is no such thing as an impartial witness. We are all interpreters of life. The gospel writers, because of the nature of their convictions, would be as honest as they knew how to be. They would not deliberately distort. They would interpret the evidence in the light of their subsequent convictions about Jesus. We shall try and understand not only what they say but why they express it in the way they do.

Note Greek was the common language for trade and government in much of the Eastern Mediterranean. The New Testament documents were all written in Greek although it was not the native tongue of most of the authors. The Jews in Palestine would speak Aramaic, although their ancient scriptures were written in Hebrew and the old language was used for worship.

Part I

The Gospel of Mark

Preface

Authorship

Although the second gospel in the New Testament is attributed to Mark, there is no internal evidence that Mark was the author's name. For centuries it was thought that Matthew's gospel was the first to be written, hence its place in the New Testament. Nowadays it is assumed, for a variety of reasons, that Mark's was the earliest account. About 95% of Mark's material is found in Matthew, 65% in Luke, so it is fair to conclude that Mark's gospel must have been known to the authors of the first and third gospels if they were able to use it in their own work.

The second gospel has been attributed to Mark because of evidence found in some early Christian writers–

1 Papias, who was Bishop of Hierapolis in Asia Minor some time around AD130, wrote 'Mark, having become Peter's interpreter, set down all that the apostle could remember of what Jesus had said and done'.

2 Irenaeus, Bishop of Lyons wrote, about AD185, 'After their deaths (i.e. those of Peter and Paul) Mark, the disciple and interpreter of Peter, himself also handed down to us in writing the things which Peter had proclaimed'.

3 A recently discovered copy of what appears to be a letter from Clement of Alexandria (about AD190) also speaks of Peter's teaching as being the basis of Mark's material.

Traditionally it has been accepted that the Mark indicated by these writers was the young man of that name mentioned in Acts. We know a few interesting facts about him: John Mark (Hebrew name John, Latin name Mark) was the son of Mary, hostess to the Jerusalem church (Acts 12:*12*), to whose house Peter went when he escaped from prison. Mark went with Paul and Barnabas on their first missionary journey (13:*5,13*), presumably because he was related to Barnabas, being either his nephew or cousin (Colossians 4:*10*). He deserted his friends at Perga in Pamphylia and returned home to Jerusalem (Acts does not mention his motives for doing so—Acts 15:*37–40*). Because of his desertion Paul refused to have him with them at the start of the second missionary journey.

Barnabas and Paul quarrelled over this, Barnabas going off to Cyprus with John Mark and Paul going with Silas to Greece. However the quarrel between Paul and Mark must have been later resolved for less than ten years after Paul speaks of Mark being with him when he was imprisoned in Rome (Col. 4:*10, 12* and Philippians *24*).

Mark is also associated with Peter in the New Testament, if the first letter of Peter is genuinely linked with the apostle and originated in Rome. 1 Peter 5:*13* speaks of 'Mark, my son'. This endorses the tradition that Mark acted as a sort of private secretary to Peter.

In Mark's gospel (14:*51*) there is a strange little story of a nameless young man who was in the garden of Gethsemane when Jesus was arrested. This incident is not mentioned by either Matthew or Luke, so it is possible that it refers to Mark himself, for otherwise there seems no point in including it. If so, Mark was a friend of Jesus during the last months of his life.

When you look at this evidence, you will see that it is not conclusive. We simply do not know for sure who was the author of Mark's gospel but I shall assume in the commentary that he was the John Mark known to us from Acts and point out the specific incidents which involve Peter.

Date and place of writing

If we can accept that Mark was in Rome with Paul and Peter, then Rome is the obvious place for the gospel to have been written. It is generally believed that both Paul and Peter were martyred by the Emperor Nero after the Great Fire of Rome in AD64, during the first Roman persecution of the Christians. Mark was clearly writing for Gentiles, for he explains Jewish customs and way of life and occasionally translates any Aramaic words used by Jesus which were of special significance. From the contents of the gospel it is possible to say that it was written *before* the Fall of Jerusalem in AD70. AD65 or thereabouts is generally accepted as a possible date. This would place the gospel after Peter's death and during the time when the Christians in Rome were going through a period of intense suffering and persecution.

Purpose and characteristics of the writer

1 The gospel is written in rough and vigorous Greek. For example, the word 'straightway' is used 41 times! In the first chapters we are swept along with a sense of urgency. Many passages contain details which might be attributed to an eye-witness to the scene (4:*38*; 6:*39*; 8:*24*; 10:*16, 21, 32*).

2

2 Another characteristic is the realism of Mark's writing. He shows us Jesus as a man with intense human emotions: anger (3:5), pity (6:34), grief or some kindred feeling (7:34; 8:12), compassion (1:41), astonishment (6:6), indignation (10:14) and deadly fear (14:33). He paints a picture of the disciples which is very convincing. They do not understand Jesus, their expectations of him are in accord with those of their Jewish contemporaries, they even get a little irritated by him (5:31). Peter attempts to rebuke Jesus for his anticipation of his own death (8:32) and in the end they forsake him and run away (14:50).

3 While he stresses Jesus' humanity, Mark was equally sure that Jesus was the Son of God. He proclaims it in the first line of his gospel, but he shows that Jesus did not claim to be so until asked by the High Priest at his trial (14:62). This is known as the Messianic Secret. His gospel falls into two parts—(a) the Galilean ministry which culminates in the climax at Caesarea Philippi where Jesus asks his disciples not only whom men think he is, but whom they think he is. Peter answers 'You are the Christ' (8:30). Even then Jesus commands them not to tell anybody because his way is quite unlike that of any messianic expectation; (b) the journey to Jerusalem and Jesus' last week there, ending with his arrest and death (chapters 9–16).

Throughout the first part of the gospel many people ask 'Who is this man, Jesus of Nazareth?' and there are many answers given. But Mark shows him as one directly inspired by God (1:11, 22; 9:7), who possesses powers which strike great awe into those who are with him (2:12; 4:41; 6:50); who is supremely conscious of what he has to do (10:45) and makes stupendous claims, even speaking of his death as inaugurating a new era of relations between God and man (12:6; 13:32; 14:24, 62).

Conclusion

If it is true that Peter and Paul's friend, the John Mark of Acts, wrote this gospel only thirty years or so after the death of Jesus, then we have here a first class interpretation of Jesus' life by a near contemporary. If you read it through in one sitting (and it will not take you very long to do so as Mark's is the shortest gospel in the New Testament) you will be struck by its vivid, direct and fresh approach.

Discussion

1 Why do you think it is important that we try and establish who wrote the second gospel in the New Testament?

2 Do you agree that all history is 'interpreted' through the mind of the historian? Take, for example, the difference which exists between the Marxist view of history and the traditional Conservative one.

Work

1 Make a short list of the facts about John Mark which are known to us from the New Testament.
2 Using both the introductory notes and this present section, summarise why you think Mark wrote his gospel.

Chapter 1

(a) Mark states his faith—Mark 1:*1*

The word gospel, of course, means 'good news'. The coming of Jesus is the good news because Mark believes he is the Son of God. This is an important declaration of faith as this particular phrase appears only three times in Mark's gospel. The titles of Jesus all indicate the different ways in which his disciples thought about him. The title 'Son of God' is a difficult one to grasp. We do not now picture God sitting on a golden throne above the sky—the supreme father-figure of Michelangelo's paintings on the Sistine chapel ceiling in Rome—although Christian artists down the centuries have depicted Jesus in glory sitting at God's right hand. Nevertheless this *is* the way those first friends of Jesus thought of their master after his resurrection from the dead. They declared that he was exalted at God's right hand and that the gift of the Holy Spirit was the external proof of this exaltation by God (Acts 2:*32–33*—Peter's first sermon after Pentecost). The phrase 'Son of God' occurs in the Old Testament where the king of Israel could be described as a son of God (2 Samuel 7:*14*, Psalm 2:*7*). Angels were sometimes viewed in the same light (Genesis 6:*2*, Psalm 29:*1*). For Mark, however, Jesus is THE Son of God in a unique sense. In him God fulfilled all his promises to his people and through him man was able to become reconciled to God. We might say that the disciples felt Jesus was of God in a very special way which they did not understand: The Father/Son relationship was one way of expressing what they experienced in their encounter with Jesus.

Discussion

1. If God is a spirit how can he have a son? Does this relationship describe a particular truth which the disciples could not express in any other way?
2. To say that Jesus was the Son of God is NOT the same as saying he was God the Son. What do you think is the difference?
3. One way of trying to resolve this problem is to say that the essence of Jesus was of God or, that Jesus was a materialisation of the Spirit of God. How do these definitions strike you?

(b) The coming of John Baptist—Mark 1:2-8; Matthew 3:1-12; Luke 3:1-20

It is difficult for us, from this distance of time, to realise the impact John had upon his contemporaries. He was the first prophet to appear in Israel for 400 years. (It is Luke who tells us that John was Jesus' cousin and gives us some details about his birth. Luke 1-2.) But he was more than a prophet, he was the Messenger foretold by scripture. Mark gives us two quotations. The first is from Isaiah 40:3. It originally referred to the return of the Jewish exiles from Babylon to Jerusalem—their way through the wilderness would be prepared. The second is from Malachi 3:1, which should be looked at in conjunction with Malachi 4:5-6. These latter references deal with the second coming of Elijah to prepare the people for the 'great and terrible day of the Lord'. From these passages we can see that John was thought of as a second Elijah and indeed Jesus referred to him as such in Matthew's gospel (Matthew 17:10-13). In some ways John was similar to Elijah—note, for example, his food and clothes. He preached repentance in view of the coming Day of the Lord, which apparently he viewed as a day of judgment. (Luke and Matthew give us a fuller account of this preaching and we shall discuss it further when we read their gospels.) John baptised with water as a sign of the forgiveness of sins but, with great humility, he prophesied the coming of one far greater than himself who would baptise with the Holy Spirit. His humility is noted by Mark in his saying that he was unworthy even to perform the slave's menial act of untying his master's sandals.

We know from other sources (The Antiquities of the Jewish historian Josephus and Luke's Acts of the Apostles) that disciples of John remained in existence for many years after his death. The first Christians saw the coming of John as the beginning of the gospel (Act 1:22) and so Mark begins at this point, although he takes the story back as far as the prophets.

Work

It would be useful if you started to make a collection of all the material relating to John Baptist from the three gospels and so build up a composite picture of him.

(c) The baptism and temptation of Jesus—Mark 1:9-13; Matthew 3:13-4:11; Luke 3:21-22, 4:1-13

According to Mark, the fact that Jesus was the Messiah was at this stage a secret known only to a few. So he tells us that when Jesus was baptised the vision of the dove descending and the voice of God came to Jesus alone.

Some time ago, the actual words spoken by Jesus in the gospels were translated from the written Greek into the original Aramaic that Jesus would have used. It became clear that Jesus was a poet, or at least that his ideas are couched in poetic symbols and metaphors. If we remember this we shall understand more fully the meaning behind his words. So 'the heavens opened'—not literally of course, but because God was 'up there'. 'The Spirit like a dove descended' is an image clarifying the character of the inspiration sent from God. In the Old Testament too, the spirit of the Lord sometimes came upon a prophet and in consequence he declared the will of God for his people, but God's message was often terrible in its denunciation. The dove however is a gentle creature, the symbol of peace, as the Flood story in Genesis demonstrates. The rabbis of Jesus' day thought of the Spirit as a dove. Moreover, if Jesus were to hear God's voice within his mind, he would naturally think of the experience in terms of the scriptures. So the words of God can be thought of as an echo of Psalm 2:7 and Isaiah 42:1. From Mark's account of Jesus' experience at his baptism, it is possible to see that this was the point when Jesus became convinced of his task and that he felt himself to be filled with the power of God to undertake it. The words of God suggest that Jesus saw himself as the servant of the Lord, also the Son of God, probably in a unique sense.

After this stirring experience, Jesus went away into the wilderness to think through exactly what kind of Messiah he was to be. Luke and Matthew give us much fuller accounts of this time of testing. The story of the temptations given by these two evangelists represents Jesus' inner conflict and his rejection of false messianic ideals. Obviously Jesus himself must have told his disciples both about his experience at his baptism and also what he went through in the wilderness. 'Forty days' is a Jewish expression meaning a long time. We find it in the account of the Israelites' sojourn in the wilderness with Moses, when 40 years stands for a generation or so. The word 'Satan' in Hebrew actually means 'opposition'. In the Genesis story it is the serpent who symbolises temptation, but Satan later became identified with the serpent. He was thought of as a fallen angel. To be a 'fallen' angel is to have known the good but rejected it, perverted it and so opposed it. Thus Satan as the Devil was the personification of evil in all its aspects and the chief enemy of God. Angels were the messengers of God, so we can understand that when Jesus had clarified his ideas about his messiahship, he in some way experienced the certainty that he was on the right lines. In scripture terms—'the angels came and ministered to him'. This passage is full of the symbolism that Jesus would use in talking about his experiences to his friends.

Discussion

Christians have always maintained that Jesus was sinless. If so, why did he come to be baptised by John in the Jordan? (For a further discussion on the meaning of sin, see 'The Call of Levi', Mark 2:*13–17*; when you have looked at this passage, perhaps it will be possible to see in what sense Jesus was 'without sin'.)

(d) Jesus begins to preach about the Kingdom and calls his first disciples—Mark 1:*14-20*; Matthew 4:*12-22*; Luke 5:*1-11*

John is now in prison (cf. Mark 6:*14–29* to find how he got there). Jesus returns to Galilee from the wilderness and begins to preach. This is a key passage in Mark because it summarises the essential content of Jesus' teaching. By comparison with Matthew (Sermon on the Mount, Matthew 5–7), Mark does not give us many details about the content of Jesus' message.

'The time has come' means the decisive hour has struck. The long time of waiting is over. The New Age, of which the prophets spoke, has begun.

'Kingdom' is not used by Jesus in either a geographical or political sense—although the Jews did conceive of the land of Israel as God's kingdom and their kings as God's vice-regents. Some of Jesus' contemporaries thought of the 'coming of the Kingdom' as a public vindication by God of his chosen people. (*cf.* p. xii). We, on the other hand, tend to think of the Kingdom of God as life hereafter—'pie in the sky' for those who have been good on earth. Yet Jesus is plainly stating here that the Kingdom *has* come. It is his ministry which has brought it. But is is not a narrow, nationalistic or materialistic ideal. For Jesus the Kingdom means the Rule or Reign of God in men's hearts and lives. Later, in reply to a question (Mark 12:*29–31),* Jesus sums up the whole of the keeping of the law (or the whole duty of man) in terms of love, so we might say that the reign of God is the reign of love in a man's heart, especially as the author of the first letter of John defines God as love (1 John 4:8). The Kingdom therefore is of universal significance because it concerns the way men and women think, feel and act, and what guiding principle they accept in their lives.

Jesus gives two clear directives for entering the Kingdom—'repent', which means a radical change of direction and 'believe in the gospel', which is acceptance of the truth of what Jesus is proclaiming.

Jesus then meets four Galilean fishermen—two pairs of brothers—and invites them to be the first citizens of the Kingdom. They are to be the new people of God, the new Israel in a different sense from the old. The power of Jesus' personality is demonstrated by the fact that these men simply leave their nets and follow him (although in the East, this would not be so strange as in our society). Jesus tells them he will make them 'fishers of men'. The metaphor is not attractive to us, for men were *not* caught in the net of Jesus' weaving. They were given the dignity of individual choice in response to his preaching. He called his friends, therefore, to help him in his mission. Their tasks would become clear as they lived and worked with him (*cf.* Mark 6:*7–13*).

Discussion

1 Before you read the above passage, what did the words 'Kingdom of God', or 'Kingdom of Heaven' conjure up in your mind? Where do you think these ideas of yours came from?
2 If you were starting a new movement, how would you invite people to join it?

(e) The First Miracle—The Demoniac in the Synagogue—Mark 1:*21-28*; Luke 4:*31-37*

In New Testament times and earlier, there was *one* central Temple in Jerusalem which was used for sacrificial worship. Although family worship took place in the home, the local community in every town and village also needed a meeting place. Any ten Jewish men could form a *synagogue*—a Greek word meaning an assembly. No priest was necessary. Every Sabbath and on other special occasions the men would meet together to read the scriptures and afterwards they might listen to someone talking about the set passage for that day. Prayer and thanksgiving were essential to the worship. The women and children were present but did not sit with the men and they took no part in the conduct of the service. The Presiding Officer, called the Ruler of the Synagogue, was probably chosen by the elders of the community. Often attached to the synagogue was a school where the boys were taught to read. When they came to manhood at thirteen years of age, they were accepted into the adult life of the community at a special service.

The synagogue was the chief sphere of influence of the Pharisees and their Scribes. Originally the Scribes were simply the copyists of the ancient scriptures, but as time went on the Law needed interpretation to fit it to present day needs. Thus the Scribes shouldered extra responsibilities and some became lawyers and rabbis (or teachers). In time there grew up an immense Oral Tradition of the Rabbis, which was eventually written down some considerable time after Jesus' day. In the lives of ordinary people, therefore, the Scribes had become much more important than the

9

priests because they taught the Law and interpreted it in all synagogues and schools. This gave them a significant role in every local community, whereas the priests were concentrated in Jerusalem, officiating at the Temple services.

Mark now takes us to Capernaum on a Sabbath day. Jesus goes to the synagogue and is presumably asked to preach a sermon (a courtesy quite frequently extended to a well-known visitor). We are not told what the sermon was about, only its effects on his listeners. They are astonished at his personal authority. The Scribe would always refer to previous rabbis, but Jesus spoke as one directly inspired by God. Here we see the beginning of trouble for Jesus as the Scribes would resent both his authoritative manner of speaking and also the people's admiring response.

In the synagogue is a 'demon-possessed' man, who is said to recognise Jesus as 'The Holy One of God'. Nowadays we might say that the man was mentally disturbed but had some kind of perception that Jesus was someone who might heal him. It was perfectly natural for Jesus' contemporaries to attribute a sickness of mind or body to 'possession' because many symptoms suggest such an interpretation. For example if a man has epileptic fits, he can behave in a way which appears to indicate that his lack of control is due to someone or something 'taking over'. If we lived in a primitive culture we would simply accept the folk-lore of our people on such matters, but it is not necessary for twentieth century minds to believe in devils in order to recognise sickness and suffering. What is more important is that we appreciate how Jesus always healed people on the level they would best understand. As we go through Mark we shall see many examples of healing. Each of them is different and individual. This man in the synagogue in Capernaum believed, as did everyone else, that he was possessed by demons. So Jesus 'cast them out' according to the man's needs and he was freed of his bondage. The technical term for expelling a demon is 'exorcism'. It is not possible for us to know whether Jesus was totally in accord with the beliefs of his particular period in history, but it is natural for us to accept that he was a man of his time and would therefore think in terms appropriate to that time. Faith is still a significant element in healing today, whether people place their trust in the doctor, the medicine prescribed, medical science, or even in the 'laying on of hands' and prayer.

Discussion

1 Do you believe in a personal devil? How would you define evil?
2 What explanation would you give for the suffering in the world? To what extent can it be attributed to man's ignorance, selfishness, greed and exploitation?

10

(f) The healing of Peter's mother-in-law and others—Mark 1:*29-34*; Matthew 8:*14-17*; Luke 4:*38-39*

It would appear that Jesus made Simon Peter's home his head-quarters in Capernaum. Mark tells us that he continued his healing work by curing Peter's mother-in-law from a fever. And then, because the Sabbath was technically over at sunset, people felt free to bring their sick to Jesus. The Scribes would not approve of people being cured on the Sabbath itself. They had a regulation that healing constituted work on the Sabbath, unless the sickness was an urgent matter of life and death. Jesus did in fact ignore this bit of scribal tradition and went ahead to meet people's needs regardless, but that is part of a later story. Mark is apparently very interested in 'exorcism' and he reports that the 'devils' recognised Jesus. Jesus however did not want to be publicly identified as the Messiah. Premature recognition of this kind would ruin his mission because popular expectation was so different from his own conception of his task.

(g) The need for solitude—Mark 1:*35-39*

This is one of the short stories in Mark's gospel which seems to indicate that Peter was the source of much of the material. Jesus had got up very early to be quiet and pray. He needed solitude. He was not inexhaustible. Here he states clearly that his primary mission is to preach, not to heal.

(h) The cure of a Leper—Mark 1:*40-45*; Matthew 8:*1-4*, Luke 5:*12-16*

Leprosy is a hideous disease, which is far less prevalent today than it was in ancient times because now it can be cured if caught in its initial stages. It was thought to be highly contagious and therefore a leprous man or woman became a social outcast, as did the victims of certain other skin diseases which were at that time confused with leprosy. Before a leper could be admitted again into the community he had to be declared 'clean' by the priest and offer the appropriate sacrifices of thanksgiving to God. It was not simply a matter of hygiene but behind it lay the concept of religious impurity which would result from contact with an 'unclean' person, whose illness might be attributable to sin and disobedience to the law of God. (See Leviticus chs. 13 and 14 for the ancient regulations about leprosy.)

The leper does not doubt Jesus' ability to cure him but only his inclination—'If only you will', he says. Jesus responds with warm compassion and touches him, thus breaking the religious law and also the social custom. By touching the leper it seems Jesus is deliberately choosing to make himself ceremonially unclean, but this act is indicative of Jesus' perception, because his very touch, with all its implications, would move the leper deeply and indeed he is cured as a result of Jesus' intervention.

Jesus tells the man very plainly to obey the law concerning his disease and cure and also to tell no one of its source. In Mark we find this request for secrecy on several occasions. There are many reasons for this–

1 Healing was not Jesus' main purpose.

2 He wanted to be able to convince men and women of the truth of his message without spectacular cures to back up his claims.

3 He did not want to be crowded out of villages and towns by excited mobs.

However in this case the man disobeyed Jesus and as a result Jesus could not enter any village or town because of the crowds. (The problems that arise from Jesus' popularity are vividly illustrated in the next story.)

Work
1 Start making a list of the healings of Jesus, with references.
2 Make a note about the distinctive features of each occasion.

Chapter 2

(a) The healing of the paralytic; the first 'Conflict' story—Mark 2:1-12; Matthew 9:1-8; Luke 5:17-26

Up to now Jesus has not come into open conflict with the Scribes and Pharisees, although the incident of the 'demon-possessed' man in the synagogue would have aroused their critical curiosity. In this chapter, Mark clearly illustrates the precise nature of the opposition Jesus encountered.

As Mark tells it, this is a graphic story which probably took place in Peter's house. One must imagine a simple, flat-roofed building with an outside staircase. Jesus is preaching about the Kingdom and the large crowd of listeners prevents the sick man, who is being carried on a rug or mattress, from reaching Jesus. On seeing that the faith of the man's friends is so strong that they are determined to reach him at all costs, Jesus forgives the man his sins. In many instances the Jews thought disease was a punishment for sin and in this case Jesus evidently discerned that some kind of spiritual or mental conflict was the cause of the paralysis.

Amongst the crowd are Scribes who are appalled at Jesus' claim to forgive sins. It was for them a blasphemous statement. Jesus reads their thoughts or perhaps sees their expressions of horror and knows their opinions on such matters well enough to deduce their condemnation of him. He then goes a step further and demonstrates how the spiritual healing or, as we might say, the release from conflict and guilt, has resulted in the man's body being made whole. The man's ability to get up and walk away with his mattress was the outward proof of the inward healing which Jesus had brought about.

According to Mark, this is the first time that Jesus clearly shows by his actions who he is. Both the forgiveness and the physical healing are demonstrations of the presence of the Kingdom. Jesus calls himself 'Son of Man'. This is a title most frequently used in Mark's gospel and must have originated with Jesus himself. It is an ambiguous phrase.

1 It can mean simply 'a man'–
'What is man, that thou are mindful of him?
And the son of man, that thou visitest him?' (Psalm 8:4).

2 In the book of Daniel, however, the phrase is used in a different sense. Most scholars agree that this book was written during an intense period of suffering when the loyalty of the Jewish people to their ancestral faith was being tested to the uttermost by the persecution under Antiochus IV (167BC) *cf* chapter 13. In chapter 7 the author has a dream of four nightmare beasts, who symbolise the four pagan empires who have tyrannised the Jews. In *v* 13 'The one like unto a son of man' represents the faithful Israel who comes 'On clouds of heaven', in contrast to the great beasts who come from the underworld. In *v* 18 the faithful minority are called 'The Saints of the Most High'. The steadfast loyalty of those who are willing to die rather than deny their faith is finally vindicated by God.

In later Jewish literature 'the son of man' came to be identified with a supernatural figure and probably, by the time of Jesus, could be a veiled name for the Messiah.

That Jesus should use this title for himself is interesting. He had the kind of courage, loyalty and moral integrity to be absolutely obedient to what he conceived to be God's will. He did not want to fight back with the physical weapons and force of his enemies but he had the conviction that in the end his cause would triumph (*cf* Mark 8:*31, 38;* 10: *45;* 13; 14: *62*). The suffering Son of Man is therefore a very different concept from the forceful rebel leader, although both are heroic in their own ways.

Work and Discussion

1 Why do you think Jesus' words and actions were a challenge to the onlookers on this occasion? In what way do you think the Scribes' reactions were different from those of the ordinary people? From the way Mark has told the story, how do you think Peter reacted to the scene (even supposing the house was his)?
2 Start making a dossier on the times when Jesus uses the phrase 'Son of Man'. Try to decide in what sense he is using the title—either as a representative of humanity, or as the Messiah with a difference.

(b) The Call of Levi—Mark 2:*13-17*; Matthew 9:*9-13*; Luke 5:*27-32*

In the first story, Mark posed the question, who was Jesus? A blasphemer? A healer? A teacher? The Messiah? Now he asks what is the nature of Jesus' ministry.

Levi was a tax collector, probably employed by Herod Antipas, Tetrarch of Galilee and Peraea (see family tree). There would be a toll house at Capernaum because the great road from Syrian

Damascus passed through the city on its way to the sea. Tax collectors were hated by the rest of their contemporaries because they were considered traitors. In any case, they were always dishonest. The job was given to the highest bidder and there was no meticulous taxation system such as we have in sophisticated western countries today.

It is not clear from the text whether Jesus had dinner with Levi in Levi's house or Peter's. It seems reasonable to suppose that when Jesus called Levi to be his disciple, Levi himself decided to entertain Jesus before he left Capernaum on a further preaching ministry. (It is another dramatic proof of the power of Jesus' personality that Levi simply got up and 'followed' Jesus.) Anyway, many of Levi's friends were gathered at the meal, much to the horror of the Scribes and Pharisees. A tax collector's friends were sure to be irreligious men, especially as they mixed with Gentiles. The Pharisees thought the way of holiness demanded segregation. It was almost as if they regarded sin as an infectious disease. They felt it was impossible to remain in a right relationship with God unless one was in a state of religious purity which for them was obtained by absolute obedience to the Law of God as found in the scriptures—the Torah. Therefore, when the Scribes and the Pharisees see Jesus actually eating with tax collectors and sinners (according to their definition of the word), their criticism takes the form of asking what kind of a prophet this is who runs the risk of such gross contamination. Mark represents them as speaking only to the disciples, not to Jesus himself.

Jesus answers the Pharisees in their own kind, as is always his way, whether with friends or critics. He quotes a proverb, probably well known in his day and adds a comment of his own. Taken together, these striking images in effect mean, 'I have come to heal the sickness of sin'. So here, for the first time in Mark's story, Jesus states the purpose of his ministry. But does 'I did not come to invite virtuous people, but sinners' really mean that Jesus is saying he has no time for good people? It all depends on how one defines sin. In ancient religions 'to sin' might merely mean breaking the ritual law and thereby bringing about the anger of the god. For the Pharisees it was disobeying or simply not keeping the Law of God which, they felt, was clearly articulated in the first five books of the Old Testament. According to the Genesis story, Adam and Eve sinned when they disobeyed the command of God. Their action separated them from direct communion with God. So it is possible to define sin as that which separates man from God or from the highest good. If God is love, as 1 John declared (cf p 8), then we could define sin as that which is unloving in thought, word or deed. In this case, sin is a universal condition from which all men everywhere need to be cured. On this basis, all men need what Jesus has to give. The trouble with the Pharisees was that they were unaware of their need of Jesus. Their blindness is well illustrated in two further stories *cf 3:22; 7: 1-23.*

Note In Matthew's gospel, Levi is called Matthew, so presumably this became his apostolic name.

Discussion

1 How would you define sin? Do you think virtuous living is simply keeping the rules or doing what you are told to do? If goodness is equated with conformity, then it is indeed very boring. How would you define goodness?
2 Do you think the Pharisees represent a type of person whom one might still meet today?

(c) The Question of Fasting—Mark 2:*18-22*; Matthew 9:*14-17*; Luke 5:*33-9*

Fasting was a sign of piety among the Jews. The disciples of John Baptist and the Pharisees fasted twice a week as an act of self-discipline. So the criticism arises, if Jesus and his disciples were really religious men, surely they would fast also?

Jesus goes to the heart of the matter. Fasting at a glad time, such as a wedding, would be totally out of place but if something tragic, such as the removal of the bridegroom, were to happen, then obviously his friends would not eat for they would be grieving too deeply. His use of specific symbols is striking. The coming of the Kingdom was sometimes referred to in the Old Testament as a marriage banquet at which God was the husband and his people the bride (Jeremiah 3: *14*; Hosea 2: *19*). The 'bridegroom' could therefore be interpreted as a veiled reference to the Messiah. There is also the underlying implication that, even at this early stage, Jesus is so conscious of hostility from the Jewish authorities that he already visualises their total rejection of him, resulting in his death. Therefore, with the courage which is so characteristic of him, he carries the conversation right into his opponent's camp. He tells two parables, both of which illustrate the point that you cannot mix the old and the new. Jesus' teaching was too radical to fit into the outward forms of Judaism, here represented by the old garment and the old wineskin. His later followers had to realise that they could not cling on to outdated customs, such as food regulations and matters relating to sabbath observance.

Wineskins were made of goat skins which had been steeped in tannin, then sewn up at the neck. The seams were pitched. As the wine fermented it would cause the hardened leather to crack and burst.

Discussion
Is it always true that you cannot mix the old and the new together without either suffering? In some cases it is necessary to build on the traditions of the past, but there must be flexibility. What outworn traditions do you think your generation has discarded and what other traditions do you think are worth keeping and building on?

(d) Sabbath Observance—Mark 2:23-28; Matthew 12: 1-8; Luke 6:1-5

It was Galilean harvest time—the month of May. The Law (Deuteronomy 23: 25) allows a hungry man to pluck the ears of corn but forbids reaping on the Sabbath. According to Luke, the disciples not only plucked the corn as they walked through the field but rubbed it with their fingers, regarded as 'reaping' by the Pharisees and so breaking the law.

Jesus' reply falls into two parts. Firstly he quotes from 1 Samuel 21: 1-6 regarding the action of David when he and his friends ate the holy bread which had lain for the previous week in the Sanctuary at Nob. They were starving and had no alternative. Jesus says—'Our great ancestor did this and you do not criticise him for it. Why do you then blame my disciples for such a trifling act?' He may be implying that as Messiah he is the son of David and therefore worthy of similar consideration, or that the ritual law is not binding. The second point is clearer and more important. Jesus states that man is greater than any institution and that the son of man is Lord of the Sabbath. The Sabbath was made for man, not vice versa. It has been argued that in this story Jesus uses the phrase 'son of man' not in a messianic sense, but to speak of humanity in general. If this is so, it bears out the same point that all institutions and regulations must serve the needs of men. There is something very wrong when men are sacrificed to maintain institutions. However it could be that Jesus was claiming messianic authority in overriding the petty scribal regulations concerning Sabbath observance.

Discussion and Work
1 Can you think of present day or historical examples of people being subordinated to the demands of an institution? Could this criticism be applied to institutional religion?

2 In these four 'conflict' stories we can see the gradual heightening of tension between Jesus and the Pharisees. The fifth story in the next chapter brings it all out into the open. Write a short summary of the causes of conflict as indicated in these passages.

Chapter 3

(a) The man with the withered hand—Mark 3:*1-6*; Matthew 12:*9-14*; Luke 6:*6-11*

This is the fifth conflict story which Mark records and it is a fitting climax to this series of incidents, for it ends with the Pharisees consulting with their traditional opponents, the Herodians, to decide on a joint plan for getting rid of Jesus. It also follows well on the controversy about Sabbath observance because here again Jesus gives a striking demonstration of precisely what he means by saying that men are of greater value than any institution.

The scene takes place in the synagogue on a Sabbath. In the congregation there is a sick man whose right arm (according to Luke) is withered. The rabbis taught that healing was permitted on the Sabbath only if life was in danger. Such was their interpretation of the Sabbath rest. Jesus challenges them on what he sees is a hypocritical attitude. Which is the better way of observing the Sabbath? By having the desire to heal as I have? Or having the desire to kill? By implication, he is saying: *You* are observing the Sabbath by harbouring the desire to kill *me*. He was both angry and sad that the religious leaders of Israel should be blind and self-willed and of course he healed the man despite their attitude.

Work
1 In the Introduction the Herodians were described as supporters of the dynasty of Herod. Add this group of people to your list of political and religious parties. Look up the family tree of Herod (*p* 185) and the relevant map (*p* 188), so that you can understand quite clearly which areas in Palestine were governed by the various members of the Herod family.
2 Also start your dossier on Jesus' teaching about the Sabbath. Make sure you are quite clear in what way his outlook was different from that of the Scribes and Pharisees.

(b) By the lakeside and the choice of the Twelve—Mark 3:7-19; Matthew 12:15-21 and 10:2-4; Luke 6:12-19

Jesus has to leave the cities and even has to cease preaching in the synagogues because of the hostility which he has aroused. In this passage we read how popular enthusiasm is still there and people come from all parts to hear him. In order to teach them, he preaches from a boat on the Lake of Galilee; otherwise he would be in danger of being crushed. Note also how 'evil spirits' call out that he is the Son of God but he does not want this kind of publicity (*cf* 1: 9–13 p 6).

The time has come for Jesus to choose from among the many who follow him a particular group of men who will be his closest friends. This is an important stage in the gospel. So far Mark has given us a few typical examples of Jesus' public ministry. Now follows a period of special training for his chosen followers. Presumably he appointed twelve men because there were twelve ancient tribes of Israel. These are to be the new Israel—the new people of God. By being in close fellowship with Jesus all the time they will learn from him so that he can send them out at a later date to be his messengers or ambassadors. These men are afterwards known as Apostles, from the Greek 'apostello'—I send. Note that Simon Peter heads the list. In spite of his failures, he was to become the spiritual leader of the Christian community after Jesus' death. The other Simon is a member of the Zealot party, the extreme nationalist group who were prepared for open rebellion and active underground resistance to the Roman occupying force. It is typical of Jesus' courage that he should appoint such a man as one of his intimate friends. Many people believed that Jesus himself was a Zealot and indeed he was crucified as such by the Roman authorities. It is clear however that although Jesus was very radical in his approach to authority, he did not believe in violence or armed resistance. This indicates that Jesus himself was almost certainly not a Zealot.

Thaddaeus is known as Judas, or Jude, in Luke's list. If he was originally called Judas, he may well have preferred to be known by another name after Jesus' death. Judas Iscariot (his name probably means 'man of Kerioth') would appear to be the only non-Galilean amongst the company. Perhaps, from the beginning, he felt something of an outsider.

(c) Jesus is accused of black magic—Mark 3:20-30; Matthew 12:22-37, 43-45; Luke 11:14-23.

Jesus comes down from the hills and again the crowds gather. His family are anxious about him because rumours are rife. People are even saying that he is out of his mind. It is in this setting that

Mark describes a further controversy with some Jerusalem lawyers who have travelled to Galilee expressly to question Jesus. They are unable to deny his power (Luke actually introduces his account of this story with Jesus casting out an evil spirit) but they attribute it to sorcery or black magic. In reply Jesus quite simply appeals to common sense. Being a man of his day, he accepts the current belief that Satan rules his own kingdom set up in opposition to the Kingdom of God, but argues that Satan's state also has its unity. Satan is not a fool – would he want civil war? Neither a divided kingdom nor a divided family will last for long. To enter into a strong man's house and take his goods, the thief has to be stronger than the owner; by implication therefore, Jesus is able to cast out demons and release a man from the bondage of evil because he has a power which is greater than the devil's.

Although Jesus answers calmly, he is angry with the Scribes. If they are so preoccupied with their own self-righteousness that they fail to recognise Jesus' healings as acts of compassion and love, then they are morally and spiritually in a very bad way. He describes their condition as a deep-seated perversity for which he sees no apparent cure. To be forgiven, a man must truly sense his need. Forgiveness is a two-way operation. Jesus forgave men for their sins of ignorance, as is demonstrated by his words on the cross (Luke 23:34); but ignorance or inability to see that one is doing wrong is altogether different from the wilful and deliberate denial of goodness by people who have had every opportunity of recognising it. Jesus is not saying that God refuses to forgive the Scribes for their remarks about him. He is talking about their spiritual blindness which arises from their arrogance.

Discussion and Work

1 People have worried, down the centuries, about the question of 'unforgivable sin'. What do you think about it? If a man said red was green, you would know he was colour-blind. So if a man describes some undeniably helpful and loving action as evil, could you justifiably say he was morally confused or psychologically sick?

2 Is the point of this story altered by the fact that our particular society does not attribute sickness of any kind to 'demon possession'?

3 Does Jesus' 'stern saying' in this story, about the unforgivable sin, bear any relation to the comment he made in the last chapter—Mark 2:17?

4 Add this further conflict story to your list of the other five. Can you begin to see how the case is being built up against Jesus?

(d) His family come to visit Jesus—Mark 3:*31–35*; Luke 8:*19–21*; Matthew 12: *46–50*

At the beginning of the previous section, Mark told us that Jesus' family were worried about him. He is working so hard that he has no time to eat and many things are being said about him. But who were his family? When Jesus returns to Nazareth (Mark 6:*1–6*), we are told the names of four of Jesus' brothers. His sisters are also mentioned. The exact relationship of Jesus to his brethren is a controversial matter depending on what you believe about Mary. If you believe the Roman Catholic and Anglo-Catholic teaching that Mary remained a virgin all her life, these brethren could have been Joseph's children by a former marriage or Joseph's brother's children, brought up by Joseph after the death of his brother in accordance with Jewish law. However, as there is no evidence in the gospel story itself to support the theory that Mary and Joseph did not have sexual intercourse with each other after they were married, it is more straightforward to believe that Jesus' brothers and sisters were the children of Joseph and Mary. (For the arguments both for and against the natural conception of Jesus himself, see notes on Matthew 1:*18–25* and Luke 1:*26–56*).

At this point in Jesus' ministry it would seem that his family did not understand either his ministry or his teaching. Presumably they come to try and take him home, but he resolutely refuses. He even takes the opportunity to declare publicly that there is a deeper relationship to be considered than the natural blood one. There is an affinity of purpose and outlook. Jesus believes that his life is dedicated to bringing in the Kingdom of God. All those who join with him in this work—who hear the word of God spoken by him and obey it—these are his true family.

This is not the end of the story because we know his mother, Mary, was with Jesus at his death and that after his resurrection, the natural family of Jesus were amongst his disciples. James, his brother, became head of the Jerusalem church and according to Josephus was later martyred for his convictions.

Discussion

In this story we have another seemingly harsh saying of Jesus. Can you think of any circumstances when loyalty to a cause is justifiably more important than loyalty to one's family?

Chapter 4

You may have noticed that Mark has arranged his material as if it could be used for teaching purposes. We might perhaps have sub-titled the first chapter—A typical day in the life of Jesus; and the second—A typical cross-section of how opposition to Jesus built up over a period of time. This is a topic which is carried over into chapter 3. In chapter 4 it seems as though Mark has given us several parables to illustrate Jesus' particular way of teaching. Of course Jesus was not at all unique in teaching through parables. Early Hebrew prophets and later Jewish rabbis had for a long time used this pictorial way of presenting truth and we have examples from other Eastern cultures of the effectiveness of the story as an aid to learning.

Note the following points:

1 A parable is a 'like' saying. 'The Kingdom of God is like . . .', says Jesus. It makes a comparison in a phrase or in the form of a picture or a story.

2 It has ONE main point, unlike an allegory where each point is important. (For example, in Bunyan's 'Pilgrim's Progress' every-thing that happens to Christian and all his encounters are intended to be related to the life of a christian in his struggles and endeavours.)

3 When truth is conveyed in picture form, the listener is then left free to interpret the matter on different levels, according to his understanding. You could take some of Jesus' parables as practical advice about everyday affairs because he always used examples which were familiar to his contemporaries, even if they are less so to us. But the parable is also challenging in that it invites the listener to think more deeply about what has been said and to try and uncover the real meaning which more often than not has some personal implication.

4 Although Jesus' parables were relevant to his own time, they have something to say to every age, even our own, because he was really talking about a certain kind of truth—the truth of human experience at its best. So in discussing them we shall try and see

what they meant for Jesus' own ministry and also what universal application they may have for us.

(a) The Parable of the Sower—Mark 4:*1-9, 13-20*; Matthew 13:*1-9, 18-23*; Luke 8:*4-8, 11-15*

Perhaps Jesus, sitting in his boat on the lake, actually saw a farmer scattering his seed on the neighbouring hillside. It would be a familiar picture to the crowds. A few verses later an explanation is given which in fact turns the parable into an allegory. Many commentators think that this explanation has been added by the Christian teacher or preacher and that it does not belong to the original words of Jesus. It is easy to see how such explanations became attached to the oral tradition and to accept that Mark included them in good faith. As the parable/allegory now stands, the quality of the soil represents people's receptiveness to the teaching of Jesus, which is the seed. The hard, the shallow, the pre-occupied man gains very little from the teaching but where a man accepts Jesus' word, then his whole life is transformed and he goes out and tells others 'the good news'. At the time when Mark was writing his gospel, Christians were going through severe persecution and difficulty. Were they going to be like the seed on the shallow or stony ground which perished when the sun blazed down because it had no roots? Or were they going to be like the seed in crowded soil, having so many cares and ambitions that there was little room in their lives for the development of their faith? Or were they going to be steadfast and through their witness bring others to a knowledge of their Lord and Master, Jesus the Christ?

(b) Parabolic Teaching—Mark 4:*10-12*; Matthew 13:*10-12*; Luke 8:*9-10*

This is a private conversation in which the Twelve ask Jesus about the meaning of his public teaching. This must have happened very often so perhaps Mark is again giving us a summary of the general situation. The Kingdom is the reign of God in men's hearts (*cf* 1:*15*). It is therefore an intuitive, inward reality or, as Jesus says here, 'a secret understanding', which can be made plain to those who want to discover its meaning. The disciples, by accepting Jesus and listening to what he says with the inward ear of comprehension as far as they are able, have thus been given 'the key' or the clue to the meaning of the Kingdom. There are others however who are not so willing or able to learn. They have doubts about Jesus himself or have reservations about putting his teaching into practice. He can still reach them through a story, to make them think,

24

even if they do not get very much out of the experience. These people are rather like the ones to whom the prophet Isaiah preached (and Jesus includes part of Isaiah 6:*9–10* in what he says); they are those who lack spiritual insight, who see and hear but do not understand. If he is to understand the parable fully, the listener must make an effort, which could lead to repentance and a renewal of his relationship with God.

It seems at first sight as if Jesus is declaring that the parabolic way of teaching is deliberately obscure so as to limit people's response. This is in direct contradiction with what we know about Jesus' outlook and treatment of others. Jesus often spoke ironically so probably the actual turn of phrase used here is meant to be ironic. According to Mark, Jesus then proceeds to give a precise illustration of how a parable can be interpreted by showing that the four types of soil are indeed four different kinds of people.

Work

1 Can you give examples of different kinds or levels of response to a particular television programme or lesson in school? Discuss the different kinds of learning that take place; you might compare learning for a test or an examination with learning from an experience that can stay with you always. Are your most vivid memories usually related to a story or an incident which stays as a picture in your mind?

2 Start making a list of parables at the back of your notebook so that you build up a picture of the teaching of Jesus about the Kingdom. Why do you think Mark put this parable first? Was it a deliberate choice on his part?

(c) A collection of sayings—Mark *4:21-25*; Matthew *5:14-16*, *7:2*; *10:26*, *13:12*, *25:29*; Luke *8:16-18*, *11:33*; *12:2*, *6:38*; *19:26*

You will see by the references above that these sayings in Mark were placed in different contexts by Matthew and Luke. In Mark they seem to be used to confirm the idea that the secrets of the Kingdom are given to the disciples in trust for the world. What they discover from Jesus they are to pass on to others, as a lamp is put on a lampstand to give the greatest amount of light. (In John's gospel, Jesus himself is called 'the light of the world'.) What is now a 'secret' will not always be so. The comment found in *v* 22 that what you put into a thing is the measure of what you get out of it, applies particularly to listening and learning. Verse 25 is simply saying that what we do not use, we lose—which is as true of limbs and muscles as of talents and skills that are buried and forgotten. Jesus is obviously referring to spiritual resources, which increase or dwindle according to the use a man makes of them (*cf* Matthew's Parable of the Talents, Matthew 25:*14–30*).

(d) The seed growing secretly—Mark 4:*26-29*

This is a parable which is only found in Mark. Because of its present context, commentators have suggested that Jesus was talking about the purpose of God which, like a seed, was sown long ago in Israel's beginnings and which has been ripening through generations until now it reaches harvest time with the appearance of Jesus.

God's purpose for Israel is fulfilled with the coming of the Kingdom in Jesus. However, it is also possible to interpret this parable in terms of the individual. The mysterious life-force in the seed itself goes on growing within the receptive and good soil of a person's mind and heart and eventually bears abundant fruit. This parable illustrates how difficult it is to be precise as to the meaning Jesus wished to convey. Is it a parable about the significance of hidden growth, or about the coming of the harvest?

(e) The mustard seed—Mark 4:*30-32*; Matthew 13:*31-32*; Luke 13:*18-19*

This parable is much easier. From a small and insignificant beginning a very great thing can develop. 'Small as a grain of mustard seed' was a Jewish proverb, yet this tiny speck can grow very quickly into a tree or shrub some 6 to 8 feet tall. 'The birds of the air', another Jewish phrase, commonly described the Gentiles. The coming of the Kingdom began in a small way with Jesus and his few friends but very soon it would grow into a new era in which both Jew and Gentile would find a place.

In *v* 33-34 Mark explains that Jesus' normal method of teaching was parabolic and so he has only included a selection of these parables. He also tells us that it was Jesus' practice to explain everything to the disciples when he was alone with them.

(f) The stilling of the storm—the first 'nature' miracle—Mark 4:*35-41*; Matthew 8:*18, 23-27*; Luke 8:*22-25*

The Lake of Galilee is subject to sudden storms which can end as abruptly as they begin. Even today experienced fishermen can be taken unawares, while inexperienced people can drown. Galilee lies at the northern end of the ravine which is called the Great Rift Valley.

Mark says that Jesus and his disciples left the crowd and went across the lake. After teaching all day Jesus is very tired and falls asleep. Note the detail 'he was in the stern asleep on a cushion'. Elemental forces were often thought of as demonic powers in Jesus' day so when Mark reports that Jesus rebuked the wind and calmed the sea, the words used could refer to the muzzling of a demon. Jesus comments on his friends' lack of faith and they ask each other in awe 'Who is this that has such power over the elements?', perhaps with Psalm 107:28–29 especially in mind.

There are several important matters to discuss here

1 We have been brought up in a culture which seeks to find a rational explanation for everything. As far as scientific observation can tell us, there are laws which govern the running of the universe. If, for example, something happened contrary to the law of gravity, scientists would try to discover why. Thus an examination of the salt content in the Dead Sea shows quite clearly why things there float which would normally sink to the bottom.

2 So far Mark has talked about the power of Jesus to heal a man's mind and even his body and we can accept this because such healings still take place even today though they cannot as yet be scientifically explained. But here he is claiming a power for Jesus which, even if we believed he were the Son of God, is still difficult to accept because it leaves us with a dilemma: Given the belief that God exists, that he created the universe and set in motion its continual survival on the basis of certain laws, is it likely that he or his accredited representatives would change or overrule those laws? So there are two questions—(i) For the agnostic—Could it happen? (ii) For the Christian—Would it happen? Is it consistent with the character of Jesus, as the Son of God, so to use his powers?

3 The disciples had no such problem. For them, Jesus' miracles were a manifestation of the power of God, of the coming of the Kingdom. Their interpretation of events was governed by a more credulous outlook. But the 'miracles' which Jesus performed never convinced his enemies of his messiahship. They were specifically 'signs' to those who already believed in him. We shall discuss this more fully when we look at Jesus' own inward struggle about the nature of his messiahship.

4 The rational explanation for this nature miracle is that Jesus calmed the storm of fear in the disciples' hearts so that they were then able to deal with the physical peril until the storm itself suddenly abated. In one sense this is a greater 'miracle' than that of stilling the storm, because it demonstrates a certain quality

of character in Jesus; by his capacity to love, encourage and understand, he enabled men to rise to the challenge of extraordinary circumstances.

We may conclude then that in the gospel a miracle is not necessarily something supernatural which goes against what we know to be true about the world in which we live, but a demonstration of the untapped resources within the human personality, for example, the courage and vision which can take advantage of the unexpected timing of events. Do you agree that a miracle will, therefore, be interpreted according to the individual's view of life?

Chapter 5

(a) Jesus heals the Gerasene Madman—Mark 5:*1-20*; Matthew 8:*28-34*; Luke 8:*26-39*

Jesus sailed with his disciples to the other side of the Lake but the actual place where they landed is not easy to locate. The area of the Ten Towns, known as Decapolis (from the Greek Deca—ten, polis—city), was east or south-east of the Lake of Galilee. The ten cities stretched from Damascus to the Dead Sea and formed a league modelled on Greek lines. In the New English Bible the spot where Jesus landed is called the country of the Gerasenes. The Authorised version calls it 'Gadarenes' because this is the name used in Matthew's gospel (8:28). The city of Gerasa was nearly two day's journey from the lake and that of Gadara was about eight miles, so neither of these two towns could have been directly involved in the story. There are however very steep cliffs on the south eastern shore of the lake; here a herd of swine could have fallen over the edge into the sea, so it is possible that the area was part of the territory controlled by the city of Gadara, hence the name given it by Matthew.

We have discussed the problem of contemporary beliefs about demon-possession in Chapter 1. At that time it was also believed that knowing the name of a demon gave you power over it.

The man whom Jesus now meets was so fierce and wild that he terrorised the neighbourhood. We are told that he lived among tombs cut out of the rocks; in the Greek and Roman period this was a characteristic feature of funeral architecture. Obviously the madman believed himself to be possessed by many devils. A legion was a Roman military unit of 6,000 heavily armed foot soldiers, but we need not suppose that the man felt precisely this number of demons in him! It is interesting that Mark records he called Jesus by his name and added the title 'Son of the Most High God'. Other demon-possessed people in Mark also called Jesus by similar titles but this instance is the more surprising because it occurred in Gentile territory, as the presence of the nearby herd of swine testifies. According to the story, Jesus restores the man to sanity by ordering out the demons, who request that they may be sent into the herd of swine; the swine subsequently stampede over the cliff edge and are drowned, thus ensuring the destruction of the demons too.

The Jews regarded pigs as 'unclean' animals and were forbidden to eat their flesh (Leviticus 11:7ff). For the disciples of Jesus, therefore, the casting out of the unclean spirits into a herd of unclean beasts which then drowned, was a perfectly logical and morally acceptable interpretation of the events they had witnessed. Because in the twentieth century we do not attribute mental illness to demon possession, we can more readily believe that the man was mentally disturbed and very sick, having been badly treated by his contemporaries who did not understand the nature of his illness. Jesus always healed people on a level they could understand. Perhaps then, obsessive illness could only be cured when the sick man actually witnessed in some tangible way what he recognised as the departure of the 'demons'.

When Jesus is asked to leave the area by the frightened townsmen (or villagers) he tells Legion, who has begged to go with him, that he must return and report to his own people how he has been cured. This is the exact opposite of what Jesus had said to the leper (1:40–45) but as this was Gentile territory and in any case Jesus was going to leave the vicinity, there was no fear that a messianic uprising would result from such publicity. How well Legion did his work is illustrated by a later story in which Jesus again comes to Decapolis (7:31–37).

Discussion

1 Do you think Jesus was willing to sacrifice a herd of swine for one man's sanity? If this is so, what implication does this story have for man's attitude to the animal kingdom, bearing in mind that we do not regard pigs as 'unclean'?

2 Even if Jesus had this kind of power (as we have discussed in chapter 4) would he have used it in this way, especially as the death of a considerable number of swine might have been economically disastrous for the nearby village?

3 What do you think of the alternative suggestion that the pigs were drowned as a result of a series of accidents, i.e. the herdsmen neglected their duties because they were curious to watch the encounter between Legion and Jesus; there was a lot of noise and shouting, which frightened the swine so that they stampeded in the wrong direction; when they were drowned the herdsmen had to blame someone and Jesus was the natural choice?

4 Jesus may have 'cast out' the demons from the man but not into the swine. This connection may have been made both by the disciples and the herdsmen, though for different reasons. What

further item of later evidence in Mark's gospel supports this view?

Work
Add this story to the list of miracles which you are making at the back of your notebooks.

(b) Jesus heals a woman suffering from severe haemorrhage and Jairus' daughter—Mark 5:*21-43*; Matthew 9:*18-26*; Luke 8:*40-56*

When Jesus returned to the west shore of the lake he probably went to Capernaum where he was well known. The President of a Synagogue (see notes on chapter 1) would be responsible for arranging the services; he was, therefore, an important man. Taking advantage of the great crowd which accompanied Jesus to Jairus' house, a woman who had suffered from haemorrhage for twelve years, dares to approach and touch Jesus. She had to do so secretly because her illness made her ceremonially unclean and a social outcast (Leviticus 15). When she touches his cloak, Jesus feels the power flow out of him; he stops and asks 'Who touched me?', much to the irritation of the disciples and the desperation of Jairus. Although the woman is very afraid to confess that she has infringed the law, Jesus speaks to her in affectionate terms and she knows the cure will not be reversed. Her faith indeed has made her whole.

When news of the child's death arrives, Jesus again stresses the need for faith. In the East it was the custom to hire professional mourners to lament the death of a loved one. These women had already moved in to Jairus' house but Jesus clears them out with calm authority, saying 'The child is not dead. She is asleep'. Note how Jesus takes with him on this occasion his three closest friends as well as the girl's parents and that Mark tells us the actual Aramaic phrase he used to rouse the child gently and tenderly. His care is also evident in the practical advice he gives the parents. In this case, the injunction not to talk about the cure was probably given for the girl's own sake.

Discussion
1 From the first story we can see that Jesus' healing work took something out of him, otherwise he would not have known that the woman had touched him. Do you find this credible? Why do you think the disciples were irritated by his question and what does this tell us about their attitude to Jesus?
2 Mark records the second story as Jesus raising someone from the dead, but what do you understand from Jesus' comment to the

mourners? Was he saying that the girl was in a kind of coma, or do you think he meant that death is but a sleep from which one could be awakened?

Work

1 In these two stories of healing the emphasis is on faith. Look up an earlier story in which faith is mentioned as a necessary ingredient of the cure.
2 Note how Mark is building up the picture of Jesus' authority in these last two chapters. He is a man with power over nature, over evil spirits, over a disease which had resisted previous attempts to cure it and even over death.

Chapter 6

(a) The Rejection at Nazareth—Mark 6:*1-6*; Matthew 13:*53-58*; Luke 4:*16-30*

Jesus now leaves Capernaum and returns to his own town. On the Sabbath he teaches in the synagogue—perhaps asked to do so by the elders, in view of his growing popularity. However the congregation is critical of him. They have known him as the village carpenter; they know his family. To stress the point, Mark even includes the names of four of his brothers. The reference to his being the son of Mary may mean that his father is now dead, or it may include a smear on his legitimacy, because it was usual to give the name of the father rather than the mother. The congregation do not understand what gives him his authority. Jesus is taken aback by their attitude and quotes a proverb, the modern equivalent of which might be 'familiarity breeds contempt'. Again in this story there is an emphasis on faith as a necessary component of healing. Jesus will not use his authority to force belief on people. He will only be followed by free choice. (Luke records this rejection at Nazareth much earlier in his gospel.)

Discussion

Does it surprise you that Jesus was rejected by his own town or that while there he seemed to experience a definite limitation to his power of healing?

How far is it true that famous people are not at first recognised by their own family and friends?

(b) The Mission of the Twelve. Mark 6:*7-13*; Matthew 10:*1, 5-16*; Luke 9:*1-6*

From a number of disciples Jesus chose Twelve to be his constant companions. After a period of training these twelve are sent out on a mission. Since Mark records it immediately after the rejection at Nazareth, it may be that Jesus now feels it imperative to test his disciples to see if they are able to put what they have learnt from him into practice and to discover how they will fare without him.

They must take only a staff, sandals and one coat, for they are to rely solely on Jesus' authority within them. The insurance of money, a supply of bread or a wallet is denied them. They are to go in pairs to support each other and rely on people's hospitality. But where they are not accepted, they must waste no time in moving on to another place, leaving that particular village or town with a solemn gesture of rejection. Their only credentials are their power to preach, heal and exorcise in Jesus' name. In fact, they are messengers of the Kingdom. We can see how successful their mission was by the way people are now talking about Jesus, as Mark reports in the following verses.

Discussion

What do you think was the real point of the strict instructions Jesus gave the Twelve? Has it any relevance to missionary work today or the work of the Christian church as a whole? What social conditions may have influenced Jesus in not appointing women?

(c) The death of John Baptist. Mark 6:*14–29*; Matthew 14:*1–12*; Luke 9:*7–9*

Herod Antipas, ruler of Galilee and Peraea, had imprisoned John Baptist for several reasons. Firstly John had condemned Herod's marriage to his brother's wife, Herodias, as adulterous. Herod had divorced his first wife (a daughter of Aretas, king of the Nabataean Arabs) in order to marry Herodias, who had left her first husband in Rome in order to come and live with Herod (see family tree *p* 185). However the Jewish historian, Josephus, implies that Herod imprisoned John because his preaching about the coming of the Messiah was stirring up messianic excitement and might lead to a revolt. Josephus also reports that John was imprisoned in the fortress of Machaerus. Mark attributes John's death to the hatred of Herodias, who used the beauty of her daughter Salome and, presumably, the drunkenness of her husband to effect her revenge.

At this point Mark gives us three current popular opinions of Jesus. To Herod's guilt-ridden imagination, Jesus was John Baptist risen from the dead. To others, Jesus was the fulfilment of a prophecy by Malachi (4:5) that Elijah would return to herald the coming of the Messiah. To another group, Jesus was simply a prophet.

Work

Look at the family tree of Herod and copy it out into your notebooks, so that you memorise it. Salome married her uncle Philip, the Tetrarch of Iturea and other regions East of Jordan.

(d) The Feeding of the Five Thousand. Mark 6:30-44; Matthew 4:13-21; Luke 9:10-17; John 6:1-15

Mark tells us that the Twelve return from their tour in great excitement but they find their master so overwhelmed with work that there is no time to eat. In this dilemma, Jesus takes them across the water to a quiet spot so that they can be alone with him and assess the results of their mission. However the crowd follow them round by the shore and Jesus cannot resist the people's need of him.

What follows is probably one of the best known stories in the gospels. It appears in all four and is the only 'nature' miracle to do so. (John also narrates the 'walking on the water' but in his gospel this is not necessarily a miraculous happening.)

Mark gives us two vivid details. The grass was green, so it was evidently springtime in Galilee, a place where the sun scorches the vegetation for most of the year. The crowd sat down in ranks—the Greek word suggests orderly beds of plants in a garden plot! Once again, it is thought that these details come direct from Peter's memory of the occasion.

Although this story is so well-known, it raises all sorts of problems for the modern reader. For Mark, however, the mysterious feeding shows Jesus' authority over material things. There was no division in the disciples' minds between the natural and the supernatural. In their eyes, Jesus, as the Messiah, the Son of God, would be perfectly capable of exercising his supernatural power to create more food out of the loaves and the fishes provided by the disciples. Note the symbolic numbers used. For the Jew, seven is a number of perfection, there being seven days in the week and the seventh day being the Sabbath. Twelve is the number of completion. There were twelve tribes of Israel. On this occasion, the twelve baskets are probably to be associated with the twelve disciples, each of whom would presumably use his basket to gather up the fragments.

In John's gospel, this event impresses the people so much that they want to make Jesus king. They want to use his power for their own ends and establish a Jewish nationalist state. Jesus realises what is happening and goes away from them into the hills, sending his disciples off in the boat across the lake. Afterwards he meets the crowd at Capernaum and talks to them about the real Bread of Life, which is himself. Consequently the Christian church has later interpreted this feeding in terms of the service of the Eucharist (the Lord's supper, Holy Communion or the Mass, according to which denomination is celebrating the rite). In the gospel story Jesus looks up to heaven, blesses and breaks the bread, hence the use of the word 'eucharist' which means 'to give thanks'.

Discussion

1 The question again arises, as in the other 'nature' miracle, did Jesus really possess this kind of power? Supposing that he did, would he have used it in such a way, even out of compassion for the crowd?

2 Since later stories show that Jesus resolutely refused to perform miracles and 'signs' that would dazzle people into believing in him (*cf* Jesus' Temptations Luke 4:*1–13*), should we not seek some rational explanation for this happening? If we accept that the most striking power which Jesus possessed was the power to understand men's minds and meet their needs, then we can perhaps see this 'miracle' in a different light. After the crowd had been with Jesus all day, listening and talking to him, they would have been deeply affected by his teaching. In such circumstances it is only natural that when the disciples pooled their resources, everyone else in the crowd who had brought something to eat during the day would put it in the pool as well. Because everyone shared what they had with each other, there would be more than enough to go round. If you had been a disciple of Jesus how would you have remembered this happening? Could it not have seemed to you that somehow, miraculously, food appeared out of nowhere and all because of the Master? Would you later associate it in your mind with the Last Supper and, even later, with the celebration of the Lord's Supper?

3 Consider the relevance of this miracle to the modern situation in which two thirds of the world go hungry whilst the rest are over-fed.

4 Do you think that belief in Jesus as the Son of God, is necessarily dependent upon his ability to work this kind of miracle?

(e) The Walking on the Water. Mark 6:*45–52*; Matthew 14:*22–36*

Like John, Mark records that after the mass excitement of the feeding, Jesus feels it wiser to go up into the hills alone and spends the time there praying. About 3 a.m. a wind arises and, seeing his friends in difficulties on the lake, he comes to help them. In Matthew's gospel we find the interesting story (which Mark omits) of Peter trying to walk on the water towards Jesus. Mark however does tell us that the disciples had not understood the incident of the loaves and fishes as their minds were closed, so they are further dumbfounded by the appearance of their Master seemingly walking on the water and getting into the boat when the wind subsides.

Discussion

1 This is the third 'nature' miracle which Mark reports; the same questions arise. Do you imagine that Jesus had the power of levitation, as some Tibetan monks claim to have? Or that, because he understood the powers of nature in some way that is closed to us, he therefore could control them?

2 The Greek phrase 'walking ON the water' which is used in John's gospel, could equally well be translated 'walking BY the water (or sea)'. Therefore it is perfectly rational to suppose that Jesus was really walking in the shallow part of the lake; the disciples' error is readily understandable, especially if they had been blown off course. In the moonlight Jesus could possibly have looked as if he were walking on water. How far do you think this view is supported by *v* 48 and also by Matthew's account of Peter's attempt to meet Jesus?

3 Assuming that Peter told him about the incident, why do you think Mark omitted the reference to Peter which Matthew included?

(d) Healing at Gennesaret. Mark 6:53–56

Mark ends his story by reporting that Jesus and the disciples crossed the lake and eventually landed at Gennesaret although they had intended going to Bethsaida. The final verse is a summary of Jesus' healing mission in and around Galilee.

Chapter 7

(a) Jesus has a controversial discussion with the Pharisees about religious purity—Mark 7:1-23; Matthew 15:1-20

In this section Mark again returns to the topic of opposition to Jesus from the religious leaders. Their antagonism must have been continually on the point of erupting because of Jesus' failure to live in scrupulous accordance with scribal custom. Although it might appear at first sight to be concerned with hygiene, the question at issue in this story is religious purity. Since Mark is writing for Gentile Christians, he explains the Tradition of the Jewish Elders to them. When they had been to the market, the Pharisees felt it imperative to remove all traces of contact with Gentiles and 'sinners' (i.e. people who did not keep strictly to the Law). They felt that if they ate with 'unclean' hands, then their food would be contaminated and they themselves would become religiously unclean (2:13-17).

Jesus is again angered by their hypocrisy and uses a quotation from Isaiah 29:13 to point out to the Pharisees that their obedience to God is on a very superficial level. They are more concerned to keep the trivial details of their own interpretation of the Law (i.e. the Oral Tradition/Tradition of the Elders or scribal custom) than the actual will of God. He illustrates his point with what perhaps may have been an actual incident in the locality. 'Corban' was an Aramaic word meaning 'dedicated' and was a formula used in the taking of vows. The rigid scribal tradition made it possible for an unscrupulous son to dedicate his money to God by use of this vow and then turn round and tell his parents that he could not support them. When the parents appealed to the lawyers, they simply upheld the binding nature of the vow. And yet the Fifth Commandment (Exodus 20:12) expressly stipulates the duty of the children to care for their parents in their need. Jesus adds that this is just one example of how the oral tradition contradicts the real requirements of God. It is clear that from then on his disciples would not feel under any obligation to be strict adherents to the Tradition of the Elders.

Mark tell us that Jesus defined the nature of religious purity on another separate occasion. The Scribes have shown that they think it is obtained by the outward observance of religious custom, but Jesus says that it is what is in a man's heart and mind that makes him right with God. This is so revolutionary a concept that Jesus has to explain explicitly to his disciples in private that food simply cannot 'defile' a man. It goes into the stomach and out into the drain. People cannot be defiled by things but only by evil thoughts which lead to evil actions. Jesus lists the wrong attitudes of mind which can lead men to exploit, kill, ravage and destroy others.

Because of Jesus' teaching on this matter, Christians do not have food and drink regulations. In this, they are unlike Jews and Muslims.

Discussion

1 How far do you think you can be 'contaminated' by false ideas? How strong-minded do you have to be, for example, if you are to mix with people who drink a lot and remain sober yourself?
2 Is a television programme or a film comparable to food in that it cannot defile? Does it pass through, leaving the mind unchanged? How far do you think people are influenced by others' behaviour? Do you think there is some truth in the Pharisaic belief that if you want to live a religiously good life, you should not mix with people whose life style is completely different? What is the relevance of this argument to the protests that some people make about television programmes or films which they regard as containing too much sex or violence?

Work

Add this event to your list of 'conflict' stories, making sure that you are clear about the reasons for opposition to Jesus and his reply.

(b) Jesus leaves Jewish territory and cures the daughter of a Syro-Phoenician woman—Mark 7:24–30; Matthew 15:21–28

Mark's Gentile readers would be deeply interested in his report of Jesus' attitude to Jewish food regulations, especially as their social contacts with Jewish Christians were often a cause of serious trouble in the early church, as is shown in Acts. Mark now tells his readers of an actual mission to the Gentiles, undertaken by Jesus. Jesus may have left Galilee because of the hostility of Herod Antipas. At any rate he evidently wished to remain unrecognised in the Gentile cities of Tyre and Sidon. The woman, who comes to Jesus with an urgent request, may have been a Greek. She is described as Syro-Phoenician because Phoenicia was in the Roman province of Syria. In the conversation which follows, it seems at first as if Jesus is refusing to help the woman. He uses conventional Jewish phrases to describe the relationship which the Jew believed to exist between himself and a Gentile—children and dogs! Jesus also implies that he has come only for Jews. However there must have been something about Jesus' manner, perhaps a half-smile or a look in the eye, which made the woman answer in like kind with wit and courage. Even a dog can belong to the family and have the children's leftovers. Jesus is very impressed by the woman's faith and tells her that her daughter is cured, a statement which the woman finds to be true on her return home.

Discussion

1 Why do you think that this healing, done at a distance in response to great faith, would have special significance for Mark's readers?
2 Why do you think that Jesus at this time thought his mission was primarily to the Jews, even though later it was the Gentiles who gladly accepted the gospel?

Work

Add this story to your list of Jesus' healings, paying particular attention to what was special about it.

(c) The healing of a deaf mute—Mark 7:31-37

Mark does not explain why Jesus returned south to Galilee via the region of Decapolis. It would have been a long and roundabout journey. In 5:17 the inhabitants of this region were hostile to Jesus, whereas now the people eagerly await him, so it is not unreasonable to suppose that Legion had done his work well. Note particularly the methods which Jesus uses in this cure–
  (i) he takes the man away from the crowd;
  (ii) because speech is useless, Jesus communicates by touch—he puts his fingers into the man's ears, as these are to be opened, and touches the tongue with saliva (which is thought to have healing properties—an animal will always lick its wounds);
  (iii) then he looks up to heaven and sighs and speaks the Aramaic word which means 'be opened'.
Jesus instructs the man and his friends to be silent about the cure but they are too enthusiastic about the miracle not to talk about it. The words Mark uses to describe their reaction are

reminiscent of Isaiah 35:4–6, a passage describing the coming blessings of the Messianic Age.

Discussion

What special significance would this healing have for Mark's readers? Why do you think Mark chose to include this particular episode from amongst many that he must have known about? Why do you think Jesus healed the man by this means rather than by his more usual methods?

Work

Add this to your list of healings, with a special note that, unlike all the others we have read about so far, this was performed in three stages.

Chapter 8

(a) Jesus feeds another hungry crowd, this time on Gentile land—Mark 8:*1-10*; Matthew 15:*29-39*

The difficulties about this story are obvious. Some people think that it is merely a variant of the feeding of the 5000, because the disciples' anxiety is hard to understand if Jesus had already fed the 5000. If this interpretation is correct, Peter must have told Mark the story of the 5000, while someone else told him of the feeding of the 4000.

On the other hand, the details of the feedings are different and, significantly, this story takes place on Gentile territory. The disciples are not sure whether Jesus will treat 'outsiders' as he treats his own people; he may react differently. But he does not. The disciples wait on the crowd. Note again the symbolic use of number: Seven is the perfect number of completion (as is twelve) and seven deacons were later appointed to help the Twelve Apostles (see Acts 6). They represented the Greek-speaking Jewish Christian wing of the Jerusalem community. Mark must have included this story because he believed it showed Jesus as the giver of the 'bread of life' to the Gentiles.

This story ends Mark's account of Jesus' mission to the Gentiles. In the next incident he has returned to Jewish territory.

Discussion and Work
Look up the notes on Chapter 6. The same questions arise about a 'nature' miracle, but you must decide for yourselves whether you think the second story is simply an alternative version of the first.

Add this incident to your list of 'miracles' performed by Jesus.

(b) The Pharisees demand a sign—Mark 8:*11-21*; Matthew 12:*38-42*, 16:*1-12*: Luke 11:*29-32*; 12:*1*

The Pharisees are in a dilemma about Jesus. They do not really believe he is the Messiah because his words and actions are so contrary to their messianic expectations. Some of their leaders have already accused him of black magic because they cannot deny his power. Now another group decide they will give him one last chance to prove himself. They want some manifestation of overmastering power. In their view, this could establish the source of Jesus' authority beyond doubt. Such a manifestation would leave them no option but to accept him and would therefore relieve them of any difficult decisions. Jesus flatly refuses, in line with his refusal to use brain-washing techniques to influence people when he was tempted in the wilderness (*cf* Luke 4:1–13). Later we shall study the relevant passages in Luke and Matthew which indicate that Jesus himself was the sign for those who had spiritual perception. His authority rested on his conviction that the God whom he called Father had commissioned him to bring in the Kingdom. Jesus' mission to show men the true nature of God was costly and difficult; on several occasions Mark records that 'he sighed deeply'.

In the next paragraph the disciples themselves are shown to lack the spiritual perception which will enable them to understand Jesus. Embarking to cross the lake, Jesus warns them of the bad influence of the Pharisees which could infiltrate a community as yeast, or leaven, permeates dough. Jesus here links the Herodians with the Pharisees, perhaps because he is aware of their intrigues against him (*cf* 3:6). Mark does not make clear which specific qualities of the Pharisees Jesus has in mind, but Matthew in his gospel explains that the leaven is the teaching of the religious leaders. In their demand for a sign, the Pharisees have exposed their own theological and moral shortcomings.

The disciples are not on Jesus' wave-length at all. They are preoccupied with the fact that they have forgotten to get any bread. The fact that Jesus has to explain precisely what he means shows how spiritually dull and blind the disciples were, in spite of witnessing the two (one?) feedings. The words Jesus uses are reminiscent of his comment in 4:11–12.

Discussion and Work

1 Even if you believe that Jesus did not possess the kind of supernatural power to write his claims across the sky, it is possible to see that he could have given the Pharisees 'a sign' that would have satisfied them. How could he have done so and would it have betrayed the essence of his own mission?
2 Was there any point of similarity between the disciples' lack of understanding and the Pharisees' insistence upon some kind of proof that Jesus was the Messiah?
3 Add this further controversy to your list.

(c) The healing of a blind man at Bethsaida—Mark 8:22-26; (Matthew 9:27-31)

Bethsaida was in the territory of Herod Philip (see map and family tree). The story of this healing is similar to that of the deaf stammerer. On both occasions Jesus takes the man apart from the crowd; he heals the sufferer in stages by outward signs, using saliva. The man's reply to Jesus' question is very vivid, indicating that Peter probably remembered his actual words. If we are looking at the artistry of Jesus' dealings with men, we can appreciate that it was for the man's own sake that he was healed in two stages. The sudden restoration of sight might have been too much for him, as the unwanted publicity could also have been.

This episode and that of the deaf stammerer are found only in Mark. There is a similar story in Matthew but the textual reference is given only in brackets because Matthew's story involves two blind men, so it may or may not have been the same incident.

Discussion and Work

Do you think Mark deliberately put this story after the two previous incidents, which highlighted lack of spiritual sight in various groups of people? If so, the gradual process of healing was also symbolic of how spiritual perception can grow. Add this healing to your list, noting its special features.

(d) Peter confesses that Jesus is the Messiah—Mark 8:27-30; Matthew 16:13-20; Luke 9:18-21

Jesus now leads his disciples to a very beautiful region north of Galilee, dominated by the snow-capped Mount Hermon. The city of Caesarea Philippi had been rebuilt by Herod Philip and named after the Emperor, Caesar Augustus; it lay some 24 miles north of the lake.

For months Jesus had been living out his messiahship in front of his disciples but he had never actually said 'I am the Messiah'. Now he asks them what other men are saying about him and receives the three most obvious answers (see notes 6:14-16). Then he confronts them with the direct question who do they think he is? This is a crucial stage of their relationship with each other, especially if you remember how disappointed Jesus had recently been about their lack of insight. This time Peter rises to the challenge and declares for all of his companions the conviction that their master is the Messiah.

The Hebrew word 'Messiah' means the Anointed One, the literal Greek translation of which is 'Christos'—Christ. If you read Isaiah

9:3–7; 11:1–10; 61:1–9, you will get some idea of the kind of expectations the disciples would have had of Jesus as the Messiah (p xii). It is important to appreciate how inevitably the disciples thought in terms of glory. The Messiah would be the bearer of God's rule for men and there would be peace on earth after he had established his Kingdom. By being the original followers of the Messiah, the disciples would receive honour and authority. Every one else had similar ideas about the Messiah, whether he was to be a mighty warrior, a priest-king, a just ruler of the line of David, or even a supernatural figure, an idea which was later associated with the writings of Daniel. Above all else, he would restore the lost fortunes of the people of Israel and reign with power.

(e) Jesus talks to his disciples about what this means to him—Mark 8:31–9:1 Matthew 16:21–28; Luke 9:22–27

Because there is such an obvious discrepancy between Jesus' own conception of his role and other people's, he immediately tells his disciples that they must not talk about his being the Messiah. He then proceeds to shatter their illusions by predicting that, because of his rejection by the religious leaders, he will be made to suffer and eventually to die. He again uses the phrase 'Son of Man' to speak about himself and in this context he indicates that death will not be the end of the story, for he will rise again 'three days afterwards' (p 13f).

Peter simply cannot accept Jesus' allusions to suffering and death; his master has somehow got it wrong. He attempts to remonstrate but receives a stinging rebuke from Jesus. To understand the depth of Jesus' repudiation of Peter's well-meant but totally misguided intervention, we must refer again to Jesus' initial conflict in the wilderness (Luke 4:1–13) when he rejected the conventional ideas of Messiahship. Peter's outlook was not God's way but simply human ambition. Perhaps it was at this time that Jesus told his disciples about the 'temptations' which followed his baptism; this would help them to understand why he deliberately resisted earthly kingship. This is the first time in the gospel that Jesus has predicted his death and resurrection. It is a distinct turning point. So far we have seen his power and authority over sin, devils, disease, death, nature, material things, Jewish food laws, regulations about the Sabbath and fasting and the Oral Tradition of the Scribes. Mark has shown him to be indeed a king. Now he begins to give his disciples a new idea of power and authority and to indicate what is required of them if they are to be truly citizens of *his* kingdom.

As Jesus was alone with the Twelve in Caesarea Philippi, the six sayings which follow are likely to have been directed specifically to the disciples. Mark reports however that Jesus 'called the people to him', which may mean that the teaching about discipleship was given on another occasion. This may perhaps be Mark's version of the Sermon on the Mount but its inclusion at this point is very appropriate. As he has spoken of his own death, so now Jesus warns that anyone who wishes to be his follower must be prepared to die for his convictions (the phrase 'take up his cross' is a specific reference to death, as crucifixion was the official Roman form of capital punishment for non-Roman citizens). The second saying (like the verses which follow) is a paradox dealing with loss and gain. It contains a fundamental truth about human experience. If a man pursues a ruthless, egotistical, selfish way of life, he will eventually be less of a person than if he had put others' interests before his own. A person's essential self will grow by consideration of others. When the immediate disciples of Jesus recalled this saying in the light of subsequent persecution, they would see a specific reference to the fact that they must be willing to suffer all things, even death, in order to be faithful to the truth they had seen about Jesus and his teaching. Death was not the end. To live Jesus' way on earth meant inheriting a life hereafter. Jesus makes this quite clear in v 36. It is a foolish exercise to deny truth in order to gain the whole world, at the cost of losing your essential self—we might call it your personal integrity or sense of identity. When you have destroyed yourself by pursuing a course of action that negates fundamental human values, how can you find your identity again? But if you give yourself in love, loyalty and faith, even though you may be betrayed as Jesus was, you still retain yourself. Your inner core is not lost in the way that a denial of your capacity to love would diminish you. The contrasting characters of Jesus and Judas show this clearly.

In v 38, we are back in the imagery of Daniel 7:*10, 13–14* (*cf p* 14). In modern terminology Jesus is saying that if a man denies instinctively what he knows to be the truth about life, then this betrayal will end in shame. As the statement stands in the gospel, it is a stern warning of the consequences of disloyalty to Jesus, but the two meanings are not unconnected. 'Adulterous' is an adjective found in the Old Testament to describe the religious infidelity of Israel to God in her worship of other things. The prophet Hosea (because of his own personal experiences) described the relationship between God and his people in terms of a loving husband and unfaithful wife. Jesus felt Israel had forgotten her devotion to God and had become obsessed by material considerations. (For a discussion on 'angels' see p.109.)

46

The last saying is apparently part of the series even though it has been included in chapter 9 of the gospel. It created some misunderstanding among the early Christians because they thought it meant that some of them would not die until they had seen Jesus return again in glory. It was a current belief that the end of the world was an imminent possibility (see *p* xiv) and that the Lord Jesus would then be established as King for ever more. There are various interpretations of what Jesus actually did mean by the phrase 'the Kingdom of God come with power'. The Kingdom for Jesus was the rule or reign of God in men's lives; we might say it was the way of compassion which Jesus inaugurated. It is possible therefore to see 'come with power' as the vindication of Jesus' teaching and life, which is what his friends experienced at the resurrection. Later they received the Holy Spirit and went out and created a worldwide community which altered the course of human history.

Discussion

1 How do you think people today would reply to Jesus' question—'who do men say I am?'
2 Think of modern examples relevant to the question—'What does a man gain by winning the whole world at the cost of his true self?'
3 From your study of Jesus' ministry so far, what kind of power do you think he exhibited? How far is this the kind of power and authority which is present to-day in the church which bears his name?

Work

The character of Peter emerges from Mark's gospel with some clarity. Start making notes about the times when he is mentioned and what you learn about him from the various incidents.

Chapter 9

(a) Jesus is transfigured before his disciples—Mark 9:*2-13*; Matthew 17:*1-13*; Luke 9:*28-36*

Jesus had shocked his disciples by what he had said about suffering and death. The idea of a suffering Messiah was very hard to grasp, but their loyalty to him held firm. Now, six days later (and Mark particularly gives us this time connection) Peter, James and John (Jesus' three closest friends) have a very strange experience. Jesus takes them up a high mountain, which is probably Mount Hermon, some thirteen miles from Caesarea Philippi (although traditionally Mount Tabor in Galilee was thought to be the site). Whilst Jesus is at prayer (according to Luke), his friends see in him a luminous quality which they can only describe as a transfiguration. Further, it seems that Jesus himself is joined by two figures, whom they identify as Moses and Elijah; these two (again according to Luke) speak to Jesus of his departure 'which he was to accomplish in Jerusalem'. Peter, in a state of high tension, impulsively suggests that they build three shelters. This was a characteristic feature of the Feast of Tabernacles, when pilgrims camped out on the Jerusalem hillsides in tents or shelters, reminiscent of the Wilderness Wanderings. The overshadowing cloud was the Old Testament symbol for God's presence and glory, known in Exodus as the Shekinah (Exodus 13:*22*; 24:*15-16*; 40:*34*). The voice confirms that their master is indeed the Son of God and that they must listen to him. Suddenly the vision disappears and the disciples are alone with Jesus.

How are we to understand this story? The following points and suggestions are offered for your discussion:

1 This experience is told from the point of view of the disciples. We know nothing of what Jesus himself saw and felt and yet in many ways it is very like the story of the baptism. In both there is a vision and a voice and even the words are similar (*cf* 1:*11*). Both events concern a striking moment of insight regarding Jesus' messiahship, especially in terms of the first Servant Song of Isaiah 42:*1*.

2 As one would expect, the experience is related to Old Testa-

ment ideas. Moses is the greatest figure in Jewish history. He is not only the supreme law-giver but to him was given the promise that God would send another prophet like him to his people (Deuteronomy 18:*15–18*)—'You shall listen to him in whatever he tells you'. Here is a direct link with the words of the vision, a link which Peter later made explicit in his speech to the Jerusalem crowds (Acts 3:*22–26*). Elijah was also a very great prophetic figure. It was traditionally believed that he had never died (2 Kings 2:*11*) and therefore it was prophesied that he would return before the coming of the Messiah, 'the great and terrible day of the Lord' (Malachi 4:*5*).

3 We know from our own experience how people's faces can be illuminated by their feelings. Love, joy and tenderness transfigure, just as the reverse emotions of hatred and revenge distort. In the past, and even to this day, people have also reported how the faces of deeply spiritual men and women at prayer have been made luminous by the intensity of their devotions. According to Exodus 34:*29–35*, for example, Moses' face shone after his encounter with God on Mount Sinai. So it is not impossible to visualise that Jesus' inner strength and commitment—the richness of his deeply-felt communion with God—was expressed by a kind of radiance in his face that was overwhelming to his three closest friends.

4 Those of you who have climbed up mountains in the English Lake District or elsewhere will know the feeling of exhilaration that comes when you reach the top. Climbers who have had to go through a curtain of clouds before reaching the summit, describe a strange experience of seeing their own shadows cast by the sun on the clouds below, each silhouette being surrounded by a halo of light—some have called it a 'glory'.

5 It is of course impossible to know what precisely happened, especially as Peter's description of it (if we agree that he is the source of Mark's gospel) is coloured by his expectations and interpretation. But the basis of the experience must have been the clearest possible recognition that Jesus was indeed the Son of God—the Christ, the Messiah, as Peter had openly acknowledged six days previously.

On the way down from the mountain, the disciples are told by Jesus not to talk about what they have seen until the Son of Man has risen from the dead. They do not understand the reference to a resurrection, although the title 'Son of Man' gives us a clue to Jesus' thinking (see *p* 13–14). However they ask Jesus a related question which obviously they must have heard from the Scribes, who implied that Jesus could not be the Messiah because Elijah had not yet returned. Jesus replies that Elijah has indeed come and the disciples understand that he has identified Elijah with John Baptist (Matthew 17:*13*). Elijah's life was threatened by the queen, Jezebel (1 Kings 19:*2, 10*) although she was not successful in her attempt to kill him. John did suffer martyrdom through the hatred of another queen, Herodias.

Discussion
What do you think might have been the experience of the disciples? How would you have described it?

Work
1 Add the John Baptist reference to your dossier about him and the part played by Peter to your study of his character.
2 Look upon the references in the Old Testament and see how men steeped in those traditions would express their own insights.
3 If you have not already done so, start making a list of the times when Jesus calls himself the Son of Man and note the implications of the title.

(b) The healing of an epileptic boy—Mark 9:*14-29*; Matthew 17:*14-21*; Luke 9:*37-43*

From the majestic beauty of the mountains, Jesus and his friends come down to a scene of human misery. The symptoms of the boy suggest what we now call epilepsy with suicidal tendencies. The disciples are helpless. Afterwards, when they question Jesus about their inability to heal the boy, Jesus says they have not prayed enough. For his own part, Jesus is saddened and angered by the whole situation but the father's courageous admission of his own limitations is rewarded by the complete cure of his son.

Work
Note the special reference to faith and add this to your list of healings, paying attention to the actual words of the father.

(c) The second prediction of his death—Mark 9:*30-32*; Matthew 17:*22-23*; Luke 9:*44-45*

Jesus is now moving south. His ministry in the north and in Galilee is over. Jerusalem is his goal. He wants to go quietly, partly because of the hostility of the authorities and partly because he wants to concentrate on his disciples, to prepare them, if he can, for what he believes to be the inevitable end of his ministry.

50

(d) True greatness; a lesson in tolerance and various instructions to the disciples—Mark 9:*33-50*; Matthew 18:*1-14*; Luke 9:*46-50*, 17:*1-3*

The disciples are still far from understanding the radical nature of the Kingdom. Jesus points out that, in his eyes, true greatness consists in service to others, a completely different concept from the world's (*cf* 10:*32-45*). In a kind of acted parable, Jesus then takes a little child who symbolises a type of helpless dependent at the bottom of the ladder of human success; yet this child is a person in its own right, worthy of respect. True greatness lies in having the perception to treat people as people, without classifying them as superior or inferior. Many people believe that Jesus' attitude towards children had a considerable influence in shaping society's future evaluation of childhood.

During the disciples' mission (6:*7-13*) John had apparently overheard another exorcist use Jesus' name and he had rebuked this man because he did not know him. But Jesus acknowledges that many do his work without necessarily understanding fully the source of their inspiration. In any case, his disciples must not be possessively concerned about their status in relation to Jesus. As he has clearly indicated, his is the way of compassion and unselfish service to others. All who walk this way walk in his company.

In sharp contrast, there is very strong condemnation of those who disturb or endanger others, especially if the victims are children or 'young in the faith'. There are seemingly harsh words too for the disciple who must be prepared to be disciplined and self-controlled about natural aptitudes and interests in order to discover the true life of the Kingdom. Of course, Jesus was not speaking literally—to lose a foot, a hand or an eye would be a great deprivation—his is the language of poetic metaphor used to point to the need to be selective, to forswear the immediate gain for the long term good. In words taken from Isaiah (66:*24*) he speaks of hell, literally 'Gehenna' a Greek term for the Jewish Valley of Hinnom to the south of Jerusalem. In Jesus' day it was an appalling rubbish tip continually burning, but it had once been a sacred site where human sacrifice had taken place to the Canaanite god, Moloch. The term 'Gehenna' had come to symbolise eternal punishment. For Jesus to use the word indicates that he believed there was a definite choice open to all men between fresh, creative life and extinction. Fire is the instrument of total destruction, so Jesus means that the man who refuses life in the fullest sense will, in the end, simply cease to exist. It is impossible to credit that Jesus meant that such a man is fated to eternal torment. (For a further discussion on hell fire, see *p* 142.)

Mark finishes these collected sayings with three more, probably grouped together because they all contain the word 'salt'. In their present context they are so enigmatic as to be almost unintelligible. One property of salt is to purify and preserve. Perhaps to be salted with fire is to experience difficulties and trials which can be used to refine one's character or which can strengthen and deepen the disciples' faith. Another property of salt is to give flavour. The disciple who has lost his point and purpose is as useless as salt when it becomes insipid. Thirdly, to the Arab salt signifies friendship, as in the saying 'There is salt between us'. So perhaps Jesus is saying in the last phrase, 'Keep your fellowship with each other in the fullness of life and peace'. In Matthew 5:*13*, there is a far easier and more relevant saying about salt.

Discussion
1 What do you know about other ancient peoples' attitude towards childhood? How influential do you consider the Christian church has been in bringing about such aspects of the welfare state as compulsory education and the protection of children?
2 How tolerant have Christians been either of each other's interpretations of Jesus' teaching or of other great world religions?
3 Can you think of modern situations to which the saying 'If your hand is your undoing, cut it off; it is better for you to enter life maimed than to keep both hands and go to hell' might be applied?
4 Is it possible to reconcile the idea of eternal torment with the teaching of Jesus; as contained in 2:*13–17*?

Work
Add to your subject list of the teaching of Jesus the references regarding true greatness and tolerance.

Chapter 10

(a) Jesus discusses the problem of marriage and divorce—Mark 10:*1-12;* Matthew 5:*27-28, 31-32,* 19:*1-12;* Luke 16:*18*

Jesus now leaves Galilee and crosses the Jordan. It is not clear where Mark intends him to be when he resumes his teaching ministry for a time. Looking at the map, you will see that the territories of Herod Antipas included both Galilee and Peraea, which lay across the Jordan. Further south lay Judaea, which was a Roman province. There were well-known pilgrim routes up to Jerusalem and it is very probable that Jesus, like other Palestinian Jews who practised their religion, went up to the sacred city three times a year for the feasts of Passover, Pentecost and Tabernacles. Mark implies that Jesus was well known both in Judaea and Transjordan as crowds gather to see him, so we deduce that this cannot have been his first visit to Jerusalem. On the other hand, Jesus by now may have been travelling with other Galileans; such pilgrims often made a detour via the Jordan to avoid Samaria, where sometimes Jews could encounter trouble. (Luke's account shows Jesus travelling through Samaria, not Transjordan, but he too brings Jesus to Jericho, in agreement with the Marcan narrative.)

Some Pharisees approach Jesus to ask his opinion on the question of divorce, a topic much debated at that time because of the divergent teaching of two famous Rabbis. In Deuteronomy (24:*1-4*) the law allowed a man to divorce his wife if he found 'some unseemly thing in her'. The Rabbi Shammai interpreted this clause to mean sexual infidelity, but the Rabbi Hillel said it could mean simply being a bad cook or some other failure of her domestic duties. According to Jewish law, a man could divorce his wife by a note of dismissal, but a woman had no legal rights in the matter at all.

The way in which Jesus deals with this question is important. It shows us that he is not interested, as a lawyer would be, in defining the terms of the law, but in rediscovering what lay behind the law—in other words, what was God's original intention in creating the sexual needs of men and women. He uses the parables in Genesis (1:*27* and 2:*24*) to show the principle underlying a real

53

marriage. In sexual intercourse two distinct individuals become one. This act of physical union is, therefore, a sacrament—an outward and visible sign of an inward, invisible total commitment of one person to another. In these circumstances, the relationship so entered into is on a permanent basis and takes priority over all other relationships, even that of one's obligations to one's parents. Moses' directive made realistic allowances for human weakness but was unjust to women, as Jesus makes clear in his conversation with the disciples afterwards.

In Jewish law a man could not commit adultery against his wife, only the woman against the man. If a man had sexual intercourse with another married woman he committed adultery against the second woman's husband but not against his own wife. Hence the inequality of the woman's status. In Roman law, a woman who was wealthy enough could divorce her husband, as obviously happened in the case of Herodias, whose second marriage to Herod Antipas aroused such bitter condemnation from John Baptist. Jesus however puts women on the same footing as men by saying that a man can commit adultery against his wife by divorcing her and marrying another woman just as a woman can commit adultery against her husband if she divorces him and marries another.

Note The terms adultery and fornication are technical ones—the first describes an act of sexual intercourse between a married person and someone who is not their wife or husband. The latter term means the act of sexual intercourse between those who are not legally married and who are therefore not breaking the formal bond of union and vow of fidelity which marriage entails.

It is important to note two points arising from this teaching of Jesus–

1 He did *not* say that divorce is always wrong. He simply stated the principle behind a true marriage according to his interpretation of God's original intention. He emphasises the act of union itself and does not mention the possible outcome of that union—children. When a marriage ceases to be the equal coming together in love of two people who share their life fully on a basis of trust and commitment, then separation can be a right means of preventing destructive attitudes such as possessiveness, exploitation, cruelty, and oppression. Jesus is emphasising that marriage should be entered into as a permanent, exclusive relationship in order to fulfil its true potentialities.

2 When Jesus is discussing adultery later with his disciples, we should be aware that he is emphasising the fundamental sexual equality between men and women; he is not giving an unnecessary further definition of adultery. If we remember that Jesus is at all

times interested in motivation and not legislation, except in the most general sense (that is, he interprets the law in terms of love), then we can more fully appreciate the revolutionary nature of his teaching. (For further discussion on this subject see Matthew 5:*31–32*.)

Discussion

Do you believe in marriage? In this so-called 'permissive' society, do you think the Christian ideal of a life-long, faithful, exclusive sexual relationship an impossibility or would you hope your own marriage might be like this?

Work

You should now be making a collection of Jesus' teaching about certain topics, so add this one to your list.

(b) The blessing of the children—Mark 10:*13–16*; Matthew 19:*13–15*; Luke 18:*15–17*

Although Jesus did not mention children in his discussion with the Pharisees about marriage and divorce, it is clear from this passage and a previous one (9:*36*) that Jesus loved children. Only in Mark is it recorded that Jesus took the children in his arms and was angry at the disciples' attempt to fob them off. After his previous teaching about the value of a child as a person, they should have known better. On this occasion Jesus goes even further. He says there is a quality in a child which an adult also needs if he is to belong to the Kingdom. Although it is not clear what Jesus meant by this it is not conceivable that he was talking about the 'innocence' which previous commentators have judged to be appropriate. For one thing, children are not necessarily innocent. For another 'innocence' is not at all a suitable adult attribute. The most outstanding quality in a child is its receptiveness. It is also, when loved, dependent and trustful in its relationships with the adult world. Perhaps Jesus is saying that the Kingdom is not for the proud and self-centred. It simply does not exist for those who have closed hearts and minds because they cannot see its implications. The next story is a precise illustration of just such an attitude.

(c) The rich young ruler and the danger of riches—Mark 10:*17–31*; Matthew 19:*16–30*; Luke 18:*18–30*

The title is a composite one from the three gospels (Luke says the enquirer was a ruler of the synagogue, Matthew that he was young). Jesus' question 'Why do you call me good? No one is good save God alone' may be interpreted that Jesus is aware of his own shortcomings. On the other hand, Jesus was probably challenging the man's conventional greeting in view of the tremendous demand which he later makes. 'Are your words flattery or do you recognise that I am from God?' The young man was an upright, zealous Jew who had kept all the commandments from boyhood but Jesus discerned his unconscious priority, as he so often did because of his compassionate response to people. He therefore suggests that the young man get rid of all his possessions, give the money to the poor and become his disciple. Unable to take this challenge, the questioner goes sorrowfully away.

Much saddened, Jesus discusses with the disciples how hard it is for a rich man to enter the Kingdom. He uses the camel and the eye of the needle as a picturesque hyperbole to describe the impossible. Riches protect and bolster one against difficulties, but they also deaden one's susceptibilities and give false security. The disciples, being very poor men, are astonished at Jesus' comment. Their own experience has led them to believe that it is far easier to be good when one wants nothing than when one is very much in need. If the rich cannot get into the Kingdom, what hope is there for the poor? But Jesus replies that this is not a question of human ability. It is God's Kingdom after all, as indeed—in Jesus' eyes at least—it is God's world. For men to enter the Kingdom and become its citizens, they must possess certain qualities which are neither the privilege of riches nor the reward of poverty as such.

In reply to a further question by Peter, Jesus reiterates that there is an essential fairness in God's dealings with men. We might say that there is a basic law of compensation which operates at the deepest level of human experience. As a man gives to life, so he receives from it, even if he does not recognise the terms of the giving and receiving. For the disciples of Jesus there will be the hardship, self-denial and persecution which come from utter dedication, but that is only half the picture. They will experience within the spiritual family which Jesus has created the love, friendship and security which the best of natural family life produces. They will also inherit eternal life. But they must remember that in the realm of God, human values as exemplified by the rich and powerful, are often reversed.

It is important to recognise that Jesus was not advocating the total abolition of wealth. He was making an immediate response to an individual's personal need. In a further story (Luke 19:*1–10*). he seems to be advising another rich man to use his riches with honest responsibility.

Discussion

1 Do you think that Jesus put too strong a challenge to the rich young ruler or can you imagine material possessions fading into

insigificance compared with the chance to take part in a decisive moment of human history?
2 Our century tends to think of achievement in technological, scientific terms such as being the first man on the moon or climbing Everest. How would you compare the distinction of being a disciple of Jesus, even if unknown by succeeding generations, to the outstanding successes recorded by twentieth century men and women?
3 How important is money to some people? Can you accept that acquiring and possessing wealth might wreck a person's chance of ultimate fulfilment?

Work
Note Jesus' stringent teaching about wealth but remember that we shall add several other incidents to the list before forming a comprehensive picture of his attitude.

(d) Jesus again predicts his death and deals with a request from James and John—Mark 10:32-45; Matthew 20:17-28; Luke 18:31-34 (Luke does not include the request of James and John but cf 22:24-27)

Somewhere along the road to Jerusalem, Jesus walks ahead of his friends. He is so wholly absorbed by his own thoughts that he is unapproachable. When he stops and talks to the disciples about his future prospects, they are quite unable to grasp the significance of his words. Even his closest companions, James and John, further sadden him by asking for the two chief places in the Kingdom—as people today might ask to become Chancellor of the Exchequer and the Foreign Secretary. Jesus uses strong Old Testament metaphors to describe the bitter suffering and death which he anticipates. Can they share in this with him? (For 'cup' see Isaiah 51:17,22 and Mark 14:36; for the general idea underlying 'baptism' see Psalms 42:7, 69:2,15, 124:4-5.) The disciples take him literally but even so the chief places are not in Jesus' gift. James was the first of the Apostles to be martyred by Herod Agrippa (Acts 12:1), but according to tradition John, after flogging and imprisonment, lived to a great age at Ephesus.

The anger of the other disciples when they heard about this incident shows that, despite his constant teaching, they also had no perception about the nature of Jesus' kingship. Jesus reiterates that although worldly greatness implies power and authority, in his Kingdom greatness means the ability to perceive and serve. Using his favourite way of speaking about himself, Jesus specifically states that he has come not to be served but to serve and 'to surrender his life as a ransom for many'. Here for the first time Jesus suggests a reason for believing that he must suffer and die. In Jesus' day a ransom was the purchase price for those condemned to slavery. Although modern kidnappings have made us familiar with the term and have highlighted the willingness of individuals to become substitute hostages so that other innocent people may go free from terrorist activity, we have to look very carefully at the imagery in Mark if we want to try and understand in what sense Jesus saw himself as a ransom. Certainly the 'many' must include Gentiles as well as Jews. However it does not seem consistent with Jesus' concept of his heavenly Father that he should think God was demanding the price of his life as a restitution for other men's sin, although he seems to have pondered much on Isaiah and sometimes saw his role in terms of the Suffering Servant of the Lord (Isaiah 53:*10*). Jesus was not prepared to stop teaching. He knew he had to declare the truth about God, his Kingdom and man's ultimate purpose and fulfilment, even if this led to his arrest and death. He believed that his willingness to give all that he had would show men the supreme importance of his convictions. He was also sure he would be vindicated in the end by the God whom he called 'Abba', Father, the creative source of life and love, if he lived out his principle of love to the ultimate. In some way, all this would act as a great liberating force for humanity, so that men could at last be free from the bondage of egotistical, blinding self-regard and passion. (For further discussion see Mark 14:*24*.)

Discussion
1 In what circumstances would you consider facing imprisonment or death for your beliefs?
2. Do you think every successful cause needs a martyr?
3 The idea that Jesus died to save us from our sins is often linked with this passage. Do you think that this link is justified and, if so, what do you understand by 'save us from our sins'?

(e) The healing of blind Bartimaeus—Mark 10:*46-52*; Matthew 20:*29-34*; Luke 18:*35-43*

Jesus has now crossed the Jordan again at the ford near Jericho. Mark tells us that he is accompanied by a great crowd, probably all pilgrims, walking the fifteen miles uphill to Jerusalem. All hint of secrecy about the messiahship has now gone and the blind man sitting in the beggars' pitch calls him 'Son of David', a definite messianic title with political overtones. Note the vivid details of this story, not least that we know the man's name, which suggests that he later became a disciple as *v*. 52 indicates. The cure is again a matter of faith and personal response to Jesus (*cf* 5:25–34 and 9:23–24).

Work
Add this healing to your list. Look up the other references to healings where 'faith' is specifically mentioned, including 2:5.

Chapter 11

(a) Jesus rides in triumph into Jerusalem—Mark 11:*1-11*; Matthew 21:*1-11*; Luke 19:*29-40*

Jesus has so far been taking every possible step to avoid a public declaration of his messiahship and yet here he is riding into Jerusalem in triumphal procession a few days before the most explosively nationalistic festival, when the city would be full of pilgrims who had come to keep the Passover. At such times the Roman garrison was at full strength in the Castle of Antonia, overlooking the temple precincts and the Roman governor was also in Jerusalem instead of at his usual residence in Caesarea. It seems Jesus has finally decided that there is nothing further to be gained by withholding his claim to be the Messiah. His task from now on is to show his people how his concept of messiahship is totally different from their own and to see whether they will then accept him as such.

Although this is the first visit of Jesus to Jerusalem recorded by Mark, it is obvious from the arrangements which Jesus makes to procure a colt from a nearby village that he has friends in the neighbourhood (*cf* 14:*3*). In the East the ass is held in high esteem. If a high official came upon a donkey, it symbolised he came in peace rather than in war, as horses were used for military purposes. The fact that the colt had not been ridden before meant that it was suitable for sacred purposes.

The great crowds greet Jesus joyfully. Their words echo Psalm 118:*25*— a psalm used at the Feast of Tabernacles when branches were waved. The Hebrew word 'Hosanna' is from the same psalm; it is really a prayer for help meaning 'save now' and addressed to God or to the King, but it could also be used as a triumphant shout of 'Hail'. Some sections of the crowd obviously see in Jesus the possible restoration of David's throne and national greatness, but Jesus is very careful to do nothing which could spark off violence. He goes straight to the Temple area, well within reach of the Roman garrison and the crowds disperse peacefully. According to Mark, Jesus is not actually staying in Jerusalem during the festival period but with friends at Bethany, where he goes that night (and so is able to return the colt as he had promised).

In Matthew's gospel, which was written perhaps some twenty years later, we can see what Jesus' disciples afterwards thought about this incident, for Matthew quotes from Zechariah 9:9 the prophecy which he considered Jesus had fulfilled:

'Rejoice greatly, O daughter of Zion; shout O daughter of Jerusalem: Behold, thy king cometh unto thee: He is just, and having salvation: Lowly, and riding upon an ass, even upon a colt, the foal of an ass.'

By choosing to enter Jerusalem on an ass, Jesus was demonstrating not only his peaceful intentions but his rejection of the Warrior King image. He is leading a revolution, but not in terms of physical armies.

Discussion

It is often said that this triumphal entry was the first of three acts of messianic symbolism (the cleansing of the Temple and the Last Supper being the other two). Looking at the text carefully, what do you think was Jesus' intention? Do you think it was a contradictory thing to do, or even dangerous in view of popular hopes and frustrations?

Work

You should make a note about the three major Jewish festivals together with information about the major religious and political parties. We shall discuss the Passover in more detail in Chapter 14.

(b) The cursing of the fig tree and the cleansing of the Temple—Mark 11:12-21; Matthew 21:12-22; Luke 19:45-48

The first story is very odd as it now stands. It seems totally out of character for Jesus to curse a fig tree petulantly, merely because it did not produce fruit out of season when he wanted it. In Israel figs are not ripe until June and this event took place in late March or early April. Mark explicitly comments on this because his Gentile readers might not know the climatic conditions of the Middle East.

Look now at the end of the section when Jesus and his friends are returning to Jerusalem the next day. The fig tree has perished.

There are two ways of interpreting this story:

1 That it was really a parable which Jesus told to illustrate the barrenness of Israel's religious practices. Jesus' strong action in cleansing the Temple (which follows this story) shows just how rotten was the Jewish religion at the very centre of its worship.

61

Perhaps a withered fig tree stood on the road from Bethany to Jerusalem. Jesus may have pointed to it when telling his story, or it may have become associated with the parable at a later date. (In Luke's gospel (13:6–9) there is a parable about a barren fig tree which is given a last chance to be fruitful before it is cut down and in Mark 13:28, Jesus uses the seasonal nature of the tree to point another lesson.)

2 Alternatively, it was a real happening when Jesus actually caused the tree to wither as an image of the unfruitful Israel. In this case, the episode becomes a symbolic act of judgment. Old Testament prophets sometimes used acted symbolism to demonstrate the righteous anger of God upon a sinful people. If this view is accepted, you must still ask the same questions as before. Did Jesus have this kind of power and, if he did, would he so have used it?

The practice of animal sacrifice was central to worship in the great Temple in Jerusalem (see sketch plan). The building consisted of a series of courtyards. First was the Court of the Gentiles, the only area where Gentiles could worship; within this area stood the temple building proper with its Courts for Jewish women, then the Court of Israel, finally the Court of the Priests and the Holy Place in which stood the altar of sacrifice. At the heart of the temple was the Holy of Holies, a perfect cube in shape, entered only once a year by the High Priest on the Day of Atonement. Within it stood the Ark of the Covenant, which contained the Ten Commandments and other sacred objects connected with Israel's past.

As sacrifices were offered daily, there was a market for the sale of animals, doves, oil and wine in the open area of the Court of the Gentiles and because the sacrificial objects could not be bought with Gentile money (especially if it bore the image of the Emperor) there were stalls of money changers. Since there was no fixed rate of exchange, pilgrims were cheated and robbed. The Temple was under the direct control of the Sadducees, the high priestly families, and they drew considerable profit from the market's operation.

Jesus is outraged both at the dishonest practices and the abuse of the Temple as a place of worship. He sweeps the Courtyard of the Gentiles clear of the traders and stops it being used as a thoroughfare. His reported spoken words on this occasion are taken from Isaiah 56:7 and Jeremiah 7:11. The moral authority required to effect such a cleansing is astonishing (only in John's gospel is it recorded that he made and used a whip). The Temple authorities were deeply angered and alarmed by Jesus' action. It was both a challenge to their position as religious leaders and a threat to their financial interests and those of the traders. Mark records it as the decisive moment when they resolve to take action to destroy Jesus, but they must wait their opportunity, for he has great popular support at this time.

In Matthew's gospel, Jesus cleansed the Temple directly after entering Jerusalem, but Mark's statement that a day had elapsed makes much better sense. With the crowds stirred to fever pitch of excitement by the triumphal entry, any immediate and dramatic act of violence by Jesus would have ended in serious disturbance.

Note Jesus' universalism. He cares that the Gentiles should have their proper place in God's house and condemns the narrow, nationalistic and materialistic outlook of the Jewish authorities.

Discussion

This is regarded by many as the second act of messianic symbolism; as it comes after the triumphal entry it could be intended to demonstrate what kind of a revolution Jesus wanted to bring about. Can you think of equivalent modern commercialisation of religion? In what ways do you think people's religious needs and hopes are exploited by some for monetary gain?

(c) Three sayings of Jesus about faith and prayer—Mark 11:22-25; Matthew 21:21-22

Possibly these sayings have been attached to the story of the fig tree at a later date. Jesus uses striking poetic imagery to express the conviction that faith can achieve the impossible and that there is no limit to the power of prayer; but he always stresses the need for the right attitude of heart and mind before we pray, pin-pointed by our willingness to forgive others and thus be forgiven by God. (Verse 26 is omitted from most manuscripts.)

Discussion

Some prayers are not answered, e.g. we pray that loved ones should get better from an illness and they subsequently die. People lose faith in consequence. What kind of things do you imagine Jesus meant us to pray for? (cf Matthew 6:9-13.)

(d) Jesus' authority is questioned by the Sanhedrin—Mark 11:27-33; Matthew 21:23-27; Luke 20:1-8

This is the first of a series of questions put to Jesus in the last days of his life. They are all interesting and significant. Having decided that they must get rid of him at all costs, the Jewish authorities first try to trick Jesus into some kind of damaging admission that could be used against him. The Sanhedrin, or Jewish Supreme

Council, was in charge of local administration in Judaea and it met in the Temple precincts. Its seventy members were made up of Sadducees, Pharisees and Scribes, who would be drawn from high priestly families and the Rabbinical schools. The Romans had given the Jews considerable independence in administering their own affairs, especially in religious matters.

The Temple authorities had every justification for asking Jesus by what right he cleared the Temple, but they hope to get from him a statement that he is the Messiah. Jesus is not prepared to given them a definite answer because he knows what they would make of it. His counter-question has direct bearing on the situation because John Baptist witnessed to the coming of the Messiah. The Sanhedrin are placed in an awkward dilemma. If they admit that John's mission was God-inspired, then they have answered their own question about Jesus. If they refuse to acknowledge that John was truly a prophet, then the ordinary people, being firmly convinced of John's mission, will turn against them. In the end they simply refuse to commit themselves either way and so does Jesus—on their terms anyway.

Work

1 Jewish religious discussion often used the method of question and counter-question; Jesus employs this way of provoking his opponents to think more deeply. Look up the other examples of this in 2:9,19,25; 3:4,23; 10:3.
2 Make a note on the Sanhedrin as part of your dossier about Jewish religious and political parties at the time of Jesus.

Chapter 12

(a) The parable of the Wicked Tenants—Mark 12:*1-12*; Matthew 21:*33-46*; Luke 20:*9-19*

Although Jesus did not directly answer the question of the San-hedrin reported in chapter 11, his reference to John Baptist implied that he considered himself to be the Messiah. In this parable he seems to make a strong attack upon the Jewish authorities on the basis of his claim to be God's Son. The details of the story suggest that it is more of an allegory than a parable (see ch. 4 for a discussion of these terms). Isaiah's song about a vineyard (5:*1-7*) was a well-known picture of Israel's religious barrenness, so Jesus' hearers would know that in his story the vineyard represents the nation and the owner is God. They would guess that the tenant-farmers to whom the vineyard was let are the religious leaders. In their less sophisticated era, rent was usually paid in kind rather than coinage. Here the produce of the vineyard stands for the right quality of life which God's people should be able to offer him in praise and gratitude but which would not be there if they were not getting the right kind of leadership. The servants are the prophets who so often were badly treated or even killed because their message was unacceptable; Jesus may indeed have had John Baptist in mind as the latest example of rejection. The owner's son is himself. Such is the Sanhedrin's hostility that Jesus senses that they are plotting his death.

The subsequent fate of the wicked tenants and the giving of the vineyard to others is an awful warning to the chief priests, the Scribes and the Pharisees. It seems that Jesus is deliberately saying—'If you proceed with your plan to kill me, disaster will fall upon you. God will end his Covenant with Israel and give it to others.' The early Christians believed they had become the new Israel, the true inheritors of the special Covenant relationship with God and they saw the Jewish revolt which ended in the destruction of Jerusalem by the Roman General Titus and his armies in AD70 as a fulfilment of Jesus' prophecy. So strong was this early tradition that some modern scholars have suggested it has coloured the narrative for later readers. Jesus may not have been alluding to himself at all in the parable, but simply issuing a stern warning to the religious leaders in view of their constant rejection of God's messengers. However Jesus was undoubtedly aware that the Jewish leaders either could not or would not accept his teaching and that the temper of his people was such that a further uprising against Rome was a strong possibility. Since he could not be party to an uprising, the disappointed hopes of many might contribute to his death.

In *v* 10 Jesus refers to Psalm 118:*22* (*cf* 11:*9*). The despised cornerstone in the original psalm was Israel, but Jesus is presumably applying the image to himself. Although the authorities may actively connive at his death, God will vindicate him in the end and upon him will be built another structure to the glory of God. At least this is how the early Christians interpreted the psalm (*cf* Acts 4:*11*, 1 Peter 2:7).

Discussion

If you look back to the beginning of ch. 11, you will see that a definite change has come over the situation. Jesus is avoiding neither publicity nor confrontation with the Jewish leaders. What do you think is his purpose in directly challenging them, even though he must know the possible outcome of such a course? (See also discussion on *p* 61.)

Work

This parable is often used as a good example of an allegory. Look up the relevant discussion (ch. 4) and compare the Wicked Tenants' story with the Parable of the Sower to see why they fall into the same category.

(b) The question about the tribute money—Mark 12: *13-17*; Matthew 22:*15-22*; Luke 20:*20-26*

In AD6 Archelaus, son of Herod the Great (see family tree) was deposed and Idumea, Samaria and Judaea, the area of which he was tetrarch, came under direct Roman rule. From that date onwards the inhabitants of Judaea had to pay a Roman tax in silver denarii which bore the name and likeness, or symbol, of the Emperor. The tax, which apparently went directly into the Emperor's private purse, was hated by the Jews and, according to Josephus the Jewish historian, had already sparked off one revolt by Judas the Galilean. The revolt was crushed but Josephus believed that Judas's followers were the originators of the extreme nationalist sect called the Zealots (see *p* xiii), who were the underground resistance movement against the Roman occupation of their country. The Zealots had strong links with the Pharisees.

The question put to Jesus was a deliberate trap. The mutually antagonistic Pharisees and Herodians had joined forces in Galilee to see how they could get rid of Jesus (see *p* 19) as they do again now in Jerusalem. If Herod Antipas had come up to the city for the Feast of the Passover, the Herodians would have accompanied him and were thus present in strength in the city at this time. They confronted Jesus with a dilemma. If he agreed it was lawful to pay Roman taxes, the Pharisees could denounce him to the people as being faithless to the cause of Jewish independence and sovereignty, whereas if Jesus declared that no tax should be paid, the Herodians could report him as a dangerous political agitator. Jesus sees their plan and skilfully avoids being wrongly compromised. He also takes the opportunity of teaching a subtle and important lesson. Man has a two-fold duty. As a member of an organised community or a citizen of a state he owes some allegiance to that community, city or state and should be prepared to be law-abiding (and pay his taxes!). However he also has a higher allegiance to God, or to his religious and ethical principles. In the Old Testament it is said that man is made in the image of God (Genesis 1:*26,27*). It is possible therefore that, with fine irony, Jesus is suggesting that man's first offering must be of himself to God. This would strike hard at the worldly Herodians, just as Jesus' recognition that law and order must be maintained would remind the Pharisees of their obligations.

Discussion
This saying of Jesus has been very much debated. People have argued about whether or not he was interested in politics and about whether it is right to oppose the irreligious claims of a state out of loyalty to man's first allegiance, i.e. his conscience. In the first centuries after Jesus, Christians found themselves having to refuse to worship the Emperor and were consequently persecuted. Christians have suffered the same fate from totalitarian regimes both in Nazi Germany and Marxist Russia. Today Christians in countries where there are oppressive governments, often join resistance movements to get rid of unjust structures, such as apartheid in South Africa. How do you interpret Jesus' meaning? Is it always right that a man should refuse to compromise his own moral and religious convictions when his government makes what he considers to be totally wrong demands upon him?

Work
Add this reference to your lists concerning the sects of Judaism and distinguish clearly the part played by the Pharisees and the Herodians.

(c) Is there a life-after-death?—Mark 12:18-27; Matthew 22:23-33; Luke 20:27-40

This is the only place in Mark where the Sadducees are directly mentioned (but *cf p*.62 and 64). Their name may have been derived from Zadok, priest in the time of David (2 Samuel 18:17). It was the custom for the priesthood to run in families and subsequently priestly lines appear to have claimed Zadok as their ancestor. The Sadducees were very traditional and old-fashioned in their religious ideas, believing only in the authority of the first five books of the Old Testament scriptures—the Jewish Torah and sacred kernel of the Law. They constantly disputed with the Pharisees over the matter of life-after-death and angels, which they could not credit; they believed a man lived on only in the blood of his descendants. As the Sadducees held office through Roman patronage, they supported a measure of co-operation with Rome and did not nurse messianic hopes. On the contrary, they feared this kind of popular enthusiasm and expectation, seeing only the ruin it could bring to the Jewish people, thus they would be both suspicious and fearful of Jesus. After his public acts of riding triumphantly into Jerusalem and cleansing the Temple, followed by the Parable of the Wicked Tenants and his veiled claim to messiahship, the Sadducees were probably the chief instigators of plans to silence him.

The ridiculous question they ask was based on Deuteronomy 25:5-10, according to which, if a man died childless, it was the duty of his brother to marry his wife. The first child born of this second marriage would be the dead brother's heir. In postulating one woman, seven brothers, no children and the question whose wife was she at the resurrection, they perhaps hope to get a cheap laugh at Jesus' expense. However he uses the occasion to make a very important statement, but first he shows the Sadducees that they are ignorant both of the scriptures and the power of God. There is a life-after-death, but conditions in that life are very different from this one. After death, the procreative side of marriage is no longer necessary. The physical body is translated into a spiritual body which presumably is of the substance of angels. And to substantiate his belief in life-after-death, Jesus quotes from the second book of the Old Testament, Exodus (3:6) whose authority the Sadducees recognised. At the call of Moses, God declares himself the God of the patriarchs. From this Jesus deduces that the patriarchs still exist for their relationship with God continued even though they had lived centuries before Moses.

Discussion
Do you believe in life-after-death? The Christian does so, partly

because of these sayings of Jesus and partly because of the evidence which convinces him that Jesus himself rose from the dead (see *p* 89f).

Work

Add the Sadducees to your summary of the various sects in New Testament times, making note of their special beliefs and the type of question they asked Jesus.

(d) Which is the chief commandment?—Mark 12:*28–34*; Matthew 20:*34–40*; Luke 10:*25–37*

The Rabbis counted 613 commandments of Law and hotly debated whether or not all were equal in merit. Roughly speaking, the law was divided into two sections. Ritual instructions dealt with such things as food regulations, priestly garments and religious rites in worship, while ethical or moral commandments concerned the prohibitions against murder, theft, adultery and so on. The Scribe may have been perfectly sincere in asking whether Jesus thought some laws more important than others and agreed with shortening the law. Certainly Jesus answers with great clarity and authority. He summarises the whole duty of man in terms of love, both in whole-hearted devotion to the one true God and in responsible concern for his fellow men (Deuteronomy 6:*4–5*; Leviticus 19:*18*). The Scribe's enthusiastic response to Jesus' declaration shows that he has the perception to understand the nature of the Kingdom as Jesus taught it.

In Luke's gospel (10:*25–28*) the Scribe asks 'who is my neighbour?' and Jesus replies with the parable of the Good Samaritan. Love dictates that anyone in need is my neighbour.

Discussion

'To love your neighbour as yourself' means that there is a proper place for self-respect and even self-love, but the value you put upon your own happiness should be the value you put upon other people's happiness too. Is the universal application of this law a practical possibility? What difference would it make to society if this ideal were realised?

Work

Add this reference to your notes about the Scribes, as this example shows how Jesus could praise a discerning lawyer even if he was critical of the class as a whole (see (f) below).

(e) Who is the Messiah?—Mark 12:*35-37*; Matthew 22:*41-46*; Luke 20:*41-44*

After Jesus has been asked all these questions, he decides to question his listeners. Using Psalm 110:*1*, which was thought to be written by David and considered to have messianic implications, Jesus asks 'how do you reconcile these two ideas of messiahship when he is described both as David's son and therefore subservient to him, and David's Lord, consequently greater than him?' When nobody answered him, Jesus left the question unsolved, although he himself was the answer. It is not quite clear why Jesus asked this question unless he wished to direct people's attention away from the political Son of David concept of messiahship.

(f) A warning against the Scribes—Mark 12:*38-40*; Matthew 23:*1-36*; Luke 11:*37-54*; 20:*45-47*

Jesus issues a strongly-worded condemnation of various habits of lawyers. They are guilty of spiritual pride and vanity, because they love the public respect which their office and dress give them and the chief seats in synagogues and feasts. But more cruelly they make a profit at the expense of the defenceless widow, whilst saying long prayers for the sake of appearances. Because they are in positions of privilege and responsibility, they will be all the more severely judged by God. Luke (11:*37-54*) and Matthew (23:*1-36*) give a more detailed account of Jesus' criticism (see p 153 and p 138).

(g) The widow's gift—Mark 12:*41-44*; Luke 21:*1-4*

It does not take too great a stretch of the imagination to understand why Jesus was aware of widows' needs and responsibilities. From all accounts, Mary was a widow when Jesus reached manhood. Here is a poignant little story which contrasts sharply with the previous incident. The Treasury, consisting of thirteen large trumpet boxes for donations, stood in the Courtyard of the Gentiles. You had to declare the amount you gave as you put in your gift. Jesus' observant gaze had spotted a very poor widow. The meaning of his comment to the disciples is crystal clear. The greatest gift is that which costs the giver most. Our generosity is measured not by the amount we give but by the spirit in which we give it.

Discussion
How would you define both hypocrisy and generosity? To what extent do you think they are present in modern society?

70

Work

Add Jesus' condemnation of the Scribes to your notes about this class of person and the comment of Jesus about generosity to your summaries on his teaching topics.

Chapter 13

The Apocalyptic Discourse—Mark 13:*1-37*; Matthew 24:*1-51*; Luke 21:*5-38*

For modern students this is the strangest chapter in Mark's gospel because it belongs to a class of literature which, although topical in its basic ideas, nevertheless has odd and unfamiliar ways of expressing them. Apocalypse is a Greek word which means an unveiling of the future; the Latin word with the same meaning, revelation, is much more widely used.

Jewish apocalyptic writing flourished for several centuries when life under tyranny and oppression seemed particularly hard to bear. The Old Testament book of Daniel (*cf p* 14) is probably the oldest complete apocalyptic writing, produced sometime between 167 and 165BC. At this time the Syrian king, Antiochus IV, attempted to stamp out the Jewish religion. He styled himself Antiochus Epiphanes ('illustrious' or 'notable') because he wanted to be worshipped as a god by his people. In 168BC he issued an edict imposing certain pagan rites on the people and he set up an image of the Greek god, Zeus, on the great altar of burnt offering in the Temple court. The sacred scriptures were destroyed and the practice of circumcision was forbidden on pain of death. This was the first real religious persecution which the Jewish people had suffered. Some reacted in open resistance and armed rebellion, others were prepared to be martyred rather than deny their ancient faith; inevitably some compromised. The book of Daniel could be described as underground resistance literature, written to give heart and courage to those who were determined to be faithful at all costs. God was still the Lord of history, even though his loyal people were suffering terrible things. He would intervene and establish his Kingdom. Those who had died in a just cause would be resurrected and live for ever.

Jewish apocalyptic writing was very popular also during the time of Roman occupation but it eventually died out after AD138, the date of the last Jewish uprising against Rome. Because the Christians suffered severe persecution at various periods from the times of Emperor Nero (AD64–5) onwards for three hundred years until the reign of Constantine, they took up this kind of writing, the book of Revelation in the New Testament being the most famous example. When Christianity eventually became the established religion of the Roman Empire, no more Apocalypses were written.

It is important to remember several points arising out of this brief historical survey:

1 Jewish ideas of the value of martyrdom first took shape under persecution. To be willing to die for your faith rather than give up its practice is quite different from being prepared to fight in armed conflict, but the former was regarded as equally effective in God's eyes and rewarded by him accordingly.

2 The final outcome of the conflict between good and evil (that is, the battle between those who kept faith and those who persecuted them for doing so) would eventually be resolved by God himself, not by human action, therefore armed resistance probably was not the way to hasten the coming of God's vindication of his people.

3 Jesus himself knew and quoted from Daniel; he identified himself with the faithful remnant, the 'Saints of the Most High' (*cf p* 14) but his views were more complex (*cf p* 57–58) and he apparently saw clearly that rebellion against Rome was doomed to failure.

4 Under martyrdom and persecution the early Christians desperately needed assurance that this was the way their master had laid down for them, not only by his own actions and death but also by his words. They had to believe that he had foreseen their troubles and knew the final outcome of their loyalty.

5 Those first Christians (*cf p* xiv) were convinced that God would act very soon—probably in their own lifetime—to bring the whole historical process to an end. Jesus would return in glory and establish his Kingdom for ever. At first this was thought to be an actual earthly Kingdom, but later it became a spiritual concept. (Two Greek words are associated with these ideas: 'Parousia' which means 'arrival' and is linked with the second coming of the Christ and his abiding presence and 'Eschatology' coming from 'eschatos'—'the end' which stands for the end of all things in the world and therefore death and judgment.)

There is a further problem connected with ch. 13. How much or little did Jesus actually say of this discourse? Some scholars think that it is all the composition of a Jewish-Christian writer, possibly Mark. Others believe that at least part of the discourse was actually spoken by Jesus, probably verses 1, 2, 9–11, 15–22, 28–37; these verses were later woven into an already existing Jewish-Christian apocalyptic writing which was included by Mark in his gospel in good faith. Others consider that Jesus said it all, just as it stands. The majority of scholars hold the middle view, which is the one I shall assume to be correct. The language of these verses fits in with the way in which Jesus talks elsewhere in the gospels. The other verses contain images and symbols very like those found in the book of Daniel. Jesus did have prophetic insight; we might describe him as an unusually sensitive and very perceptive man. He saw that if his people rejected the way of moral and spiritual change and chose instead war against Rome, the consequences would be disastrous. He also knew that if he himself were killed, his disciples would inevitably be persecuted. It is hard to credit that he prophesied his own 'second coming in glory' in the materialistic way his disciples mistakenly anticipated or that he felt the end of the world was near.

(a) **Verses 1–4: (probably authentic).** When the disciples admire the Temple building, Jesus tells them that it will be destroyed. Begun in 20–19BC by Herod the Great and not completely finished until AD62–64, it was destroyed after the siege of Jerusalem in AD70 (*cf p* 65). When his four closest friends ask Jesus for the sign that will herald these events, he does not answer directly.

(b) **Verses 5–8: A warning about false Messiahs who will lead men astray.** The last of several uprisings (AD132–138) was led by Bar Cochba, a messianic claimant, called by his followers 'Star out of Jacob'. Wars, earthquakes (AD61, 62) and famines (AD46, Acts 11:28) were numerous in the first century AD. Here they are all linked with the coming of the New Age.

(c) **Verses 9–11: (probably authentic).** The disciples will suffer severe persecution from both the civil authorities and the Jews but it will be an opportunity to witness to the truth of the gospel and they will be given the courage and the ability to do this by the indwelling Spirit. The mention of 'the end' which would not be reached before the gospel had been proclaimed to all nations may perhaps indicate that Jesus did visualise a sudden ending of the world by an act of God. Beyond doubt it shows his concern for all men.

(d) **Verses 12–13:** Families will be split in two by divided loyalties but faithfulness to Christ will bring its own reward.

(e) **Verses 14–23:** The term 'abomination of desolation' comes from Daniel (9:27, 11:31, 12:11) where it refers to the outrage to the Temple by Antiochus IV. The warning of a further desecration could refer to the attempt by the Roman Emperor, Caligula, to put a statue of himself in the Temple in AD38–40, in which case it is an addition to Jesus' actual words. However it could possibly refer to the total destruction of the Temple by the Romans at some future date. The time of disaster will come suddenly and will bring intense suffering. In vivid poetic metaphors, Jesus warns his disciples to flee to the hills. (In fact Christian Jews did leave Jerusalem at the outbreak of the Jewish war and so many of them were saved.) For the sake of those who have responded to God through the challenge of Jesus, the time of intense suffering will be shortened. This echoes the theme found in the Suffering Servant Songs of Isaiah—by their quality of life, the few upright good men can affect the fate of the many.

(f) Verses 24–27: A prediction of the end of the world and of the second coming of the Son of Man taken from Daniel 7:*13* (*cf p 82*).

(g) Verses 28–37: The theme is watchfulness in view of the crisis created by the rejection of Jesus. Just as the disciples can observe the coming of spring through nature, so they must interpret the political signs, because disaster will strike in their lifetime. However in *v.* 32, Jesus emphatically disclaims personal knowledge about when the end of the world will come. Such knowledge belongs only to God, the Father.

Then the theme of alertness returns and the passage concludes with the parable of the absent householder whose servants must always be ready for his homecoming, as the disciples also must be prepared for the return of their master.

Discussion
1 No doubt many of you read your horoscopes or are interested in science fiction. What are the differences and similarities between the modern 'unveiling of the future' and the ancient Jewish-Christian method?
2 At least two contemporary religious sects believe the end of the world will come before the turn of the century. Do you know anything about them and on what they base their ideas about the future?

Chapter 14

(a) The Sanhedrin conspire to arrest Jesus—Mark 14: 1-2; Matthew 26:1-5; Luke 22:1-2

Mark reports that on the Wednesday of this momentous week, when all their other plans to entrap Jesus have failed, the Sanhedrin decide to make a private arrest of him. An open arrest would have been unwise because many of Jesus' Galilean sympathisers were in Jerusalem for the Passover Festival. In these circumstances a public seizure might provoke a riot or worse, thus involving the Romans. However due to the treachery of Judas, the Sanhedrin are able to take Jesus sooner than they had anticipated.

(b) The anointing at Bethany—Mark 14:3-9; Matthew 26:6-13

There are difficulties about this highly emotional story. The textual problem is that Luke does not mention this story at all but includes a different version which occurs early in Jesus' ministry. The woman concerned is a prostitute and furthermore Jesus is in the house of a Pharisee called Simon who is very critical of him (Luke 7:36-50). On the other hand John tells us (John 12:1-8) that Mary the sister of Martha and Lazarus, anointed Jesus' feet at their home in Bethany six days before the Passover. In this story it is Judas who grumbles about the waste. Mark does not name the woman who anoints Jesus' head in the house of Simon the leper (presumably he has been cured by Jesus). Jesus answers the disciples' angry comment by praising the woman for her courageous, costly and intuitive act of love. Somehow she has sensed that his death is imminent. (It was customary to anoint the body for burial.) In this special context it is not meaningful to contrast her extravagant gesture of love with the continuing plight of the poor. When love discerns an individual's specific need, it will endeavour to meet it.

(c) Judas' treachery—Mark 14:10-11; Matthew 26:14-16; Luke 22:3-6

Judas' betrayal is starkly portrayed in direct contrast to the woman's love. He probably told the Council where and when Jesus might be taken secretly and also that Jesus had privately admitted to being the Messiah. Matthew tells us that Judas was paid 30 pieces of silver (the possible price of a slave) for the information. No indication of Judas' motives is given, although John says Judas was a thief and Luke attributes his treachery to Satanic possession. He may have been disillusioned because Jesus was not turning out to be the kind of Messiah he expected, either as a rebel leader or as a righteous keeper of the law. It has also been suggested that by bringing about a direct confrontation between Jesus and the authorities, Judas was trying to force Jesus into definite action. If this is correct, Judas in no way meant Jesus to die and was filled with bitter remorse when things did not turn out as he had anticipated. Certainly according to Matthew (Matthew 27:3–10), when Judas realised Jesus was going to die, he went to the Council and tried to 'buy Jesus back'. When he failed, he committed suicide.

Apparently, Judas was the only non-Galilean member of the twelve. Perhaps he felt obscurely jealous, resentful or even confused as to the nature of Jesus' messiahship. Some people have believed that he was fated or 'pre-determined' to betray Jesus, but to accept this view is to deny that man has free-will.

Discussion

1 Did you think Jesus' comment about the poor sounded rather cynical? Did it surprise you? How would you have reacted to the situation had you been there? Can you think of a contemporary parallel where an extravagant personal gesture might be justified?
2 Why do you think Judas betrayed Jesus?

(d) Preparations for the Passover—Mark 14:12–16; Matthew 26:17–19; Luke 22:7–13

Luke tells us that it was Peter and John whom Jesus sent into the city and it is probable that the Last Supper was held at the house of Mary, mother of John Mark. It was important to Jesus that Judas did not know beforehand where the festival was to be held. He did not want to be arrested before the Last Supper. Women were the water-carriers, so the unusual sight of a man doing that task would be a prearranged signal. Preparations would also involve obtaining the paschal lamb (one for each household) from the Temple, where it would have been ritually killed.

(e) The Last Supper—Mark 14:17–25; Matthew 26:20–29; Luke 22:14–38

The Passover meal is presided over by the master of the house before whom are placed four cups of wine. The first is called the

Cup of Consecration and when it is blessed, it is passed round to all present. On the table are the roasted lamb, the unleavened bread (rather like water biscuits because no yeast has been used), bitter herbs, and the charoseth or sauce. The master dips morsels of bread into the sauce dish and gives a portion to each member of the family. The second cup of wine is then poured out and the youngest person present asks the meaning of the festival, to which the master replies by telling the story of the Exodus. This is known as the 'Haggadah' or 'showing forth'. The Passover Hymn or 'Hallel' consists of Psalms 113–118, the first part of which can be sung during the meal. Grace is said over the unleavened cakes which are broken and handed round; the lamb is eaten and then the third cup—that of Blessing—is shared. After the thanksgiving, the fourth cup—of Joy—is drunk and the rest of the Hallel is sung.

Possibly the Passover Festival goes back to very ancient times when shepherds offered the first-born of their flocks to God as a thank-offering in the Spring. In later Israelite history this feast became associated with the deliverance of the Hebrew tribes from Egypt. The earliest Old Testament account of the institution of the festival is in Exodus (12:*1–28*) from which can be seen how the Feast of Unleavened Bread became associated with the Passover, although they must once have been quite separate. In Jesus' day the two Feasts were celebrated during the eight days from 14th–21st Nisan, Nisan being the first month in the Jewish calendar.

There is some difference of opinion over whether or not the Last Supper was a Passover meal. On this occasion the Passover fell on a Sabbath, so strictly speaking the meal should have been eaten on the Friday evening. (The Jews counted the beginning of a new day from after sunset at 6 p.m.) Some Jews might have preferred to keep the Passover separate from the Sabbath and therefore would have eaten the meal the day before, which is what Jesus may have done. At first it seems surprising that the lamb is not mentioned in the synoptic gospels, but John's gospel clearly indicates that the Last Supper was held the day before the lambs were ritually killed in the Temple. It has therefore been suggested that what Jesus and his disciples celebrated was a Chaburah meal, when a group of friends met together for social and religious fellowship. The synoptic gospels however all strongly indicate the Passover setting for the Last Supper.

In Mark, Jesus simply says that the traitor is in the room with them, much to the dismay of the disciples. In telling Judas that he knows (in Matthew the reference is quite specific) and in warning him of the terrible consequences of such a betrayal, Jesus is making a last appeal of love to Judas, while leaving him free to act as he wills. When Jesus interprets his forthcoming death as foretold in the scriptures he has the Suffering Servant Song of Isaiah 53 in mind (cf p 58).

In describing the bread and the wine as his body and blood, Jesus in using sacrificial language which would be less strange to a Jew at Passover time than to us. For the Jew the blood of the animal is sacred because it contains the life principle (cf Genesis 9:4) and therefore may not be eaten but must be offered to God, hence 'kosher' (purified) meat, from which the blood has been drained. Nevertheless, Jesus must have deeply disturbed his friends for they would realise he meant that the giving of himself—in ritualistic terms as a kind of sacrifice—would establish a new relationship between man and God.

When Moses brought the Israelites out of Egypt to Mount Sinai, they entered into a solemn Covenant with God. On this occasion the Ten Commandments were given (or so we read in Exodus 20) and in the actual Covenant Ceremony described in Exodus 24:1–8, the blood of a sacrificed animal was used as a symbol binding God and Israel together. The Israelites continually failed to keep their part of the Covenant and, as Jesus warned in his Parable of the Wicked Tenants, if the Jewish leadership persisted in their plan to kill him, God would end his special relationship with Israel and give it to others.

Jesus now clearly saw that his ministry was going to end abruptly by his being put to death but he believed it would inaugurate a new era between man and God. This does not imply that Jesus actually thought of his death as a restitution for his people's sins (cf p 57–58) as the Jewish sacrificial system and laws attempted to deal with the nation's shortcomings. It means rather that through his life, teaching and his courageous acceptance of his death, men would better understand the true nature of God and his expectations of them, leading to a new orientation of their lives. If God is love, then love is the creative principle in the universe and God's total law could be summed up in terms of love (see p 69). In his willingness to die for what he believed to be the truth and by overcoming hatred, fear and envy in himself, Jesus demonstrated the power of a sacrificial love that was prepared to give everything for the sake of others. It was this kind of love which must become the basis of the new community which Jesus founded and the terms of the new relationship between man and God. By asking his friends to accept the consecrated bread and wine as a symbol of his self-offering, Jesus was inviting them to share in the inauguration of this new Covenant. Then, finally, in this tense situation, he makes a solemn vow, the purpose of which is not clear, that he will not touch wine again until he drinks it new in the Kingdom of God.

The early Christians met together regularly on the first day of the week—the day of Jesus' resurrection—and 'broke bread' together (see Paul's letter 1 Corinthians 11:23–26) probably repeating Jesus' own words. This is the origin of the Christian sacramental service variously called The Lord's Supper, Holy Communion, the Eucharist and the Mass (from the Latin words at the end of the service, when the congregation is 'sent out' to do God's will).

Discussion

1 All Christian denominations, except the Quakers, keep the Lord's Supper in some way. The Quakers believe that Jesus did not mean to institute a separate religious rite, but that every time his followers meet together to 'break bread' he is there. How do you think Jesus intended his disciples to remember the occasion?
2 This service is the source of fellowship between Christians and their Lord, but it has also been the keenest controversial issue in the church, splitting Catholic from Anglican and Anglican from Free churchman. In what way do you think these divisions might now be healed?
3 Animal sacrifice is no longer part of Judaism. It disappeared when the Temple was destroyed. But Christians have never felt it had any part in their worship. What aspect of Jesus' teaching was responsible for this conviction?

(f) On the way to Gethsemane—Mark 14:26–31; Matthew 26:30–35; Luke 22:39

After singing the rest of the Passover Hymn, Jesus and the disciples go out of the city to the Mount of Olives, which lies across the Kedron Valley, not far from the walls of Jerusalem. Jesus seems to know that all his friends will desert him at the final confrontation with the Jewish leaders and he quotes from Zechariah 13:7; they will be like sheep when the shepherd is struck down. Nevertheless Jesus had the courage and faith to predict his own return to them in Galilee. Peter valiantly protests his undying loyalty but Jesus knows both the strength and weakness of Peter's character. Cock crow came at the first sign of dawn.

(g) The Garden of Gethsemane—Mark 14:32–42; Matthew 26:36–46; Luke 22:39–46

As they near the olive grove called Gethsemane Jesus feels intense need of prayer. He leaves eight of his disciples on the fringe of the grove and takes with him his three closest friends. A deadly desolation of spirit comes upon Jesus, something of which he shares with the other three men, perhaps expressing it in terms of Psalm

88:3–4. Asking them to stay awake, he moves away to pray, but not too far, for they hear his words. In a desperate appeal to God, who is addressed very intimately as Father (Mark gives us the Aramaic word—Abba) Jesus asks for another way to be found to avoid the agony ('cup' 10:39). This is the return of an old temptation, messiahship without suffering and death (cf Luke 4:1–13) but even at this lowest ebb Jesus accepts the Father's will. When he comes back the three friends have fallen asleep (Luke says they were worn out by grief). He wakes them up and goes away again to return once more and find them sleeping. The third time he hears the approaching soldiers and summons his disciples to go forward to meet them.

(h) The arrest—Mark 14:43–52; Matthew 26:47–56; Luke 22:47–53

The Jewish council—the Sanhedrin—possessed the power to arrest and they had collected together an armed band of men led by Judas. In the darkness Judas must have said, 'The one I kiss is your man'. Jesus offers no resistance, but one of his followers (John says it was Peter) draws his sword and cuts off the ear of the high priest's servant (John gives his name as Malchus). Jesus' words imply that he has been teaching for quite some time in the Temple, but they did not then regard him as a guerilla leader. He sees his arrest as a fulfilment of scripture—possibly Psalm 41:9 regarding the desertion of the disciples and Isaiah 53 regarding the general situation.

Neither Matthew nor Luke thought it worthwhile to include v 51–2, probably because the incident seemed so trivial. The only reasonable explanation for Mark's inclusion of it is that he himself was the young man in question. If the Last Supper had been held in his mother's house, Judas might have taken the soldiers there first, thus rousing Mark who had run to the garden to warn Jesus.

(i) The trial before the Sanhedrin—Mark 14:53–65; Matthew 26:57–68

The whole question of Jesus' trial by the Jewish authorities is of difficulties which are too complex to go into thoroughly Briefly, according to Jewish law the Council could meet only the hours of daylight. It is probable that in Jesus' day they even have the authority to try serious offences without permission and that only the Roman Governor had the execute the death sentence. According to Deuteronom man could not be convicted on the unsupported evidenc witness and, strictly speaking, a prisoner could not be condemned on his own admission alone.

Luke tells us that the Sanhedrin did not meet until the following morning (Luke 22:66) and John simply reports a private investigation conducted by Annas (the deposed High Priest) and a further reference of the case to Caiaphas, the actual High Priest at the time and son-in-law of Annas (John 18:12–24). It is probably most reasonable, therefore, to describe the Jewish leaders' action as a preliminary enquiry in order to have something definite to present to Pilate for the official trial, although Mark (followed by Matthew) depicts the proceedings as a full Council meeting.

According to Mark, Jesus had predicted the destruction of the Jerusalem Temple (13:2), while John says (John 2:19) he invited the authorities to destroy the Temple and he would raise it up in three days but he was referring to himself, not the Temple building! According to Matthew, when the High Priest finds the investigation getting nowhere, he puts Jesus on oath and asks him the direct question about his claim to messiahship (Matthew 26:63). Jesus acknowledges that he is the Christ but expresses his messiahship in terms of the 'Son of Man' and using words taken from Daniel 7:13 and Psalm 110:1 he declares his faith that God will entirely vindicate his cause even though everything is apparently in ruins. This admission is enough for the High Priest to go through the formal act of condemnation when a man is convicted of blasphemy. The Council now feel they have a case to present to Pilate since the claim to be King of the Jews could be turned into a political charge. Jesus is then blind-folded and mocked by the guards.

(j) Peter's denials—Mark 14:54, 66–72; Matthew 26:58, 69–75; Luke 22:54–62

This story must originate with Peter himself. If he had wounded the High Priest's servant, it needed considerable courage to follow Jesus into the courtyard of the High Priest. He first sits by the fire in the courtyard then, after the servant girl's challenge, he moves into the porch where it would be darker and colder but the girl sees him again and again he denies all knowledge of Jesus. Finally he is recognised as a Galilean by his accent and challenged by a group of bystanders, whereupon his self-control breaks down and he begins to curse and to swear that he knows nothing of Jesus.

Discussion

~hat way does the scene in Gethsemane help to deepen your
`·~n of Jesus' humanity?
`'s actions in this chapter fit in with the impressions

you have formed about his character so far? To what extent do you sympathise with or despise him?

Work
1 Make a note of the Passover Festival and also the various Jewish legal points surrounding the details of Jesus' interrogation by the Sanhedrin.
2 Look up the Old Testament references to the Passover and also the account of Jesus' 'trial' by the Jewish authorities in John's gospel.

Chapter 15

(a) The trial before Pilate—Mark 15:*1–20*; Matthew 27:*11–31*; Luke 23:*1–25*

The Sanhedrin meet again at dawn, thus legalising their decision of the previous night. The charge of blasphemy is turned into one of treason, the only one in which a Roman governor would be interested. (According to Luke 23:*1–5*, the Sanhedrin meet only once, at dawn. He gives details of the specific charges laid against Jesus by the Jewish authorities.) When Pilate questions Jesus, he gives a non-committal answer—'I would not express it like that,' which is made clearer by John's account of the proceedings (John 18:*36*), 'My kingdom is not of this world.' Pilate is astonished that Jesus makes no further attempt to answer the accusations brought against him. (For further discussion of this scene see Luke 23:*1–25*.)

According to Mark, on a great occasion like the Passover it was a usual custom for the Roman Governor to grant a favour to the subject people by releasing a political prisoner. There is really very little external evidence to support Mark's statement. Maybe the particular case of Barabbas' release was later construed as a general practice. It has been suggested that the crowd assembled before the governor's palace had actually gathered to petition for Barabbas' release. According to Matthew (27:*17*), the rebel leader's name was Jesus, son of Abbas (Bar meaning 'son of'). Mark seems to take for granted that his readers know not only who this man was but also the insurrection with which he was associated. He also indicates that Pilate was aware of the malice of the chief priests and made some weak attempt to protest that Jesus is innocent but gave in to the clamour of the mob. Pilate was procurator of Judaea from AD26–36 and, according to Jewish writers of the New Testament period, was 'inflexible, merciless and obstinate'. However for political reasons, it was important for Mark to blame the Jews, not the Roman Governor, for the death of Jesus. Luke makes this same point even more strongly.

A Roman flogging was a terrible ordeal as the leather thongs were weighted with bits of metal or wood. John represents Jesus as being flogged *before* Pilate's final condemnation—a usual procedure with slaves. Before they reclothe Jesus, the soldiers dress him up in mock regalia, probably a soldier's red cloak and a crown made of thorns.

Discussion

1 How would you account for the changed attitude of the people welcoming Jesus on Palm Sunday and then crying out for his crucifixion? Bear in mind that Jesus' Galilean supporters were probably not present at the governor's palace.
2 A Jewish historian recently maintained that the gospels deliberately white-washed the Romans' part in the trial and death of Jesus and that the Jews were far less responsible that is suggested. After looking at all the mixed motives in the case, who do you think was to blame for Jesus' death?

(b) The crucifixion, death and burial of Jesus—Mark 15:*21-47*; Matthew 27:*32-61*; Luke 23:*26-56*

The Romans customarily executed slaves and criminals by crucifixion. (A Roman citizen had the right to die by the sword!) The criminal carried the cross-bar to the place of execution. He was then nailed or fastened by ropes to the upright post and left to die of exposure. Like the old English practice of hanging a man on a gibbet at a cross roads, crucifixion was meant as a horrible deterrent. The nature of the crime was written on the cross.

Simon of Cyrene, in North Africa, may have been visiting Jerusalem for the Passover. As Mark names his two sons, they were presumably well-known to the Christian church in Rome, which suggests that Simon himself became a Christian.

Jesus is crucified at Golgotha (Latin name—Calvary) a skull-shaped mount outside the city; it is impossible now to be sure of the site. The drugged wine was a gift from some charitable women of Jerusalem to convicted criminals, but Jesus refuses to drink it, perhaps because he wants to keep his mind clear. He is crucified at 9 a.m. and, according to custom, the soldiers cast lots for the criminal's clothes as a man was crucified naked. It is likely that the two hanging on either side of Jesus were accomplices of Barabbas. The passersby, the chief priests, the Scribes and even the two crucified men, jeer (although according to Luke one turns to Jesus). Their taunts are echoes of the trial scene and the claim to messiahship. The mockery contained bitter truth. Jesus had visualised the purpose of his ministry as saving others and it must have been his chief temptation to save himself although to do so would have been a betrayal of his task.

The black sirocco, or sandstorm, is not uncommon in Jerusalem in April. Matthew 27:51 suggests it was followed by an earthquake. For Mark the darkness between noon and 3 p.m. symbolised desolation of spirit. Jesus cries out, 'My God, my God, why hast thou forsaken me?' (Mark gives the actual Aramaic phrase.) It is difficult for us to try and penetrate Jesus' mind at this terrible moment, especially as Mark does not give us any of the other words from the cross (cf Luke 23:43–46), but it would seem that for a time Jesus felt himself completely isolated from the Father. Intense suffering of body, mind and spirit can bring with it this sense of dereliction or even desertion. Psalm 22 opens with such a note of anguish but ends with one of triumph and consolation. Taking into consideration the evidence of the other gospels, we may suppose that Jesus lived out the psalm in his suffering and final renewal of confidence in the love of God.

The bystanders' comment about Elijah only really makes sense as a piece of mockery, although it was sometimes believed that Elijah came to the assistance of those in distress. The vinegar (sour wine) could have been brought out of pity, as Matthew suggests, but we do not know whether the giver was Roman or Jewish. The bitter taste caused Jesus to draw in a sharp breath. Since it is likely that once the lungs were thus fully extended they could not easily contract because the body was taut against the cross, death may have resulted from this action.

The innermost shrine in the Temple—the Holy of Holies—was curtained off from the Holy Place. This was the veil which Mark reports was torn in two at Jesus' death—a symbolic piece of writing, unless the darkness did really precede an earthquake which damaged the temple. For Christians the symbolism served to underline their belief that through the death of Jesus the barriers between man and God have been removed. By his total obedience to the demands of Love Jesus had demonstrated how a man could achieve a right relationship with God.

Mark began his gospel with the statement that Jesus is the Son of God and he ends it with a Roman centurion's remarkable tribute to a man of an alien race.

The Sabbath day began at 6 p.m. so there were only a few hours left for burial. It would be a concession to Jewish feeling for the Romans to allow the body of a criminal to be taken down from the cross. Often they were left to rot, or sometimes buried in a common grave. It required great courage on the part of Joseph of Arimathea to ask for Jesus' body. Mark says he was a member of the Sanhedrin, therefore of good social standing and probably a secret disciple of Jesus. According to Jewish law, a criminal could not be buried in his family's grave as he was rendered 'unclean' by his manner of death. Pilate was surprised that Jesus had died so quickly. It is

John who reports the spear thrust into his side to make sure Jesus is dead.

The faithful women who had been present at the crucifixion see that Joseph has laid the body of Jesus in a rock tomb whose entrance is closed by a stone. They will come there after the Sabbath to anoint the body.

Discussion
1 What does the centurion's comment suggest to you about the manner of Jesus' suffering and death?
2 What do you think about the bystanders' mockery? How does this link with Jesus' temptations, Luke 4:1–13?

Work
1 Read Psalm 22. You will see why it has been linked with Jesus' suffering and death.
2 Make a note of the people involved in the death of Jesus and later compare the other two evangelists' account of events and people.

Chapter 16

(a) The empty tomb — Mark 16:*1-8*; Matthew 27:*62*-28:*8*; Luke 24:*1-12*

The women are not able to do anything on the Sabbath but at sunset they bring aromatic oils for the anointing of Jesus' body. The oils are never used of course, because when they get to the tomb, they find the stone rolled away and the body gone. A young man in a white robe tells them that Jesus has risen. They must return to tell the disciples, especially Peter, that Jesus will meet them all again in Galilee. This echoes Jesus' last words to the disciples (Mark 14:28). Overcome with terror, the women flee from the tomb saying not a word to anyone.

It is generally agreed that Mark's gospel ends here. The second part of *v* 8 and the *v* 9–20, known as the shorter and longer ending or Epilogue respectively, are thought to have been added at a later date because of the unsatisfactory nature of the abrupt ending in *v* 8. There are three reasons for thinking that these verses do not belong to the original manuscript:

(1) The two oldest Greek manuscripts omit these verses.

(2) The style is quite unlike the rest of the gospel; for example, 21 words in this passage are not found elsewhere in Mark.

(3) The contents of these verses are really a summary of material drawn mainly from Luke and John, thus: *v* 9–11 are an abridged version of John 20:*1–18* — the story of the risen Jesus meeting Mary Magdalene in the garden.

v 12–13 summarise the graphic story told in Luke 24:*13–35* when the risen Jesus walks and talks with two disciples on their journey to Emmaus.

v 14–16 are more fully covered by Luke 24:*36–49* and Matthew 28:*16–20*.

v 17–18 summarise the miracles reported in Acts.

v 19–20 record the Ascension of Jesus as told in Acts 1:*9–11*. They also echo Luke's account in Acts of the spread of the Church.

Why does Mark's gospel end with the words 'for they were afraid . . .'? Various explanations have been offered. Some scholars believe that the sentence was not finished, indicating that Mark was interrupted, perhaps arrested and finally martyred. Possibly the end of the papyrus scroll was torn and subsequently lost. It would appear that neither Matthew nor Luke knew of the lost ending, for their resurrection narratives would not differ from one another if they had a common source. Of course, Mark may have meant to end his gospel where he did, but this appears very unlikely in view of the young man's words; Mark obviously considers him to be God's messenger, i.e. an angel. A further explanation of the problem is that John 21 may contain the essence of what Mark intended to write or indeed did write. Many scholars regard this chapter as an appendix to John's gospel.

Discussion

Looking at the evidence given above, what do you think about the 'end' of Mark's gospel?

Work

Look up all the references given in this chapter so that you can be clear about their bearing on your views about the longer ending to Mark's gospel.

Evidence for the Resurrection

1 Paul's letter to the Corinthians, written about AD55, contains the earliest account of belief in Jesus' resurrection. In 1 Corinthians 15:3–11 he records that Jesus appeared six times; firstly to Peter, secondly to the twelve, thirdly to about five hundred people, many of whom were still alive when Paul wrote the letter, fourthly to James, Jesus' brother, fifthly to all the apostles and finally to Paul himself.

2 All four evangelists talk about the empty tomb and Matthew, Luke and John witness to the risen Jesus.

3 How can we interpret this evidence that at the least there appears to have been an empty tomb? Here are some suggestions as to what might have happened to the body.

(a) That it was stolen: But by whom? It was not in the best interests of the Jewish or Roman authorities to dispose of the body. In fact Matthew reports that they asked for a guard on the tomb precisely because they did not want rumours of Jesus having risen. If they had the body, they would surely have produced it as evidence that the Christians were spreading a lie. If the disciples had stolen the body — as the Jews later said — it would mean that they then lived the rest of their lives on the basis of a lie. It is hard to credit that men and women would be prepared to suffer imprisonment, torture and death for a known and deliberate lie. The subsequent behaviour of those first friends of Jesus indicates that they, at any rate, believed that he had overcome death. If the body was stolen by an unknown person, what was the motive? It is also difficult to envisage that the theft could remain a secret for all time when one considers how small a community was involved. Would not the authorities have offered a large reward and made every effort to recover the body?

(b) That the body was disposed of in the usual way by being thrown into a common grave. But all the gospels specifically mention the part played by Joseph of Arimathea, a fact which surely could have been refuted if not true. John adds the name of another influential Jew — Nicodemus — who helped Joseph of Arimathea to bury Jesus privately.

(c) That Jesus did not die on the cross but regained consciousness in the tomb and walked out later. However even if Jesus did not die on the cross, he would certainly be a very sick man, rather like someone suffering from a stroke and therefore incapable of much speech or action. Who rolled away the stone? In any case, if Jesus had not died, where did he go to later? Would he not have attempted to go on preaching? What happened eventually to his body when he did die? Where was it buried? Why was this spot not known to Christians? Mark tells us that Pilate was surprised at Jesus' early death and John reports on the spear thrust into Jesus' side to make sure he was dead.

(d) That the women made a mistake and went to the wrong tomb which was naturally empty. The young man was no angel but simply a gardener who redirected them but they were too frightened to look further. Once again the question arises — if the body was available as evidence of death and decay, why was it not produced?

(e) That Jesus did in some way rise from the dead. What this means may be understood in various different ways: (i) That the resurrection was a physical reality, as is suggested by Luke, where the risen Jesus actually eats some fish before the disciples. (ii) A spiritual transformation of the physical body took place. Jesus is reported as disappearing at will. Both Paul and John indicate that Jesus' physical body was in some way changed to a spiritual one. (iii) A spiritual resurrection happened through which the disciples became conscious of their Lord's presence among them even though they did not see him, touch him or experience him with any of their five senses. Although this last interpretation is the most credible to modern minds, it is not the way in which the gospels describe the resurrection appearances.

4 The three pieces of evidence for the belief in the resurrection are:

(a) The emergence of the Christian church. It is difficult to account for the change in Jesus' first disciples unless something startling happened to them on that momentous first day of the week after his death. They changed from frightened, heart-broken, even disillusioned men and women into people of courage, resolution and extraordinary power who went out and spread the good news of their Master's life, death and resurrection to the Roman world. The theme of the resurrection was central to their teaching about Jesus and the proof in their eyes that he was the Christ.

(b) The New Testament documents, all of which arose within the first century AD and all of which are concerned to proclaim a faith about Jesus of Nazareth and to train those groups who based their lives on belief that he was their risen Lord.

(c) The first Christians were all Jews to whom the Jewish Sabbath was sacred, yet it soon became apparent that these people met also on the first day of the week and kept that as the Lord's day (Revelation 1:*10*), commemorating his rising from the dead until eventually the Lord's day took precedence over the Sabbath and became our Sunday — the holy day of the Christian church.

Discussion

Consider the arguments both for and against the resurrection. What do you think might have happened?

Part II

Selected passages from the Gospels of Luke and Matthew.

Preface

(a) Discussion on possible sources of these gospels, including the 'Sayings of Jesus' (the document Q) and each gospel's own particular material, known as L and M respectively

When you look at the gospels of Luke and Matthew, you will notice how much longer they are than Mark. In fact they incorporate most of Mark, although each treats his gospel in a slightly different way. Apart from Mark's contribution, these longer gospels agree in other respects. This has led scholars to suggest that both Luke and Matthew used a further independent source which they incorporated into their work. This is known as 'Q' (from the German Quelle, meaning source) or 'The Sayings of Jesus' because it contains practically no narrative but consists almost entirely of moral and religious teaching.

If Mark and Q are subtracted from Luke and Matthew, there is still quite a chunk of material left which the gospel writers must have obtained from their own independent sources. That which is found only in Luke is known as L and that which is peculiar to Matthew as M.

(i) The document Q As we have seen from Mark's gospel, Jesus himself spoke Aramaic (Mark 5:*41*, 7:*34*, 14:*36*, 15:*34*). This was the common language of Palestine although the synagogue services would be conducted in Hebrew. Since Jesus quotes from the Old Testament in his teaching, it is probable that he knew Hebrew well; he was certainly able to debate with the Scribes and Pharisees on points of the law. Greek was the universal language of the Roman Empire, although Latin was used for official purposes. Jesus may even have known some Greek and Latin as he was able to talk to Pontius Pilate.

The teaching of Jesus fell into three categories. Firstly he spoke to crowds of people; secondly he engaged in controversy with the religious leaders, especially the Scribes and Pharisees; thirdly he taught his close disciples in private. Collections of Jesus' sayings were probably made at an early stage in the life of the Christian community. Perhaps they were first arranged chronologically and later according to topic. For easy recall, sayings might be grouped by a verbal link, as for example 'salt' in Mark 9:48–50.

It has been suggested that such a body of teaching was in existence when Paul wrote his first letter to the Corinthians (I Cor. 7:10; 9:14) about the middle of the first century. These collected sayings of Jesus would be written first in Aramaic and later translated into Greek. A great deal of Jesus' teaching was in poetic form, like the oracles of the Hebrew prophets. His use of metaphor, parable and allegory was all part of his poetic inspiration (see p 7).

We need not go into verse details about which passages in Luke and Matthew scholars attribute to Q. In outline the main contents are as follows:

The mission of John Baptist, the baptism and temptations of Jesus.

The Sermon on the Mount (Matthew) and the Sermon on the Plain (Luke).

John Baptist's message from prison and Jesus' tribute to him.

The disciples' missionary tour, the story of the centurion's servant, various parables, the lament over Jerusalem and the Coming of the Son of Man.

(For specific references see text of Luke and Matthew gospels.)

There is no Passion narrative in Q.

The apostle Matthew could have been the person who edited Q; Papias (see p 1) stated 'So then, Matthew compiled the oracles in the Hebrew language' (probably Aramaic) 'but everyone interpreted them as he was able' (i.e. translated them as best he could). For various reasons (see p 97) it is not possible to credit Matthew the apostle with the gospel which bears his name, but Q is exactly the kind of document which fits Papias' description. In the Old Testament, Papias' word 'oracle' stood for the inspired message of the prophet of God. Assuming it existed, Q was certainly translated into Greek, as it is found with only slight variations in the gospels of Luke and Matthew.

Since it seems that Q was composed primarily as a teaching manual for Christian converts, it has been associated with Syrian Antioch, the first great centre of Gentile Christianity.

(ii) The L material A great deal of Luke's gospel comes from his own particular source. Although he uses 65% of Mark, this only comprises 30% of his own gospel and the contribution of Q, despite being vital to our understanding of Jesus' teaching, accounts for only approximately 200 out of the 1149 verses which make up the gospel. The following are the chief passages found only in Luke:

Stories about the birth and childhood of John Baptist and Jesus chs. 1 and 2.

A great deal of chapters 7:*1*–8:*3* and 9:*51*–19:*44*.

Certain sections of the Passion narrative chs. 22–23.

The Resurrection narrative ch. 24.

It is generally agreed that the basis of this material was not a written source but oral tradition which Luke must have collected himself. According to Acts (21:*8, 15*) Luke and Paul stayed with Philip the Evangelist at Caesarea and again with Mnason, an early disciple, during Paul's last visit to Jerusalem. Presumably Luke was again with Philip when Paul was imprisoned for two years at Caesarea, so he had plenty of time to hear about Jesus from these early Christians. It is even conjectured that Luke met Mary, the mother of Jesus, or those closely associated with her.

(iii) **The M material** Matthew's gospel has been described as an enlarged edition of Mark's. It contains approximately 95% of Mark's gospel, plus Q; the M material therefore, although important, is much less significant than the L material in Luke's gospel. The verses which are thought to compose M are made up of four different strands as follows:

> A narrative section comprising both the birth and infancy stories and stories about the last days of Jesus in Jerusalem, including the Resurrection narrative.
>
> A collection of Christian 'proof-texts' from the Jewish scriptures, which aim to show that everything which happened to Jesus was in fulfilment of Old Testament prophecy. Statements such as 'all this happened in order to fulfil what the Lord declared through the prophet' occur twelve times throughout the gospel, followed by an Old Testament passage or illustration (1:*23*; 2:*6, 15, 18, 23*; 4:*15–16*; 8:*17*; 12:*18–21*; 13:*35*; 21:*4–6*; 26:*56*; 27:*9, 10*).
>
> Certain teachings in the Sermon on the Mount and elsewhere, together with parables (which will be noted as we come to them) not found in Mark or Luke.
>
> Editorial matter.

Study of the gospel indicates that M originated in Jewish Christian circles of Judaea, having their centre at Jerusalem.

Discussion

This has been a rather complex section to study. Remember that we do not know for sure whether Q, L and M existed, but the majority of scholars think they probably did. At any rate they are sensible propositions. How does analysis of this kind affect your assessment of the gospels' worth?

Work

Spend time looking up the references in this section and seeing their significance, especially the Matthew passages concerning the Christian 'proof-texts'.

(b) Clues as to authorship, date and place of writing, purpose and characteristics of Luke and Matthew's gospels

(i) Luke's gospel

Authorship   As far back as the second half of the second century, Luke has traditionally been regarded as the author of the third gospel. There are two sources of evidence. Firstly Irenaeus who refers to this gospel and secondly the Muratorian Fragment (c.AD200) which gives a list of New Testament books accepted by the Roman church in about AD190 —

'The third book of the Gospel, that according to Luke, was compiled in his own name on Paul's authority by Luke the physician, when after Christ's ascension, Paul had taken him to be with him like a legal expert. Yet neither did *he* see the Lord in the flesh; and he too, as he was able to ascertain events, begins his story from the birth of John.'

Luke is mentioned by Paul in three letters, all written when he was in prison:

Colossians 4:*14* — 'our dear friend Luke the doctor'.
Philemon *24* includes the name of Luke amongst Paul's fellow workers.
2 Timothy 4:*11*, when Paul is awaiting his death 'only Luke is with me.'

The third gospel is part of a two-volume work, of which the Acts of the Apostles is the second book. The number of 'we' passages Acts 16:*10–17*; 20:*5–15*; 21:*1–18*; 27:*1–28:16* imply that Luke kept a travel diary, joining Paul at Troas in Asia Minor (probably about AD50) and accompanying him on his missionary work.

Date and place of writing   It is impossible to be precise about these matters. Two facts are important (1) presumably Luke wrote his gospel after Mark wrote his in AD65 (2) Luke's own gospel had become sufficiently well-known to be mentioned by Clement of Rome in AD96. A third factor arises from 21:20 'But when you see Jerusalem encircled by armies, then you may be sure that her destruction is near.' The fall of Jerusalem took place in AD70 when the Roman armies under Titus crushed the Jewish revolt. Luke is reporting a prophetic warning by Jesus who foresaw the disastrous course upon which his nation was set but it is possible he wrote his account after the event had taken place. The majority of scholars date the third gospel between AD75–80, although it has recently been attributed to the AD60s.

Purpose and characteristics Luke dedicates his work to Theophilus, saying in his introduction that he wants Theophilus to have *true* knowledge about the faith in Jesus Christ. Theophilus seems to have been a high-ranking Gentile as Luke calls him 'your excellency'. Possibly Theophilus, which means 'Friend of God', was not the Roman's real name as it is an unlikely one for a first century Roman. It may have been his baptismal name or even a pseudonym. Thus Luke, writing for educated Gentiles, is presenting Jesus as much more than the Jewish Messiah. In this gospel Jesus is the Saviour of the World. He uses 'the Lord', his favourite title for Jesus, at least twelve times, and in his two volume work Christianity is recommended as the religion for the Roman Empire. Note the following points about the gospel:

1 In giving Jesus' family tree, Luke traces Jesus' ancestry to the start of the entire human race, beginning with Adam, whom he probably believed to be a real historical person.

2 Luke also puts Jesus into history by giving dates for events according to Roman emperors and Jewish officials.

3 There are special references to Gentiles (4:*20–27*; 24:*47*) and he omits specifically Jewish terminology such as rabbi and scribe, substituting teacher and lawyer.

4 Luke has marked social sympathies. He is deeply aware of the humbler members of society, such as women, the poor and the outcast.

5 Even if he is not himself a poet, he has sensitivity and appreciation of poetic imagery. In the early part of his gospel we have four songs, which some scholars believe to be his own composition. He is also particularly aware of the workings of the Holy Spirit, of prayer, joy and thanksgiving.

6 It is possible that his pro-Roman sympathies may have influenced his presentation of the trial and death of Jesus.

We do not know the order in which the gospel was written. Did an original draft, complete in itself, consist of Q plus L, to which Mark was added later? Or was the non-Marcan material built into the Marcan framework? Close study of the gospels shows that Luke handled his sources with care, correcting only Mark's grammar and style and alternating passages from Mark with those from Q and L, except in the Passion story where some mingling was inevitable.

(ii) Matthew's gospel

Authorship   While we call the first gospel in the New Testament by his name, there are strong reasons for thinking it highly unlikely that the apostle Matthew wrote it.

Although the first gospel reproduces some 95% of Mark's gospel, using Mark's order and much of his language, the vivid and realistic detail is missing and remarks, especially about the Twelve, are toned down. If the Apostle Matthew were the author, he would not need to use Mark as his framework and his gospel would be full of eye-witness accounts. Furthermore the gospel was written in Greek and it includes quotations from the Greek Old Testament.

The mistaken view of authorship could have arisen from a misunderstanding of the words of Papias. 'Oracles' were taken to mean 'the gospel'. Scholars are now sure that the present form of the first gospel was never written in Hebrew before being translated into Greek. Matthew might have been the author of Q — 'The Sayings of Jesus' or he could have collected together the Old Testament texts which were such an important feature in Christian preaching to Jews, to convince them that Jesus was the long-awaited Messiah, despite evidence to the contrary.

The author of the first gospel therefore is unknown but he was a Jewish Christian who used Mark, Q and his own material M, some of which may have been the original work of the apostle Matthew. For the sake of convenience we shall continue to call the first gospel and its author, Matthew, as it has been so known since the middle of the second century AD.

Date and place of writing   Matthew was composed later than Mark and probably after the fall of Jerusalem, which some commentators think is mentioned in 22:7 — 'the king was furious, he sent troops to kill those murderers and set their town on fire'. Two other references which indicate Jerusalem has already fallen are 22:38 and 24:15.

By the time of writing, the Christian community seems to have developed its own organisation and discipline (cf 18:15–18) which suggests a late date. In 28:19 a late baptismal formula is used. For these reasons it is believed the gospel was written not earlier than AD80 and possibly at Syrian Antioch.

Purpose and characteristics   The aim of the author is to show Jesus as the long-awaited Jewish Messiah. He traces Jesus' lineage back to Abraham, strictly limits Jesus' ministry to the Jews and makes several early references to people calling Jesus 'Son of

David' (9:27; 12:23; 15:22), unlike Mark who introduces this title with the late story of Blind Bartemaeus at Jericho.

Although Matthew shows great respect for the Jewish law, he presents Jesus as greater than Moses and as the giver of the highest perfect law. He has arranged his gospel in five books or discourses by Jesus. His readers, being Jewish Christians, would be accustomed to the Pentateuch. The endings of these five sections in the gospel are clearly marked by the phrase 'when Jesus had finished this discourse' (7:28; 11:1; 13:53; 19:1; 26:1).

The word 'church' (Greek 'ecclesia') occurs twice in this gospel (16:18; 18:17) and in no other.

The author is especially concerned with the discipline, organisation and life of the Jewish Christian community and his gospel has been regarded as the great teaching manual of the Christian church down the centuries although in several matters his treatment of subjects is open to criticism. Note the following:

1 The decidedly anti-Jewish tone (3:7; 21:43 and 23). The Jewish Christian would suffer more from Jewish attacks than the Gentile Christian.

2 The strong interest in rewards and punishments, the urgency of the times (because the Jewish rejection of their Messiah has brought disaster on the nation) and the belief in the Second Coming of Christ and the final Judgment. Mark 13, for example, is considerably expanded in Matthew 24. Hell-fire and 'wailing and grinding of teeth' are often mentioned (8:12; 13:50).

3 Points 1 and 2 reflect the interests of a small, rather isolated community, with its back against the wall in a hostile climate of opinion, clinging desperately to its convictions about Jesus and openly expecting vindication by God for its faithfulness.

Matthew, like Luke, alters Mark's grammatical constructions and tones down Mark's abrasive treatment of matters (compare Matthew 13:58 with Mark 6:5, 6 and Matthew 8:25 with Mark 4:38). However his treatment of Mark is different from Luke's in that he abridges Mark quite considerably in order to add his own source which he combines with the Marcan material. He also tends to heighten the miraculous, for example, by having two mad men at Gerasa and two blind men at Jericho and so on.

Conclusion to Preface   Although we shall not be studying Luke and Matthew's gospels verse by verse because they often duplicate, we shall still be able to get the feel of these two great ancient documents which are full of individual interpretation of the person of Jesus. For the sake of revision, an index is given at the back of the book showing the gospel passages omitted from the contents.

(There are 661 verses in Mark, 1068 verses in Matthew, 1149 verses in Luke. Scholars disagree about the number of verses in the possible document Q but they range from 200 to 250.)

Discussion

1 Most people today believe that the story about Adam and Eve in the Garden of Eden is a parable explaining the origins of the human race, not historical fact. What difference do you think it would have made to Luke's presentation of Jesus if he also had believed Adam was part of an ancient Hebrew myth about creation?

2 How far has Matthew's intense preoccupation with Jesus' fulfilment of Old Testament scriptures led people to think Jesus acted as he did simply because it had been ordained? In what sense do you think Jesus was free to make his own decisions about his life?

Work

1 Note the characteristics of Luke and Matthew's gospels so that you get a clear picture of the chief points of each.

2 Copy the diagram into your note books and learn its structure.

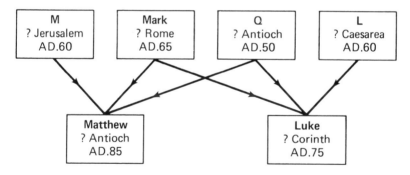

Diagram of Synoptics and their sources (after B.H. Streeter's 'The Four Gospels').

Chapter 17

(i) Stories about the birth of John Baptist: The birth and childhood of Jesus according to Luke—Luke 1-2.

(a) The author's preface: Luke 1:*1-4* Luke probably meant this preface to be for the whole two-volume work (Gospel and Acts of the Apostles). It is written in good Greek and follows the custom of his day in its dedication. Although not a first-generation Christian himself, he has had access to those who were eye-witnesses to the events of Jesus' ministry. His special contribution is to write about truth of the faith in a consecutive narrative from the beginning, having verified all the facts.

(b) Zachariah in the Temple: Luke 1:5-25 John Baptist is an important, if secondary, figure in Mark's gospel, but Luke gives us a great deal more additional information about him. It is apparent that even so many years after his death, the Baptist had his followers and those who venerated his memory. Great as he was however, the gospel writers are anxious to show right from the beginning that the Baptist was only the forerunner of Jesus, the Christ.

Both Zachariah and his wife Elizabeth were of priestly descent. Abijah was the eighth of the twenty-four rotas or courses into which the Jerusalem temple priests were divided and which came in turn to the Temple for a week's service (1 Chronicles 24). Incense was offered at morning and evening sacrifice and the ascending smoke was a call to prayer to the worshippers in the outer courts.

In New Testament times, the forces of good and evil were personified as angels and demons, at least by the Pharisees and the ordinary people (see *p* 10). Gabriel appears in Daniel 8:*16* and 9:*21*. In 1 Enoch 9, he is one of the four arch-angels, but in the book of Revelation he is one of the seven great angels (8:2) who stand before the throne of God. Their names are given in 1 Enoch 20:*1-8* and they are thought to have originated from Ezekiel 9:*2-11*, although probably the prototype of these were the seven planets, which the Babylonians believed to be divine beings. In later Judaism, Michael is described as the prince or guardian angel of Israel and next to him in rank comes Gabriel.

The prophecy regarding John is important. To abstain from strong drink might mean that he became a Nazarite (Numbers 6 and Judges 13) or Rechabite. These were protest groups following in the tradition of the prophets who blamed the ills of the Israelite nation on too much settled agricultural life and the products of the vine. The Nazarites also refused to have their hair cut. John will also receive the spirit and power of Elijah, the prophet whose return was believed to herald the coming of the Messiah according to Malachi 4:5. It was possible for the Jews to conceive that Elijah might return as he was believed to have been translated up to heaven and not to have died (2 Kings 2:11).

Zachariah's subsequent dumbness which made him unable to bless the people outside in the courtyard, was interpreted as a reproof of his doubt regarding Gabriel's prophecy, but it could equally well have been the result of shock. Anyway, Elizabeth did conceive in spite of her age and having been barren for so long—a condition regarded at that time as a sign of God's displeasure.

(c) The visit of Gabriel to Mary: Luke 1:26–38 According to Luke (but not to Matthew) Nazareth was the home-town of Joseph and Mary. For the significance of Jewish betrothal see notes on Matthew 1:18–25. Gabriel's words to Mary summarise current Jewish hopes of the Messiah—an eternal, mighty Davidic king. Jesus is a late form of the name Joshua, which means 'God is salvation'. As Mary is a virgin she is puzzled as to how she can be the mother of the Messiah but she is told that she will conceive through an action of the Holy Spirit. Luke deliberately uses language which is reminiscent of the Old Testament account of Creation (Genesis 1:2). The conception of Jesus will be a new creative act of God. Mary accepts her vocation, although her words imply that she could have refused it.

(d) Mary's visit to Elizabeth—Luke 1:39—56 Gabriel had told Mary that her cousin Elizabeth was also pregnant. When Mary enters Zachariah's house, Elizabeth's baby stirs in her womb and Elizabeth intuitively knows that Mary is the mother of the Messiah. Thus, even before his birth, John Baptist is credited with recognising Jesus. Mary's song is known as the 'Magnificat' from the first word of the Latin translation and has been regularly used in Christian worship since the early days of the church. It is based on the song of Hannah after the birth of Samuel (1 Samuel 2:1–10) but has other Old Testament ideas in it. Many people think the 'Magnificat' is Luke's own composition, others that it was a Jewish hymn known to Mary, or one which Luke adapted. At any rate there are strong social sympathies in it as the humble, the poor and hungry will be helped and the rich and arrogant punished. Thus God's mercy and justice will be vindicated; he will fulfil his promises to Abraham and his descendants, while Mary herself will be remembered for all time as the mother of the Messiah.

We will postpone a full discussion on the virgin conception until we have read Matthew's account of it. Meanwhile note the similarity between Luke's presentation of Gabriel's visit to Zachariah and his visit to Mary. Like Zachariah she is distressed at the visitation; she receives reassurance and the promise of a son; she expresses doubt as to how this can come about and she receives a sign from the angel—that her cousin Elizabeth is also pregnant through the intervention of God—as a confirmation of the angelic words about her own virgin conception through the action of the Holy Spirit.

(e) The birth of John Baptist—Luke 1:56–80 It seems Mary stayed with Elizabeth until John was born. Eight days after birth a boy was named and circumcised, this rite being a symbol of the Jewish covenant relationship with God, according to Leviticus (12:3) and the story of Abraham (Genesis 17:11), although it was not an exclusively Jewish custom. Its Christian counterpart is baptism. As John was not a family name the relatives did not understand why Elizabeth declared her son should be so called and went to Zachariah for confirmation. Apparently he was deaf as well as dumb, but when he wrote the name John, meaning 'God is gracious', a miracle happened and he was able to speak. His song is called the 'Benedictus' and, like the 'Magnificat', has been constantly used in Christian worship. As with the 'Magnificat', many people believe that Luke composed this hymn of thanksgiving; on the other hand it is not difficult to imagine that the priest Zachariah, versed in the sacred scriptures, could have uttered some such psalm. Verses 76–7 describe John as 'the prophet of the Most High' and claim his work will bring to God's people 'salvation through knowledge of him by the forgiveness of their sins'; this precise account of John's actual adult work may have been written after his death, rather than at his birth. The image of the new era coming as sunrise after night echoes Malachi 4:2.

It was presumably after John's parents had died that he went off into the wilderness. Since the Dead Sea Scrolls have shown that an Essene community existed at Qumran, it has been suggested that John might have been attached to the Essenes. Certainly, like Elijah and Amos, he was in the wilderness until he returned to proclaim his message.

(f) The birth of Jesus—Luke 2:*1-20* For Luke, of course, Jesus was a definite historical figure as well as being Saviour of the World, so he endeavours to place Jesus' birth in the context of Roman history. The difficulty about his dates is that we know insufficient about Quirinius, governor of Syria. Josephus (see *p* 6) wrote that Quirinius carried out an enrolment of Judaea in AD6, which provoked a desperate rising of the Zealots under Judas of Galilee (Antiquities xviii.2.1), but this is an impossibly late date for Jesus' birth as Herod the Great died in 4BC. It appears, however from inscriptions, that Quirinius might have been involved in military operations in the Syrian province between 10 and 7BC and even held office as governor twice.

According to information from Egypt, it was a Roman practice to hold a census or enrolment every fourteen years and this was done by households. This practice had been instituted by Augustus, the first Roman Emperor, as a means of obtaining useful information for governing the Empire. 'All the world' is a technical impossibility, nor is there any record of such a census taking place for the whole Roman Empire. Another difficulty arises from the fact that under Herod, Judaea was semi-independent, therefore unlikely to come under direct Roman rule. The census in AD6 took place when Herod's son Archelaus had been deposed and a Roman Procurator was appointed to his tetrarchy (see *p* 186). A possible explanation may be that Luke got his facts right and that there was a first enrolment fourteen years earlier than that recorded by Josephus; assuming that this was begun about 8BC, Herod could have complied with this prior enrolment. Alternatively, Josephus implies that an oath of allegiance to Augustus and Herod was required of 'all the people of the Jews' about this time (Antiquities xvii.2.4), so Luke may have confused the census of loyalty with the later enrolment under Quirinius.

Western historical dating is based on the conventional assumption that Jesus was born in AD1. This arises from the fact that Constantine the Great, on his accession to the throne in the fourth century AD, made Christianity the official religion of the Roman Empire. Several centuries later, attempts were made to ascertain the exact date of Jesus' birth, using all the information then available. Having calculated the year, history was divided in BC and AD at that point (Before Christ and After, Anno Domini meaning 'In the year of our Lord'). Although scholars now agree that 7, 6 or 5 BC would be a more accurate birth date, it would of course be quite impracticable to alter the whole of western historical dating at this stage.

Why Joseph had to go to Bethlehem is also not clear as Roman enrolments did not insist on a return to the place of origin but the tribal system was very important to Jews so this may have been a special local feature. Certainly Joseph must by this time have married Mary (see Matthew's account *p* 106), as Jesus was born the legal son of Joseph and therefore of the tribe of David.

Bethlehem is six miles from Jerusalem. It was David's birthplace. David himself had been a shepherd (*cf* 1 Samuel 17), so it is appropriate that shepherds are the first to hear of the birth of the Messiah. Again Luke uses angels to bring 'the good tidings of great joy' that a deliverer has been born. 'The Lord', always Luke's title for Jesus, was probably commonly used in the Christian communities of his day rather than the Jewish term Messiah. The angels' song speaks of peace on earth for all men of good will.

Note the reference to Mary in *v* 19; this together with verses 33, 34, 48 and 50–51, has led to the suggestion that the birth stories came from Mary herself.

Ever since the 4th century AD, the birthday of Jesus has been celebrated on December 25th. Christian festivities replaced the more ancient Winter Solstice festival.

(g) Circumcision and presentation at the Temple—Luke 2:*21-40* Shortly after birth Jesus was circumcised according to the Law and his mother went through the rites of purification (Leviticus 12:*1-8*). Childbirth and menstruation were surrounded by mystery amongst ancient peoples. According to the Law, after the birth of a male child the mother was 'unclean', that is to say 'untouchable', for seven days and was confined to the home for a further period of thirty-three days. After this she had to bring her offering to the priest in the sanctuary. A third ceremony concerned the firstborn male child who, according to Exodus 13:*1-2*, belonged to God. Therefore the child was solemnly offered to God and then 'redeemed', i.e. bought back by making a substitute offering in his place. If the family were not very rich, a pair of turtle-doves or two young pigeons would do in place of a lamb.

Simeon's song of thanksgiving is known as the 'Nunc Dimittis', again from the first words in the Latin version. It has been used in Christian churches since the 5th century. Simeon says four things:

1 that deliverance or salvation will come through this child;

2 that the mission of Jesus is not only for the Jews but for all the world;

3 that Mary will suffer greatly because many will deny and revile Jesus;

4 but that the state of men's hearts will be shown by whether they reject or accept Jesus.

The aged prophetess, Anna, complements the aged priest. Together with the simple shepherds, they both represent the best of Judaism at that time, indicating that many were looking for the Messiah.

Compare Luke's comment that Jesus 'grew big and strong and full of wisdom; and God's favour rested upon him' with his comment on John Baptist (1:*80*).

(h) Jesus in the Temple—Luke 2:*41-52* The Law prescribed that all male Jews should attend at the central sanctuary for the three great feasts of Passover, Pentecost and Tabernacles (Exodus 23:*14-17*), but by the New Testament period it had been accepted that one visit to Jerusalem could suffice. As Nazareth is 70 miles distant from Jerusalem, Joseph apparently chose to go up for the Passover. Every Jewish boy receives special instruction between the ages of 12 and 13; the process culminates in his reading from the Law and the prophets for the first time in the synagogue and being received as a fully adult member of the congregation. Jesus is of an age to go up to Jerusalem with his parents in a pilgrim caravan and spends the time there listening and talking to the rabbis. For Luke the central point of the story is that Jesus was aware even at this early age, of a unique relationship with God, the Father, a relatively rare way for a Jew to address God, although not unknown. If there had been unusual circumstances surrounding his birth, presumably Mary had not told Jesus about them, only so could one account for her surprise at his behaviour.

Luke ends his narrative of the birth and childhood of Jesus by stating that Jesus was obedient to his earthly parents even though a possible conflict of loyalties had arisen. Luke only mentions Mary once more in his gospel (8:*19f. cf* Mark 3:*31-35*).

Discussion
We do not believe that barrenness is a sign of God's displeasure, but in ancient times, when at last a child was conceived, it is easy to see how it was regarded in a miraculous light. How would you interpret the story of Zachariah and Elizabeth?

Work
You should look carefully at the four songs in these chapters and make sure you understand their meaning.

(ii) Stories about the birth and childhood of Jesus according to Matthew—Matthew 1-2

(a) The family tree of Jesus—Matthew 1:*1-17*; (*cf* Luke 3:*23-38*) Technically the clue to this genealogical table lies in *v* 17. One cannot expect from Matthew the exactness of a modern genealogy which is based on accurate research through church and national registers; the point of Matthew's presentation is to answer the question, probably much debated in his circles, of Jesus' identity. Matthew proclaims that Jesus was the Christ. As son of David he was heir of the royal house and as son of Abraham he was the inheritor of God's promise (Gen. 22:*18*; 12:*1–3*) and in *v* 20 Matthew declares Jesus to be the son of God.

Many commentators interpret *v* 16 as an implicit belief in the virgin conception. The most reliable manuscripts describe Joseph as the husband of Mary, so obviously Joseph had married Mary before Jesus was born, thus making Jesus his legal son.

(b) The supernatural conception and the birth of Jesus—Matthew 1:*18-25*

In Jewish circles betrothal was a solemn and legally binding undertaking almost amounting to marriage, which usually took place a year before the wedding. (In fact the Mosaic punishment for adultery, death by stoning (Leviticus 20:*10* and Deut. 22:*21*), was really only applicable to a betrothed virgin!) The breaking of an engagement could only take place if the man served a writ of divorce upon the woman. When Joseph discovers that Mary is pregnant he is very troubled but decides to have the marriage annulled privately. He is told in a dream not to do this and subsequently believes that Mary has conceived by a supernatural act of God. He marries Mary, yet both *v* 18 and *v* 25 affirm that Jesus is not the natural son of Joseph as he did not have intercourse with Mary before Jesus was born.

In *v* 23 we have the first of Matthew's many quotations. In Isaiah 7:*14* the word 'maiden' simply means 'a young woman'; there is no hint in Isaiah of a virgin conception and the text was not regarded as messianic.

The story of Jesus' conception and birth is told from Joseph's point of view (as Luke's is from Mary's). There is no textual reason for supposing that Joseph and Mary did not live together as man and wife and that Mary did not bear Joseph children (*cf* Mark 3:*31–35*).

(c) The Wise Men—Matthew 2:*1-12*

Matthew agrees with Luke that Jesus was born in Bethlehem, although he assumes that this was the home of Joseph and Mary.

The subject of the star has always aroused great interest. The great 17th century astronomer Kepler thought he had solved the mystery by noticing in 1603 and 1606 a rare conjunction in the sign of Pisces of the planets Saturn and Jupiter, which were later joined by Mars. A new, bright star then occurred which shone for about a year before finally disappearing. Kepler reckoned this particular conjunction only happened about every 800 years and would have been visible three times in 7BC. In December 1977, three English astronomers published a paper about some research they had undertaken into Chinese and Korean astronomical records, where sightings of a 'nova' (a so-called new star) were reported about 5BC in positions tallying with Matthew's statement.

Jesus was born in an age of conflict and disorder and consequent expectation of some kind of deliverance. As the Babylonians were great astrologers the appearance of a star would have been considered to have great significance in human affairs. Herod was both angry and afraid to hear that a possible rival had been born. He would interpret messiahship completely in terms of political power. Any messianic uprisings against Rome would be disastrous for the Jewish nation. It has been suggested that the prophecy (Micah 5:2), like other 'proof texts' found in Matthew, might have been taken from an Aramaic paraphrase translation of the Old Testament for use in synagogues, as this particular quotation differs slightly both from the Greek and from the Hebrew Old Testament.

The gifts of the wise men to the child are highly symbolic; gold stands for kingship, frankincense for priesthood and prayer, myrrh for love and sorrow. The fact that Mary and Joseph are now in a house (v 11) as opposed to the stable in Luke 2:7, *13*, suggests that the wise men arrived on the scene somewhat later than the shepherds. Notice that a dream is again used as a medium of divine revelation (v 12).

(d) The flight to Egypt and the murder of the children of Bethlehem—Matthew 2:*13-18* Once more the warning comes in a dream. It was natural that Joseph should think of travelling along the Gaza caravan routes to Egypt as there were many Jewish communities there. The third Old Testament reference (v 15) is taken from Hosea 11:*1* where the prophet is writing about the Hebrew rescue from Egyptian captivity in the time of Moses (see Introduction). In Hosea 'my son' refers to Israel but Matthew sees Jesus as the one greater than Moses and he here parallels the way in which both were saved from death in infancy.

We do not know any contemporary account of the Bethlehem massacre but it is not uncharacteristic of Herod's last years, judging from his treatment of his own family. He put to death his favourite wife, Mariamne, because he thought her unfaithful, and her two sons, Alexander and Aristobulus, because he was led to believe they were plotting against him. Five days before he died he received permission from Rome to execute another son, Antipater, for treason. Although we may assume that there would be no more than two dozen or so boy babies under two years old in Bethlehem, the crime was very terrible and probably prevented Joseph and Mary from returning to Bethlehem at a later date.

In *v* 17 and 18 Matthew quotes from Jeremiah 31:*15*, written during the conquest of Judaea by the Babylonian king Nebuchadnezzar. Jeremiah was describing the deportation of hundreds of Jews to captivity in Babylon, especially from Rama, an Ephraimite town 8 miles north of Jerusalem. Rachel was the favourite wife of Jacob, patriarch of the twelve tribes of Israel. Her sons were Joseph, from whom came the tribes of Manasseh and Ephraim, and Benjamin. Rachel's tomb is at Ephrath near Bethlehem, and the prophet imagines her weeping in her grave at the sight of her descendants being taken into captivity. Matthew uses this passage as a lament for the children of Bethlehem, because of the proximity of Rachel's tomb. It is not strictly speaking an appropriate reference, as Bethlehem was 'the city of David', a descendant of Judah, whose ancestress was Leah, sister of Rachel!

(e) Return from Egypt and settling in Nazareth—Matthew 2:*19-23* In his will, Herod left his kingdom to three of his sons (see *p* 185). Archelaus was removed by Caesar for brutality, so Joseph's fears about him were not unfounded. The dream motif is twice mentioned in these verses and is given as the reason for Joseph settling in Nazareth, an obscure Galilean town in the area governed by Herod Antipas. This time Matthew rather overstates his case (*v* 23) as no such prophecy 'He shall be called a Nazarene' can be found in the Old Testament. According to Acts (24:5), the Christians were later known by this nickname.

Concluding comments on this section

Luke and Matthew are so different in detail that they must have got their information from *separate* sources:

1 Luke says Mary and Joseph were at Bethlehem because of the census but Matthew assumes Bethlehem was their home.

2 Luke tells us of the visit of the shepherds, Jesus in a manger, the visit to the Temple and the words of Simeon and Anna.

3 Matthew reports the visit of the astrologers or wise men, the star, the massacre of the Bethlehem children and the flight to Egypt, Joseph and Mary eventually settling in Nazareth.

4 For Luke it is simple Jewish shepherds who first see the child; for Matthew it is wise Gentiles.

The two evangelists do *agree* on the following:

1 Birth of Jesus was at Bethlehem and his upbringing was at Nazareth.

2 His parents were named Joseph and Mary.

3 He was born during the time of Herod the Great.

4 His birth was accompanied by supernatural signs and was itself of a miraculous character.

Discussion on the use of angels and dreams as a means of communicating God's will

1 Luke is interested in angels and Matthew in dreams as a means of divine revelation. Victorian pictures of winged creatures have made it very difficult for us to conceive of angels! However, we can see how men's intuitive perception or what we might call their 'higher consciousness' could be attributed to spiritual beings. Judaism thought that the angels' primary function was to praise God before his throne and to carry out his will on earth, in particular bearing his message to men and interceding with God on their behalf. In view of the comments on Luke 1:5–26 it is interesting that Muhammad, the prophet of the Islamic faith, believed the inspiration of the Qur'an (the Muslim sacred scriptures) was given to him by the angel Gabriel and that he also taught that Michael fought for Islam. How would you analyse Luke's use of angels?

2 So far as dreams are concerned, modern psychology has put a very different interpretation on them, although there are still people today who claim some kind of extra-sensory perception and who feel that dreams can be warnings about future actions or events. Do you think it is necessary to take Matthew's use of dreams quite literally or can you envisage some quite rational explanation for the decisions taken by Joseph and the wise men?

3 Do you think that long usage has made the Christmas story more of a fairy tale than anything real? Can you pick out the probable or even possible facts which lie behind the poetic imagery?

4 What do you think about astrology?

Discussion on the arguments both for and against the virgin conception

Arguments against 1 A virgin conception is a physical impossibility. Even if it were medically possible, the child would have to be female.

2 Belief in a virgin conception appears only in Luke and Matthew and not elsewhere in the New Testament. In fact Jesus is sometimes referred to as the son of Joseph (John 1:45). The obvious difficulty about Luke's presentation of Jesus' conception lies in the contradiction that Jesus is to be an heir to David's throne, yet not the child of Joseph, who was of the royal line. Nothing is said of Mary's

lineage, but it would be likely that she was of Levitical descent (i.e. priestly), not royal, as was her kinswoman Elizabeth.

3 Other ancient religions have myths and legends associated with great men; e.g. many Greek heroes were supposedly the products of a god mating with a mortal woman and it was traditionally thought that stars announced the birth of Alexander the Great.

4 It would be more in keeping with what is known about God's ways of revealing himself through ordinary men and women to suppose that Jesus, although of God in a special sense, was conceived in the normal marriage relationship.

5 A virgin conception implies that the sexual relationship between husband and wife was the means whereby the taint of 'original sin' was transmitted but as Adam was not an actual historical person the latter doctrine is out of date anyway and the former idea is degrading to married love.

6 The belief that men must follow Jesus' example becomes invalid if he was a supernatural being; was he truly man? The reality of his death is vital to the Christian faith; does not a supernatural conception cast doubt on a natural death?

Arguments for the virgin conception attempt to answer these criticisms as follows:

1 The virgin conception, although an unnatural occurrence, may not be the physical impossibility once believed.

2 Silence in the rest of the New Testament may arise out of consideration for Mary. Luke and Matthew's gospels were written after her death when any chance of personal ridicule and scorn would be over. In any case, Jesus was the legal son of Joseph, if not his natural one.

3 Although myths and legends about mortal women conceiving through intercourse with a god abound in other religions, there is actually no record of a virgin conception without some kind of physical contact. In any case, it was completely alien for the Jews to think of Yahweh in sexual terms and they had long since passed the stage of deifying forces of nature. The first Christians were Jews and for them Jesus was not a remote figure in a distant past, but someone they knew personally.

4 The Bible has a healthy view of sex. There is nothing in the New Testament to suggest that Mary herself was immaculately conceived, i.e. without sin, or that she stayed a virgin all her life, although these have subsequently become doctrines of the Roman Catholic church and many other Christians also believe Mary did remain a virgin.

5 Both Luke and Matthew stress the beginning of a New Age:

Luke presents the conception of Jesus by an action of the Holy Spirit as a New Creation, similar to that brought about at the beginning of the world (Gen. 1:2).

Matthew thinks of the conception of Jesus as constituting a definite break in the chain of sinful human life, so he also has Genesis in mind.

For both evangelists the virgin conception was a unique event because Jesus the Christ was and is unique.

To sum up, the basic argument for the virgin conception is, 'why should those early Jewish Christians have invented it if it were not true?' And the argument against it is 'why was it necessary?' Before you decide what you think about it yourself, be clear that Jesus was either the product of Mary and Joseph's love or the product of a supernatural event. It is not possible to believe that Mary had sexual intercourse with another man, as Joseph would then certainly not have married her, so strict was Jewish sexual morality and the idea that the betrothed virgin had already been committed to the man as his wife. It is fashionable today to speculate whether Jesus was the product of a liaison between Mary and a being from outer space; but this is nothing very new as Muhammad wrote in the Qur'an that Jesus was the product of a relationship between the angel Gabriel and Mary.

It is often conceded that belief in a virgin conception is not an essential to being a Christian; do you agree? Looking at all the evidence, what do you think about the question?

Work

Be clear about the differences between Luke and Matthew. Make a brief summary of the stories and memorise the arguments for and against a virgin conception.

Chapter 18

(i) The Ministry of John Baptist and the baptism of Jesus— Luke 3; Matthew 3

(a) The Ministry of John Baptist—Luke 3:*1-20*; Matthew 3:*1-12*; Mark 1:*1-8* In keeping with his stated purpose, Luke gives as accurate a date as he can of the preaching of John:

1 As Tiberius became joint Emperor with Augustus AD11–12, the fifteenth year of his reign would be AD26–7. If sole succession is meant (AD14) then the date would be AD29.

2 Pontius Pilate was Procurator of Judaea AD26–30.

3 Herod Antipas was tetrarch of Galilee 4BC–AD39.

4 Philip was tetrarch of Iturea and Trachonitus 4BC–AD34.

5 The dates of Lysanias are unknown.

6 Annas was succeeded by his son-in-law Caiaphas as High Priest AD18–36 but retained the courtesy title.

Note the phrase 'the word of God came'. For Luke, John is a prophet, similar in calling to the Old Testament men of God. Unlike Mark and Matthew, he does not emphasise the second Elijah aspect. John's baptism was much more significant than the Jewish ritual of purification which was undergone by converts to Judaism; by cleansing from sin, it could mark the renewal of life. It was an act in preparation for the coming of the new age.

The passage from Isaiah (40:3–5), quoted in all three gospels, is extended by Luke to include 'all mankind' as the recipients of God's deliverance brought about through his Messiah.

In Luke, John calls the multitude 'You vipers' brood' but, characteristically, in Matthew it is the Scribes and Pharisees whom John addresses as Satan's children. The Jews considered themselves exempt from any coming judgment as they were God's children through their great ancestor Abraham. John however points out that the physical descent of Israel is meaningless unless it is backed up by a quality of life. He is terrible in his denunciation of a spiritually unfruitful people.

Luke alone (*v* 10–14) gives John's practical advice as to how the repentant person must act. Firstly there is a general lesson in unselfishness; considering that most of the listening crowd were poor and would only possess two shirts each at most, John is demanding a costly standard. Secondly, specifically to the tax-collectors (see Mark 2:*13–17*) John does not suggest a change of job, but the harder path of honesty in it. Thirdly, to the soldiers (who would be Jewish not Roman), he again highlights the relevant temptation to exploit others which their job would provide.

John is in the great tradition of the prophets of old who, in exposing the wickedness of their age, declared its offensiveness to God. It is in keeping with Luke's strong sense of social justice that he should concentrate on this aspect of John's word.

John thought of the coming Messiah as a Judge; this is perhaps emphasised in the phrase 'baptism by Holy Spirit and fire'. For Luke what happened at Pentecost (Acts 2:*2–4*) was the fulfilment of John's prophecy, although the image has nothing to do with judgment on that occasion. A winnowing fan or fork (shovel) was the implement used by a farmer to throw the grain against the wind to separate it from the chaff. This also is a symbol of judgment.

The early Christians regarded John Baptist's ministry as the beginning of the Christian gospel. Jesus himself later drew attention to the significance and importance of John (Luke 7:*30* and 20:*4*). For Luke the crowning misdeed of Herod Antipas was to imprison John Baptist (for fuller discussion see Mark 6:*14–29*) and it was after this that Jesus began his own ministry.

Discussion

What ills of modern society do you think a modern John Baptist would condemn? Are there such 'prophets of doom' around today?

Work

At the beginning of Mark's gospel, I suggested you should start making a dossier of John Baptist. Add this new material to it and look up the relevant passages in Mark.

(b) The baptism of Jesus—Luke 3:*21-22*; Matthew 3:*13-17*; Mark 1:*9-11* In Luke the baptism of Jesus is not quite the personal experience found in Mark's account (see *p* 6). It is interesting that Matthew adds a brief conversation between John and Jesus, probably to explain how it came about that Jesus, who was regarded as sinless by the early Christians (2 Cor.5:*21*; Hebrews 4:*15*,7:*26*; 1 John 3:*5*) should contemplate baptism by John. But John was creating a new Israel and Jesus would want to identify himself with John's work. It is also clear from all three gospels that Jesus' baptism marked a turning-point in his life. At it he became convinced of his messianic role based on his relationship with God, the Father, although according to Luke (2:*49*) he had been conscious of this special relationship from an early age. For Luke's genealogy (3:*23–28*) see *p* 96.

(ii) The temptations of Jesus—Luke 4:*1-13*; Matthew 4:*1-11*; Mark 1:*12-13*

Luke and Matthew agree about the three temptations, but have a different order and a slight variation in the dialogue between Jesus and the devil. Jesus himself must have provided the details, perhaps after Peter's confession of his messiahship at Caesarea Philippi (Mark 8:*29*). Jesus must have explained his conflict to his friends in easily recognisable terms even if they did not then see its full implications. Mark has Jesus in the wilderness for forty days during which he is tempted by Satan. The wilderness was thought of as the home of evil spirits. Matthew has altered this so that Jesus is led into the wilderness to be tempted; there he fasts for forty days and then the temptations begin. Luke combines the two versions.

The first temptation The current belief about the Messiah was that he would bring in an age of prosperity and plenty, so the thought of feeding the hungry occurs to Jesus, no doubt sparked off by his own hunger at that time. This course would gain him great popular support. But when Jesus considers the matter further, he realises that man has spiritual as well as physical needs. Material prosperity is not the real source of happiness. In the text Jesus answers Satan by quoting from Deuteronomy 8:*3*. 'Man shall not live by bread alone'. Matthew completes the verse. Note that all Jesus' replies to the tempter come from Deuteronomy, Moses' farewell sermon to the Israelites as they were poised to take Canaan, the 'promised land'. Evidently Jesus was thinking of his great predecessor and wondering what kind of a Joshua he was to be as he endeavoured to lead his people into the Kingdom.

The second temptation according to Luke, the third according to Matthew This is a visionary experience in which Satan shows Jesus all the kingdoms of the world; presumably they are the pagan kingdoms headed by Rome, since they are supposedly under Satan's jurisdiction! The tempter assumes the right to strike a bargain. In modern terms we might express this as the idea of compromise, employing evil means to achieve a noble end. It is the temptation to take the short cut, perhaps through war and certainly through the abuse of power. But Jesus is clear that he must not confuse messiahship with dictatorship. Man worships power and becomes corrupted in the process. Jesus remembers Deuteronomy 6:*13*: 'You shall do homage to the Lord your God and worship him alone.' God, and all that the concept of God the Father personifies, must come first.

The third temptation according to Luke, the second according to Matthew From the kingdoms of the world, Jesus moves to the Jewish Temple, the heart of Israel's ancient faith. In one sense this is the subtlest of the three temptations because it is twofold. Firstly there is the drama of producing a tremendous sign which will convince men beyond any shadow of doubt. In modern terms this would be to brainwash people into acceptance of Jesus by propaganda or unscrupulous advertising. The second element is the temptation that Jesus should himself ask God for a sign, a tangible confirmation that he is God's son in a special sense. That Jesus may have had moments of selfdoubt is perhaps indicated by the wording in the first and third temptations, '*If* you are the Son of God', so the final temptation is to put God to the test and is even supported by a passage of scripture, Psalm 91:*11–12*. Jesus' answer comes from Deuteronomy 6:*16*—testing God in such a way is really a refusal to trust him.

Luke and Matthew record different words for the devil's departure. Matthew adds the details of angels coming to minister to Jesus (as in Mark). Luke says the devil left him for a while. He would return later!

All these temptations give us a vivid picture of the mind of Jesus and the clash between what he believed himself to be called by God to do and Jewish aspirations about the Messiah.

1 The people hoped for a king who would establish the former glories of David. In their poverty and oppression, the concept of a messianic feast was a symbol of the good time coming. In John's gospel, when Jesus feeds the 5,000, the crowd want to make him king.

2 Many believed the only way to establish a Jewish national state was by war. If Jesus had wanted to raise a revolt he would have had an instant response as can be seen by the various Jewish uprisings during the period of Roman occupation; all of these were harshly crushed. The irony of this situation lies in the fact that Jesus was ultimately put to death as a Zealot, even though he had rejected political intrigue backed by military force.

3 Men craved for a sign. In Mark 8:*11* the Pharisees wanted a display of supernatural power; even on the cross Jesus was challenged to show who he was by coming down. A truly spectacular event would have absolved men from the responsibility of making their own choice about Jesus.

Amongst Jesus' friends there were dreams of glory and prestige (see notes on Mark 8:*27–30* and 10:*35–45*) whilst John Baptist pictured the Messiah as a kingly Judge who would destroy the wicked and reward the righteous.

This story shows us very forcefully that Jesus' concept of his role was quite distinct from all these ideas. He was God's servant, he did not want to take the centre of the stage. In his reading of the scriptures he had obviously pondered much on the Suffering Servant Songs of Isaiah (Isaiah 42:*1–2*, 49:*1–6*, 50:*4–9* and especially 52:*13*–53:*12*), the servant of God who endured much for the sake of others but who was eventually vindicated by God. So Jesus chose the way of sacrificial love, showing men the truths of the Kingdom by example and teaching but giving them the dignity of individual choice. To seduce men by material prosperity, to exploit and oppress them by political and military means or to fool them by clever techniques, robbed them of their freedom to apprehend and follow the right path and subsequently to grow in stature to become responsible human beings.

Discussion

How does Jesus' conflict relate to the dilemmas which have confronted humanity down the ages in its attempts to create a just and peaceful society? What methods do you think twentieth century man should employ to build a better world and how far do you think he has faced the implications of past mistakes? Has he learnt anything from history?

Work

1 You should look up the three occasions in Mark where Jesus gives a specific reason for his coming and refer again to the Marcan discussion about the Kingdom.
2 Make a note of the times when the ideas represented by the three temptations are present in Jesus' ministry, e.g. the feeding of the 5,000.

(iii) The Ministry in Galilee, Luke's account of the rejection at Nazareth, the call of the first disciples—Luke 4:*14*–5:*11*; Matthew 4:*12-25*; Mark 1:*14-39*

Matthew records the public ministry of Jesus in Galilee but abbreviates the Marcan narrative. He sees it as a fulfilment of prophecy (Isaiah 9:*1–2*) although scholars think his actual wording is based on an Aramaic paraphrase of the Old Testament. Because so many Gentiles lived in Galilee it was despised, but it became the area from which Jesus drew most support.

Mark mentions a visit to Nazareth at a later date in Jesus' ministry (Mark 6:*1–6*). Matthew follows Mark's order although he implies an earlier visit to Nazareth in 4:*13,* before going to Capernaum. For his own reasons, Luke puts Jesus' rejection at Nazareth at the beginning of his public ministry. Note how Luke also mentions the activity of the Spirit in Jesus' life.

Jesus attends a synagogue service in his home town and is asked to read the lesson, showing that even at this early stage he is regarded with respect as a rabbi. The passage appointed for that day was taken from Isaiah 61:*1–2* (although Luke suggests that Jesus chose it). Jesus then identifies himself with this prophecy. He has been anointed by the Spirit and his mission is to the poor and oppressed, the imprisoned and the blind. He is to proclaim (as in Mark) the 'coming of the Kingdom' or 'the year of the Lord's favour'. When the congregation react with a mixture of admiration and conjecture that one of their own people should claim to be the fulfilment of scripture (note the comment 'Is not this Joseph's son?'), Jesus replies with a proverb and then refers to two great Old Testament prophets, Elijah (1 Kings 17–18) and Elisha (2 Kings 5), who worked miracles for aliens rather than their own countrymen; by implication, this is what he will also do as his own countrymen ignore him. This arouses the congregation to fury and they thrust Jesus out of the town, perhaps with the intent of murdering him. For the present Jesus escapes unharmed, although some three years later he was killed on a hill outside a city.

Discussion
Why do you think Luke puts this story at the beginning of Jesus' ministry? What significance to you think his readers would see in Jesus' sermon and further comments?

The call of Simon Peter—Luke 5:*1–11*

For the rest of ch 4 Luke follows Mark both in order and content, but he has a different setting for the call of the first disciples. This passage, like the rejection at Nazareth, has a symbolic purpose. Peter, who is to become the leader of Jesus' disciples, is specifically called to become a fisher of men (*cf p* 8f). The success of the disciples' mission is foreshadowed by a miraculous catch of fishes. The account of the miracle leads scholars to suppose that there is some connection between it and John 21, which is very like it except that it happens after the resurrection! Some think that Luke got the story from a tradition that might have been incorporated in the supposed lost ending of Mark. Peter's strange words 'Go, Lord, leave me, sinner that I am!' would be much more in keeping as the reaction of Peter to the first appearance of the Risen Lord whom he has denied. The rather clumsy introduction of Jesus' preaching to the multitude, and the inclusion of James and John in the story, suggests that Luke compiled it from different sources.

From 5:*12* to 6:*16* Luke follows Mark and then from 6:*17–49* he gives his version of the teaching of Jesus found in Matthew 5–7. For Luke the setting of the sermon is not at all important. Jesus has been at prayer, he has chosen the twelve from amongst many disciples and now he comes from the mountain and talks to the crowd gathered 'on level ground'. This is why Luke's account is often referred to as the Sermon on the Plain.

Work

Note the specific examples of the special characteristics of Luke's and Matthew's gospels shown in the passages we have studied.

Chapter 19

The Sermon on the Mount—Matthew 5:*1*-7:*29* (Luke 6:*20-49*)

This is the first of the five great discourses which characterise Matthew's gospel (see *p* 98). The sermon takes place on a mountain, thus Matthew points to the similarity with Moses on Mount Sinai when the Law was given to the Israelites (Exodus 19–20). Both Luke and Matthew appear to have a common source which is probably 'Q'. Jesus may have originally delivered these various teachings at several different times and places. As it now stands in Matthew (and Luke), the sermon is primarily addressed to his disciples, because in it Jesus is saying, 'If you are citizens of the Kingdom, this is the quality of life you must have.'

1 The Beatitudes—Matthew 5:*3-12;* (Luke 6:*20-26*)

A beatitude is not quite the same thing as a blessing. It is really an expression of happiness. These eight (some commentators count nine or ten) epigrammatic statements are condensed and enigmatic but they do portray a quality of character, like that of Jesus himself, from which inevitable results follow. Jesus is not talking about heavenly rewards or punishments but of what he considers to be the natural consequences here and now of a certain way of life. He is stating a truth about human nature at its best. Luke balances four beatitudes with four woes and lays greater emphasis on the social aspects of Jesus' teaching.

(i) Those who know they are poor— During times of oppression by a foreign power, riches became associated with compromise; those who remained poor were therefore regarded as saintly (*cf* Psalm 69:*29*). It is certainly possible to follow a way of life which does not put material prosperity and worldly success first, yet to find happiness nevertheless.

On a spiritual level, there is a divine discontent which is the opposite of that arrogance which leads to the unforgivable sin (*p* 21). We need self-knowledge to be aware of and express what we lack in quality and character, then there is a chance of our growing in wisdom and understanding.

In Luke 'poor' is specifically related to material possessions and there is a corresponding 'woe' against the rich.

(ii) The sorrowful— If we are indifferent to finer feelings, we can know neither sorrow nor joy. But if we have a sensitivity to others and to God, so that we can identify with others in their distress, we can also share in their happiness. The capacity for suffering brings with it its own compensatory opposite emotion.

(iii) Those of gentle spirit— The world acknowledges the proud, self-assertive and aggressive as successful, but for Jesus humility is a sign of strength not weakness and true greatness is measured by humble service to others (Mark 10:*44* cf also Psalm 37:*11*). By saying that those of a gentle spirit will inherit the earth, Jesus highlighted the futility of aggressiveness, which leads eventually to war and despoliation. His words are particularly relevant in the atomic age, for unless we can learn to live by mutual co-operation rather than mutual aggression we shall end by destroying our species and our earth.

(iv) Those who hunger and thirst to see right prevail— Jesus' imagery implies that the passion for justice and harmony on the social, political and spiritual level is as fundamental to the human spirit as food and drink is to the body.

(v) Those who show mercy— Forgiveness is a characteristic theme of Jesus, particularly brought out in the Lord's Prayer (see *p* 125f). But to show mercy can equally mean to show compassion, as in the Parable of the Good Samaritan (Luke 10:*37*). It also links up with Jesus' comments about judging others; these remarks come later in the Sermon (Matthew 7:*1–5*, also Matthew 18:*21–35*; 25:*31–46*).

(vi) Those whose hearts are pure— For Jesus the ultimate aim of all life was union with God and he is talking here of a single-minded devotion which is not distracted by material things, but pursues the vision of the Blessed One. Even if one does not believe in a personal God, the principle applies. An ardent desire for wisdom and the highest good uncluttered by other considerations, will achieve its object.

(vii) The Peacemakers— It is the positive virtue of reconciliation which, says Jesus, is the truly God-like quality. This must

120

not be confused with compromise or peace at any price. If a man is to be in reality the son of God, he must exercise power to bring about peace and end the injustice, conflict and tension that exist in himself, his family, his society and his world.

(viii) Those who suffer persecution for the cause of right— When men and women exhibit true nobility of character, they are often disliked and persecuted by their contemporaries, because they constitute such a direct challenge. By the time the gospels were being written, Christians were persecuted both by Jew and Roman and Jesus himself had died because the religious leaders could not accept the truth which he proclaimed. And yet his way of compassion and forgiveness leads to peace and fulfilment and his disciples must have the courage to live and declare it openly, even though men, with tragic perversity, so often ignore or destroy those who might resolve their fundamental problems.

2 Salt and light—Matthew 5:*13-16*; Luke 14:*34-35*; 8:*16-18*; Mark 4:*21-23*; 9:*50*.

Citizenship of the Kingdom of God means commitment to the world. Salt acts both as seasoning and as preservative. The Christian therefore must give both flavour and stability to society; without these qualities stagnation and corruption can set in.

Light has to be seen to be effective. The task of the Christian is to illuminate society, but the motive must be selfless not self-regarding (*cf* Isaiah 42:*6* and John 8:*12* 'I am the light of the world').

Discussion

1 The law of cause and effect is an established part of scientific procedure. Can you see how it might work out also in a moral and spiritual sense? Take any of the beatitudes and apply it to a familiar situation, seeing if you agree with Jesus' analysis.

2 Do you think Christians do act as 'salt' and 'light' in modern society? What problems would you expect them to be tackling if they were following Jesus' directives?

3 The New Law—Matthew 5:*17-48*

Jesus did not legislate about every detail of life as did Moses before him and Muhammad after him. His genius lay in giving certain graphic examples of the re-orientation of the human personality when motivated by love. The difference between his teaching and that of the orthodox Jewish rabbi is clearly defined in the six brief statements this passage contains. For Jesus, it was always the *inner*

121

disposition which was of primary concern, whereas the Scribes and the Pharisees were more attentive to the external act and outward observance (*cf* Mark 7:*6–13*, 12:*38–40, p* 70).

Since Matthew was writing for Jewish Christians, he was concerned to show that Jesus was not downgrading that which was most sacred to the devout Jew; the Law which had been given to them by God was of necessity perfect. Even so, taken literally, verses 18 and 19 contain words which are so contrary to what we know about Jesus' treatment of Sabbath observance and Jewish food laws that, if he did express himself as Matthew has reported, he spoke with biting irony. He had in fact come to fulfil the law by his deeper interpretation of it and in *v* 20 he makes it plain how he regarded the Scribes and the Pharisees. In their emphasis on the letter rather than the spirit, they so often wrongly interpreted God's Law. (See Mark 7 for a clear illustration of this, *p* 38.) The examples which follow show what Jesus means by the higher righteousness which his disciples must have.

(i) Murder (*v* 21–26)   Jesus first states the law, which in this case is the sixth commandment (Exodus 20:*13*) and the subsequent trial and punishment of the crime. Then he comments, contrasting the outward act which is judged by men, with the inner disposition which is judged by God. So often it is anger or hatred which causes a man to murder. If we deal with the anger, contempt and hatred within ourselves, then murder will not arise.

Matthew adds two further sayings of Jesus which point firstly to the need for reconciliation before one attempts to worship God and secondly, the common-sense approach to personal relationships as unresolved anger may lead a man into a situation from which he cannot extricate himself. There is a parallel passage in Luke (12:*57–59*) where the parable relates material to spiritual bankruptcy. Men must repent before it is too late.

(ii) Adultery (v 27–30)   After referring to the seventh commandment (Exodus 20:*14*), Jesus again distinguishes between the outward act and the inward disposition. More often than not, it is lust which leads to adultery. The difference between love and lust is not a matter of sexual passion but of one's attitude to the other person. Lust simply regards the other as an object to satisfy a desire. Love always looks at the other as a person to be reverenced, respected and considered. In poetic language, Jesus points to the difference between self-discipline and self-indulgence. Self-discipline leads ultimately to self-fulfilment—self-indulgence to disaster. Matthew has added these words to Jesus' teaching about lust but Mark puts them in a different context (Mark 9:*43–47, p* 51), indicating that they need not only be applied to sexuality. The eye signifies the way we regard people and life in general, while the hand represents the action which follows.

(iii) Divorce (v 31–32)   In Mark (10:*1–12, p* 53) when Jesus was discussing divorce with a group of Pharisees, he emphasised the original nature of the marriage relationship. Later, commenting to his disciples, he placed men and women on an equal basis with each other, a view directly contrary to Jewish custom. The point which is made here is that a marriage should only be dissolved when it has ceased to be the true union of which the sexual act is a symbol. Many scholars believe that the clause 'for any cause other than unchastity' is an addition by Matthew put in to bring Jesus' teaching in line with that of the great Rabbi Shammai. But if we keep in mind the principle of inner motivation, we can see that this clause is entirely in keeping with the spirit of marriage. If men or women cease to feel sexual love for their partners and have extramarital intercourse, then the relationship is no longer a real marriage and divorce may be the only possible solution.

(iv) Vows and Oaths (v 33–37)   The third commandment is 'Thou shalt not take the name of the Lord thy God in vain' (Exodus 20:7). This is not a prohibition against bad language but against calling on God to witness the truth of a statement (although the original commandment had much more depth as it concerned the misuse of God's name in magical incantations etc.). Leviticus 19:*12* expressly forbade perjury, which means making a false statement under oath, an offence punishable by law to-day. Jesus however comments that oath-taking is an outcome of evil; what is needed is inward honesty. If you are in the habit of speaking the truth, then it is quite unnecessary to swear an oath that something is so. Apparently this did not apply to a Court of Law as Jesus himself respected the High Priest's oath and answered to it (Matthew 26:*63*).

(v) Revenge (v 38–42) (Luke 6:*29–30*).   In very ancient days injury was repaid with interest (Genesis 4:*15* where vengeance was taken seven-fold, *cf* Matthew 18:*21–35, p* 135). The Mosaic regulation of an 'eye for an eye' (Exodus 21:*23–25*, Leviticus 24:*20*, Deuteronomy 19:*21*) was an advance on this habit and constituted strict justice, although by the time of Jesus fines could be imposed by way of punishment. Jesus however cancels out revenge altogether. He advocates a complete change of attitude. In the three examples which follow, it must be remembered that Jesus was speaking to Jews who were living under hated foreign oppression.

The slap on the cheek, the robbery of a garment (in Luke) or a legal action as in Matthew, must not be taken literally. The average Israelite only had two articles of clothing—his shirt and an outer cloak, which served as a blanket at night—if he gave up both, he would be naked! Jesus is talking about a spirit of active love that will not be overcome by evil but which is able to overcome evil with good, because it will not respond to injury with a desire for revenge. Jesus is not saying that we must passively accept anything that is false, cruel or unjust. He himself acted against exploitation by clearing the Temple. He is not saying that we must lie down under oppression and violence, but that we should deal with these evils by not becoming part of them because we have the capacity to endure suffering without being contaminated by the spirit of bitterness, resentment and revenge.

His third example relates to a Roman practice. For purposes of rapid communication a state courier could requisition transport especially horses. His illustration means that a disciple of his should give double what is required of him. Finally, to those who beg or borrow, practical help must be given in a compassionate, sensitive way.

(vi) Love (v 43–48) (Luke 6:27-28, 32-36) To the Jew neighbour meant fellow-Israelite. The Law which Jesus quotes (Leviticus 19:18, 32) did not specifically state 'hate your enemies' but every loyal Jew would feel justified in hating the Romans. However when Jesus says 'love your enemies as well as your friends' he is meaning that we should regard all others—whether friend or foe—as people worthy of consideration and understanding. This is precisely what he did himself even when undergoing the agony of crucifixion (Luke 23:34, p 177). He makes an appeal to his disciples to walk the God-like way. It is not in the least extraordinary to love those who love you, but it does require a quite exceptional quality to be compassionate to those who wrong you. Luke includes more examples than Matthew of the enlightened self-interest of human affection. Genuine love however is selfless. This is the way to love as God loves.

Discussion

1 Do you think that Jesus is presenting an impossible ideal?
2 Do you consider that a forgiving character is a weakness because it might lead others to exploit you? Is forgiveness the same as forgetting? Can you forgive and still punish? Is there any justification for thinking that Jesus is advocating the lenient treatment of people who have committed terrible crimes against others, such as brutal murder?

4 The New Worship—Matthew 6:*1-18*

Jesus again stresses the importance of the inner motive and contrasts those who do things simply to gain public admiration with those who are completely sincere. With challenging clarity he gives three examples showing how the hypocrite simply gets exactly what he is looking for and the truly religious man finds a closer relationship with God.

(i) **Charity or almsgiving** The hypocrite is the man who gives his money so that people may say how kind and generous he is. He is not concerned primarily with the cause he is supporting but with his own reputation. Well, says Jesus, he gets what he is paying for! The disciples on the other hand must be motivated by unselfishness and therefore no one need know anything about it, not even one's intimate friends. (To the Arabs the right and left hand typified a very close relationship.) The fact that God is said to know about the latter kind of giving does not imply that the motive should be to win the approval of God, because this is only one step better than the hypocrite. True generosity does not seek for any reward other than that of helping the particular person or situation.

(ii) **Prayer** The devout Jew practised a number of private acts of worship as well as attending services in the synagogue and the Temple. It was not difficult for a man whose priority was to gain a reputation for piety to do so. However this attitude has nothing to do with real prayer. Communion with God takes place in the deep recesses of the mind and heart. It is essentially a personal matter. It is the genuineness of the prayer which is all-important, not its length or the repetition of endless phrases. The pagans are cited as an example not to be followed because they worshipped many gods with innumerable titles and ritualistic incantation was more important than conscious thought and meaning. By contrast the disciple of Jesus is to think of God as his loving father who knows his needs precisely. Nevertheless prayer is essential to the disciple as the means by which he becomes more self-aware. Jesus then gives the concrete example of how to pray. Familiarity with this prayer must not be allowed to rob it of its originality and conciseness. Jesus is portraying an attitude of mind, a way of looking at life.

Firstly there is a statement of the Fatherhood of God. To the Jew the name of a person signified his character, so God is our heavenly Father and as such we must honour him, especially by working for the coming of the Kingdom. The Kingdom is present wherever the reign of God or of Love is a reality in men's hearts and lives. It is both a present, earthly concept and also something which operates in a different sphere and will be finally fulfilled at some future date.

Secondly there is a realisation of our daily needs on every level of existence; of the need both to forgive and be forgiven; of the reality of suffering and difficulty, that we may not be overcome by extreme distress of evil but find sufficient strength to cope with what the day brings (*cf v* 34). A literal rendering of 'do not bring us to the test' could imply that God deliberately tests faith, which is absurd. Life itself tests to the uttermost if it is to be experienced to the full.

So Jesus' prayer emphasises a sense of perspective which embraces both world issues and the individual responsibility. The doxology (giving glory to God) which is found in the Authorised Version and which ends the prayer in common usage is not found in the best manuscripts of Matthew's gospel. Luke's version of this prayer (Luke 11:*1–4*) is shorter and appears in a different context, when the disciples, finding their master at prayer, ask Jesus to teach them how to pray.

(iii) Fasting The Pharisees and the disciples of John Baptist regularly fasted and were critical of Jesus' disciples for not doing so (Mark 2:*17*). Like charitable gifts and public prayer, fasting in such a manner as to draw attention to oneself could be undertaken simply for its effects. By contrast, if Jesus' disciples wished to exercise religious and moral self-discipline, they must not let other people know anything at all about it. Only thus would it achieve its proper aim.

5 The Two Ways—Matthew 6:*19–34* (Luke 11:*34–36*; 12:*22–31, 33–34*; 16:*13*)

Matthew now collects together a series of Jesus' sayings in which two different approaches to life are sharply contrasted. Luke has included these sayings at different times in his gospel.

(i) Earthly and heavenly treasure (*v* 19–21) (Luke 12:*33–34*) There are two kinds of treasure. One is worthless because impermanent and a man is consumed by anxiety to retain it. The other is a permanent possession because it results from the quality of life. In the medieval morality play 'Everyman' the only things a man could take with him when he died were his good deeds.

(ii) Light and darkness (*v* 22–23) (Luke 11:*34–36*). If your eye is healthy, you can see clearly. If your eye is diseased, you may be in blind darkness. If that is your only kind of light, then the outlook is indeed grim. A false perspective about life's values is like physical blindness.

(iii) God and money (v 24) (Luke 16:*13*).

In what does a man put his trust? He is bound to choose as he cannot serve two masters at the same time. This is strongly linked with the preceding saying as the false security of wealth can blind a man's judgment on ultimate issues (*cf* Luke 12:*13–21 p* 219).

(iv) Trust and anxiety (v 25–34) (Luke 12:*22–32*).

Food and clothing are not to be taken as ends in themselves. They are but means whereby we maintain life. If we have the wrong perspective we become very anxious, which is futile because worrying about a matter will not change it. Jesus uses a man's height as a measure of the unalterable. In this passage he is not preaching asceticism (i.e. a disregard for bodily needs and pleasures) or recommending a fine careless attitude about the future, but is again searching for inner motivation and a proper sense of proportion. Birds and the slender purple anemones which grow wild in Israel, have their grace and beauty because they are content simply to be. Man however is capable of planning for the future and it is quite right that he should do so, but not at the risk of the present or of the quality of life itself. Jesus puts first the Kingdom of God and his justice. If we have that perspective, then everything else will fall into its proper place.

Because *v* 34 can be taken pessimistically and has no parallel in Luke, some commentators think it was added by Matthew from a Jewish source. On the other hand it can be seen as endorsing Jesus' sayings about anxiety. It is foolish to worry about tomorrow because we simply do not know what tomorrow may bring; in any case, we need our energies to deal with today's problems. The Authorised Version of this verse reads, 'Sufficient unto the day is the evil thereof' which, linked with Jesus' prayer, could imply that if we have faith in God we will be able to deal with the present problems, especially if we do not worry about something which may never happen!

To sum up this chapter, Jesus is presented as talking about the generous spirit which lies behind true charity, the attitude which is involved in true prayer and the self-discipline (which in his day was often expressed by fasting) which is a necessary quality of the spiritual life. All this points to a certain detachment from material things and a consequent freedom from worry, which results in a sense of harmony and well-being.

Discussion

The sayings of Jesus have often been interpreted on a far too literal level as if he were advocating an impractical other-worldliness which could lead to nakedness and starvation. How would you apply them to twentieth century Western man? What is the difference between the happiness one can get by going for a springtime walk with a friend and the pleasure one can experience from a good meal?

Work

Look up the passages in Luke and note the different setting of these sayings.

6 Right judgment—Matthew 7:*1-11, 13-27* (Luke 6: *37-42*, 11:*9-13*, Mark 4:*24-25*, Luke 6:*43-49*, 13:*22-30*).

(i) About men—v 1-6 (Luke 6:*37-42*; Mark 4:*24-25*)

We are not to judge others because the whole question of judgment belongs to God. However there is also a law operating in human relationships. If we forgive, we shall be forgiven; if we condemn, we shall be condemned. Jesus uses a ridiculous example of a splinter and a plank of wood to point to the absurdity of criticising another for a minor fault when we have a glaring flaw in our own character.

The 'pearls before swine' verse is difficult. For the Jew, a dog was a wild animal and a pig an unclean one. If Jesus did make this comment he was pointing to the need for discrimination, which is not quite the same as judging. We must not press on people more than they can take either in a spiritual or worldly sense as they will hate us for giving them something which is totally indigestible (*cf* Mark 6:*7–13*).

(ii) About God—v 7-11 (Luke 11:*9-13*)

We must also have a right attitude towards God, whom Jesus has revealed as a loving Father. Ask, seek, knock, for God will always respond. The door to be opened is that of the Kingdom, so all requests and seeking are to be directed towards that aim. Jesus uses another absurd situation to point the lesson. No affectionate human father would give his son a stone or a snake when the child had asked for bread and fish. God is all that is best in human relationships and much more.

(iii) The narrow and the wide gates—v 13-14 (Luke 13:*22-30*)

There is a choice to be made between two ways of life. One is seemingly attractive and easy, because it is the way of compromise and self-indulgence, but it leads to self-destruction. The other way looks narrow and unattractive because it is the way of self-discipline and even self-denial, but it leads to fulfilment and life. Jesus sadly reflects that fewer people take the latter way because it appears to be so hard and demands much of a man.

(iv) False prophets and false disciples—v 15–23 (Luke 6:43–46) There are false guides as well as true ones and the Christian must learn to distinguish between the two. The only way to judge the value of what a leader has to say is to look at how he lives. What is the quality of his life and by what is he governed—love or greed? A good tree cannot bring forth rotten fruit and vice versa. Similarly, the acid test of discipleship will be the disciple's motive. 'That day' is the Day of Judgment when all men will be assessed on how they have lived their lives.

(v) The parable of the two believers—v 24–27 (Luke 6:47–49). In countries like Israel and Jordan it is necessary to dig down to rock for the foundations of your house, because heavy rain can very quickly turn the dry river beds into raging torrents, sweeping away sandy levels. So, says Jesus, we must be wise builders. Not only listen to my words, but carry them out, then you will have a firm foundation which will stand you in good stead when crisis hits you.

In the conclusion of the sermon (v 28–29), Matthew comments on the authority of Jesus which is in sharp contrast to the method used by the Scribes (cf p 10). In all the passages we have studied Jesus is laying down general principles which are timeless in their application, even if his examples belong to his own day.

7 The Golden Rule—Matthew 7:12 (Luke 6:31). This is really out of place as in Luke's version it is included in the section on 'love'. It makes more sense to add this verse to Matthew 5:42. It should also be linked to Mark 12:28–34 (p 69).

The negative principle of not treating others as you would not like to be treated yourself is found in the teaching of Confucius 500 years before Jesus, and the great Rabbi Hillel offered his disciples very similar advice. Jesus puts the matter in a positive way. Thus his words are more creative and far-reaching.

Discussion

1 People have often found that their specific prayer was not answered and so have become disillusioned. But Jesus did not suggest that prayer and God worked like a coin-in-the-slot machine into which you popped the prayer and out came the bar

of chocolate. How would you describe real prayer and how do you think it might be answered?

2 Do you think the choices life is always presenting you with are simply a matter of right and wrong?

3 What does it mean to be governed by a principle of compassion and forgiveness and how would this affect your choice?

Work

Make a list of topics about which Jesus taught in the Sermon, such as money, prayer, charity etc. and add these to your list of his teachings which you started from your reading of Mark's gospel.

Chapter 20

The Teaching Ministry of Jesus according to Matthew.

This section deals with the chapters which are in the main peculiar to Matthew and illustrate his particular purposes and characteristics. For the chapters not covered by this section see reference index at the back.

(i) Matthew 13—A Discourse in Parables, *cf* Mark 4.

This chapter, an extension of Mark, includes seven parables, four of which are found only in Matthew's gospel.

(a) The Parable of the Sower, its explanation and the reason for speaking in Parables—Matthew 13:*1-23*; Mark 4:*1-20* In Mark, the disciples ask Jesus the meaning of the parables, but in Matthew they ask him why he uses parables as a teaching method. Matthew's version is thought to be a later addition by the evangelist, for the disciples, being Jews, would be familiar with rabbinical use of the parable. In Mark it is also clear from the explanation that the different kinds of soil represent people while the seed is the word of God, but Matthew has confused the issue by stating that the seed illustrates the different kinds of hearer. By the time the gospel was written, some of the parables were not at all clear to the early church because they had been removed from their original context. Also the fact that Jewish Christians were singularly unsuccessful in converting Jews to their faith may explain why Matthew presented Jesus as being at times deliberately obscure.

(b) The Parable of the Good Seed and the Weeds (tares or darnel) and its explanation—Matthew 13:*24-30, 36-43* This is more of an allegory than a parable. Many scholars believe that the original words of Jesus have been added to and in fact what we have here, as in the explanation of the Sower and the Dragnet (*v* 10-17, 49-50), is more likely to be a recollection of a Christian sermon preached on the original teaching of Jesus, rather

131

than the teaching itself. As it now stands the story and its explanation is an allegory concerning the Last Judgment. The wheat is the righteous servant and the weed (tares) the false or evil man. The weed is probably darnel, which is poisonous. To begin with it grows very much like wheat, reaching about the same height. So good and evil men exist side by side not only in the world but even in the Christian community. God alone will judge at the end of the age, when the wicked will be consigned into 'the blazing furnace' and the good will be received in heaven. This phrase 'blazing furnace' occurs in 13:*50* and nowhere else in the gospel. However the rabbis thought of hell as a furnace of fire (*cf* Mark 9:*45*, *p* 51). Reference to 'wailing and grinding of teeth' *v* 42 is a characteristic of Matthew (*cf* 8:*12* and 13:*50*).

(c) The Parables of the Mustard Seed and Leaven—Matthew 13:*31-35*, Mark 4:*30-34* Note how Matthew makes the exaggerated claim that Jesus always spoke in parables. This is to explain why he was not always either accepted or understood. Matthew also supplies, in support of Jesus' authenticity, an Old Testament verse, which is not from Isaiah but Psalm 78:*2* (cf Luke 13:*18–21*).

(d) The Parables of the Hidden Treasure and the Pearl of Great Price—Matthew 13:*44-46* The same point is made in both these vivid stories. When once he has seen the Kingdom's true worth, a man will not consider any price too high to attain it. Of course, one must not take the story literally and quibble over the legal rights to the treasure; Jesus is showing that as men will devote great time and energy to obtain riches, so must his disciples exert every effort to gain spiritual ones. Furthermore they must convince other men by their preaching of the supreme value of the Kingdom.

(e) The Parable of the Dragnet—Matthew 13:*47-50* As presented by Matthew, this parable is very similar to that of the Wheat and Weeds, but there is some discrepancy between parable and explanation. In the story it is the fishermen who sort out the fish. In the explanation it is the angels. The parable itself seems to be about missionary work (*cf* Jesus calling his disciples to be 'fishers of men') but one does not win a person and then reject him. Possibly the original words of Jesus are contained in *v* 47 which applies to the universal character of the Kingdom. However the additions turn it into a Parable of the Last Judgment which will take place at the Second Coming of the Messiah.

132

(f) Conclusion to the Parables—Matthew 13: *51-52*
Matthew is here expressing the Jewish-Christian ideal as embodied in his gospel. If a rabbi becomes a disciple, he has not only the riches of the Old Testament to draw upon but also the vitality of Jesus' new concepts.

(g) The Rejection at Nazareth—Matthew 13:*53-58*, *cf* Mark 6:*1-6* Note how Matthew softens Mark's statement in 6:*6*. Once again the closing formula is used to end the great discourse (*cf* 7:*28*, 11:*1*, 19:*1*, 26:*1*).

Discussion and Work

1 From Mark's gospel (2:*18-22*, *p* 16) it would appear that Jesus realised his own interpretation of the Law was very different from that of the rabbis. From a study of this chapter, how far would you think that Matthew's own situation coloured his interpretation of Jesus?
2 What kind of difficulties does it raise for you when there are contradictory reports of Jesus' teaching?
3 Look up all the relevant Marcan references in this chapter.
4 Start making a dossier of examples showing Matthew's characteristics and purposes.

(ii) Matthew 17:*24-27*—The Coin in the Mouth of the Fish

This is a very strange story. It is hard to credit that it reflects an actual episode in Jesus' life where a miracle is performed simply for the sake of money!
Every male Jew over nineteen was expected to contribute towards the upkeep of the Temple (*cf* Exodus 23:*15*, 30:*13*). As the yearly tax was one-half shekel, two Jews would usually combine to pay a shekel or its Greek equivalent which was a much more common coin. Jesus implies that as true citizens of the Kingdom of God, they should not have to pay taxes for the upkeep of their father's house. However for Matthew and his contemporaries a real problem arose about the Temple tax because they considered themselves both Jewish and Christian and would not wish to give unnecessary offence to the authorities. Although the Jewish Temple was destroyed in AD70, the Romans continued to exact the tax.
Note how Peter features prominently in the story.

(iii) Matthew 18:*1-35*—The Nature of Christian Fellowship

(a) Humility and Responsibility—Matthew 18:*1-14,* cf Mark 9:*33-50,* Luke 9:*46-50,* 17:*1-3*

In Matthew the question as to who is the greatest in the Kingdom is asked by the disciples, thus softening the effect of Jesus' rebuke as reported in Mark. Matthew also omits (as does Luke) that Jesus put his arm around the child. The narrative is expanded here but conflated later in 19:*13-15* when Matthew is following Mark 10:*13-16*. The Marcan narrative is much clearer (see *p* 51 and 55).

In the gospels 'little ones' refers not only to children but to the young in faith; on other occasions Jesus called his disciples 'children'. As the early Christian community were more concerned with the disciples than with Jesus' attitude towards children, important though this was, in the course of time 'little one' was thought to apply to the believer. The saying in *v* 10 may originally have referred to children, although the majority of Jews strongly believed that all men had their guardian angels (*cf* Psalm 91:*11* and discussion, *p* 109).

The parable of the Lost Sheep (*v* 12-14) concerns sinners (*cf* Luke 15:*3-6* where the context is different). The image of the shepherd resolutely searching for his lost sheep is a familiar one, but the comment that he is more delighted over the regained sheep than over the other ninety-nine can strike us as unfair to the faithful disciples. Presumably the lost sheep assumes special significance because of the costly time and energy spent on its recovery. It is not God's will that men should 'stray from the right path', although human freedom means that some will do so.

(b) Church Discipline—Matthew 18:*15-20,* Luke 17:*3-4*

In order to make them applicable to the Christian community of his day, Matthew probably collected together various teachings of Jesus, uttered on different occasions. In this passage there are specific instructions about resolving inter-fellowship quarrels. Firstly the two people concerned must attempt a reconciliation; if this fails, then objective witnesses must be called in and in the last resort even the whole congregation should become involved. Finally if the offender does not repent, then he must be regarded as having left the church. The word 'pagan' or 'tax-gatherer' to describe the unrepentant sinner clearly shows that Matthew was writing for a Jewish-Christian community, not a Gentile one. If notice was taken of Jesus' own attitude to pagans and tax-collectors, then there was always hope of ultimately resolving the dispute. Matthew reports (in *v* 18) that the Twelve are given the same authority that previously had been conferred on Peter at Caesarea Philippi (Matthew 16:*19*). Some commentators think that the 'forbidding' and 'allowing' refer to the community's earthly life. Hence the Pope's prerogative of excommunication and the practice of absolution by priests of the Roman Catholic and Anglican communion (*cf* John 20:23 'If you forgive any man's sins, they stand forgiven; if you pronounce them unforgiven, unforgiven they remain'). However, as time and time again Jesus specifically refers judgment to God, it is fair to assume that *v* 18 and similar references belong to Matthew's day rather than that of Jesus.

In *v* 19–20 corporate prayer is said to be doubly effective, but Christians are bound together solely by concern for the Kingdom, so their prayers and work should be in total accord with Jesus himself, then truly his spirit is with them. It is possible that Jesus adapted a rabbinical saying to give his disciples the assurance of his continuing presence with them.

(c) The Parable of the Unmerciful Servant—Matthew 18:*21-35*, Luke 17:*4*

Continuing the theme of community life, Peter asks Jesus about the difficult question of forgiveness. The rabbis taught that a man must be willing to forgive if the offender truly apologised and made restitution for his misdeed. Behind Peter's use of 'seven times' lies Genesis 4:*15*, when vengeance was taken seven-fold, rather than the strict justice of the Mosaic regulation 'an eye for an eye'. In his reply, Jesus picks up this connection because in Genesis 4:*24*, Lamech the descendant of Cain, says—

'If Cain shall be avenged seven-fold,
Truly Lamech seventy and seven-fold.'

which means without mercy or limit. So, says Jesus, the Christian must be prepared to forgive in a limitless, merciful fashion.

The famous parable that follows is all the more interesting because it does not quite illustrate the point which Jesus has made. It is however characteristic of his teaching that only those who are willing to forgive will themselves receive forgiveness. A hard and revengeful spirit shuts out the possibility of forgiveness and reconciliation.

In the story, a certain king decides to settle his affairs and discovers that one of his servants has grossly mismanaged his charge. In his generosity the king eventually forgives the servant his enormous debt. This good example is not followed, as the servant goes out from his master's presence and exacts a due penalty from a comrade who owes him a trifling amount. The other servants, incensed by this lack of consideration, report the matter to their master who takes appropriate action. The king is very angry to see the servant's debtor callously treated and this time the servant is fearfully punished.

Matthew has probably added *v* 35 which ostensibly points the moral of the tale but embodies a kind of threatening attitude that is not characteristic of Jesus. Presumably Matthew is saying that Christian discipline within the community can only be properly exercised if the leaders know how much they too need to be forgiven by God. From the description of the punishment it seems that Matthew is referring to torment after death.

Note the characteristic formula ending the discourse (19:*1*). N.B. In Jewish law a man could not be sold into slavery if his debt was less than his price as a slave.

Discussion and Work

1 The contrast between the teaching in *v* 22 and that of the parable is stark. How important is it to demonstrate that 'forgiveness' is not weakness? If a man continually exploits another, should he not be punished? (*cf p* 21) To what extent should motivation be taken into account?

2 Certain sections of this chapter illustrate Introductory points about Matthew's gospel; be sure you have noted them in your dossier about Matthew's characteristics.

(iv) Matthew 20-*1-16*—The Parable of the Labourers in the Vineyard

The central point Jesus is making is that fortunately for us, God's love is such that it is not nicely portioned out according to what we think we deserve. It is a generous, over-flowing love which embraces all men. In the story 'first and last' have no meaning at the end of the day, therefore we must presume that *v* 16 is another Matthean insertion which does not make much sense in its present context.

According to Jewish law, the working day was from sunrise to sunset when a labourer was entitled to his pay (Leviticus 19:*13*). A usual day's wage was one denarius. In Jesus' day four denarii would buy a lamb, a hundred an ox, so one denarius was a good wage. At nine, noon, three p.m. and five p.m. the owner of the vineyard does not stipulate a wage, but promises to pay fairly. At the end of the day the steward deals with the wages, beginning with the last employed. Quite naturally, those who have worked twelve hours in the sweltering heat feel they ought to receive more than those who have simply worked for one hour. The owner's reply is based on two considerations. He has justly paid what he promised and he has a right to do what he wants with his own money. If he chooses to be generous, the first employed men should not let jealousy prejudice them against the others, especially as it was presumably not their fault that they were unemployed throughout the major part of the day.

As the vineyard was often a symbol of Israel (Isaiah 5:1), Matthew could have thought of 'the day' as being the whole of Israelite history, the successive summons to work as the repeated prophetic call, the steward as the Son of Man (cf Matthew 25:31). On this interpretation the 'last being first' fits Matthew's concept that the Christian community will have pre-eminence over the old Israel.

Discussion and Work

1 Do you think the master was just? Is it appropriate to interpret the story in terms of human economics?
2 Make a note of this parable as an example of how Jesus' teaching was re-interpreted by the evangelist, but do not ignore the central point.

For the rest of the chapter Matthew follows Mark, but note two points:
(1) In the request of James and John (v 20–28, cf Mark 10:35–45), Matthew softens the story by making the disciples' mother ask Jesus for the favour although Jesus answers the disciples themselves.
(2) In the healing at Jericho (v 29–34, cf Mark 10:46–52) Matthew leaves out the vivid details but adds that it was *two* blind men who were healed.

(v) Matthew 21:28–32—The Parable of the Two Sons

This story is obscured by different textual versions. We have been using the New English Bible throughout but if you are reading the text from the Authorised Version, the Revised Version or the Revised Standard Version you will notice that it is the first son who says 'no' and then changes his mind and goes to work; the second son says 'yes' and does nothing. In either case the meaning reminds us of Jesus' comment in Mark 7:6–7 'Lip-service, not heart-service, is what you give God'. The son who promised to work and did not, stands for the religious leaders, especially the Scribes and Pharisees. The son who appeared to be difficult and yet in the end did what his father asked, represents the 'sinners' who have listened both to John Baptist and Jesus and consequently repented and changed their way of life. Matthew has linked this parable to the religious leaders' challenge to Jesus about his own actions in cleansing the Temple.

(vi) Matthew 22:*1-14*—The Parables of the Marriage Feast and the Wedding Garment, *cf* Luke 14:*15-24*

While the first part of this story is much the same as the one recorded by Luke (see *p* 159–160 for full discussion), Matthew has added confusing material in *v* 5–7 and 11–14. The latter seems an independent fragment of another story as a guest brought in unexpectedly could hardly be blamed for not wearing the right clothes! As a separate story, 'not having the right clothes at the coming of the King' stands for being spiritually unprepared at the end of the age. Note the characteristic appearance of Gehenna, 'the place of wailing and grinding of teeth' (*cf* 8:*12*; 13:*42, 50*; 22:*13*; 24:*51*; 25:*30*). In contrast there is only one such reference in Luke (13:*28*).

Although *v* 14 does not really fit the parable it may have been a genuine saying of Jesus insofar as it reflects his own experience. It is true that comparatively few Jews responded to his teaching.

Work
Make a note of the three parables mentioned above and also how Matthew has changed the story as recorded in Luke.

(vii) Matthew 23:*1-36*—Condemnation of the Lawyers and Pharisees, *cf* Luke 11:*37-54*, 20:*45-47*; Mark 12:*38-40*

Although very similar criticisms are found in Luke (and to a lesser extent in Mark), Matthew has his own way of emphasising the religious leaders' basic faults.

The 'chair of Moses' (*v* 2) was so called because those who sat on it in the synagogue (the lawyers) were regarded as dispensing and interpreting the Law. Jesus however comments on the discrepancy between what is said, (which is often praiseworthy) and what is done, which should not be followed.

A 'phylactery' (*v* 5), a small leather box containing four scriptural passages, was worn by pious Jews on the forehead and the left arm during morning prayers; the 'fringes' or 'tassels' were prescribed by Law (Numbers 15:*38*, Deuteronomy 22:*12*) and were ornamentations on the prayer shawl.

The early church regarded Jesus as their only teacher, so *v* 8–10 may have originated from Matthew's time rather than Jesus', although Jesus himself constantly taught that true greatness in the Kingdom was humble service (*v* 11–12, *cf* Mark 10:*43-44*).

The seven lamentations (*v* 13–32) are addressed to the lawyers and Pharisees. In the *first* one there is a double meaning. By their literal interpretation of God's law, the lawyers and Pharisees actually prevent men from entering the Kingdom and in Matthew's day the Jews themselves prohibited others from becoming Christians. (Verse 14 is omitted from most manuscripts.)

The *second* condemnation refers to the brief period in the first century AD when Jews throughout the Roman Empire made a determined effort to win Gentiles to their faith. Gentiles were attracted to the ethical monotheism of Judaism but were unwilling to submit to circumcision and the strict keeping of Jewish ritual and food regulations. According to Matthew therefore, if a Gentile did convert to strict Judaism his last state was worse than his first!

The Scribes enforced petty regulations about an oath's validity; for example, it was only valid if sworn by the Temple gold, not the sanctuary itself. Their hypocrisy is condemned in the *third* example. Jesus believed in a more searching honesty (*cf* Matthew 5:33–37).

The *fourth* criticism deals with a preoccupation with trivialities (*cf* Luke 11:42). The tithe demanded by the Law (Leviticus 27: 30–33, Deuteronomy 14:22) was a tenth part of the harvest on flocks and cereal produce. Zealous for the letter of the Law, the Scribes and Pharisees extended the regulation to herbs such as mint and rue, which were probably not subject to the tithe and even strained their wine to avoid a drowned midge; contact with the dead insect would bring about ceremonial uncleanness. Jesus points ironically to the absurdity of such practices.

The lawyers and Pharisees were obsessed with ritual purity (*cf* Mark 7:1–23; Luke 11:39). Their lack of self-knowledge about their own inner impurities constitutes the *fifth* lamentation. Jesus' own emphasis was always on the priority of inner motivation. Graves were white-washed to warn people of their presence as contact with the dead ceremonially defiled a person (Numbers 19:16 *cf* Luke 11:44 but Matthew has slightly changed the sense in the *sixth* woe. The lawyers and the Pharisees are themselves so hypocritical as to appear good (i.e. clean) outside despite the rottenness within.

Prophets were only honoured when they were long dead and had ceased to be challenging (*cf* Luke 11:47–48). The Jews of Jesus' day were following in their father's footsteps by rejecting and persecuting Jesus himself. Note the bitter irony (*v* 32) in the *last* of the lamentations.

'Vipers' brood' (*v* 33) is a phrase used by John Baptist (*cf* Matthew 3:7; Luke 3:7), which has probably become attached to Jesus at a later date. Certainly *v* 34–36 read like an oracle relating more to Matthew's circumstances rather than Jesus', as the persecuted prophets, sages and teachers seem to represent the Jewish Christian leadership. It is possible that Luke has the original saying (Luke 11:49). In both gospels the reference to Abel and Zechariah, the first and last recorded martyrs in the Hebrew scriptures, (Genesis 4:*10*; 2 Chronicles 24:*22*), is intended to span Jewish history. In the coming judgment all martyrs' deaths will be avenged.

For the **lament over Jersusalem** *v* 37–39, *cf* Luke 13:*31–35*.

Work
Read through the chapter again and then add to your dossier about the lawyers and Pharisees, the essential points in Jesus' criticism of them.

(viii) Matthew 25:*1–46*—Parables of Judgment and the End of the World
Jesus' life had reached its time of supreme crisis. That being the setting for these parables, there was urgent necessity for his disciples to be alert and on their guard. For Matthew the parables all point to a different crisis, that of the Son of Man's Second Coming in judgment. He places the first parable immediately after Jesus' teaching about the Second Coming.

(a) The Parable of the Ten Girls—Matthew 25:*1–13*
According to Jewish custom, the bride waits for the bridegroom to come to her home, then the wedding party is escorted through the streets to the groom's house where the wedding feast is held. In this story certain details are obscure, for example, the absence of any mention of the bride and the uncertainty about the girls; were they bridesmaids—in which case why were they not inside the house?—or simply friends of the bride? However the interpretation of the story as it now stands in Matthew's gospel is that the girls, sensible and foolish alike, are the Christian church awaiting the Second Coming of their Master. Those who are found ready are received into the Kingdom, those who are not remain outside. In the other New Testament passages the Messiah is depicted as the bridegroom of the church (*cf* Mark 2:*19–20*; 2 Corinthians 11:*2*; Ephesians 5:*25*). The 'oil running out' could represent lack of staying power, as Christians were required to be faithful until the end. Matthew 5:*16* may suggest an appropriate image of the brightly burning lamp.

Discussion
1 On an everyday level, this story can point to the moral of being prepared, or even that you should live each day as if it were your last! Is the latter a sound philosophy?
2 Can you think of examples when being alert to every opportunity that presents itself is necessary to success?

3 Do you find Matthew's sharp division between those who are accepted in the Kingdom and those who are rejected really typical of Jesus' teaching? Other parabolic examples from this gospel are—the wheat and weeds, the two sons, the marriage feast. Some scholars suggest that this teaching is more characteristic of John Baptist than Jesus (*cf* Matthew 3:*12*). Would you agree?

(b) The Parable of the Bags of Gold or Talents—Matthew 25:*14–30*; Luke 19:*12–27* The central point of this story is like that made in Mark 4:25. If you do not use, you lose (*v* 29). Possibly when Jesus told the parable he was thinking of the priceless religious heritage of the Jewish nation. If the leaders were not prepared to share this gift with the rest of humanity, they would have it taken away from them. As Matthew now presents it, the story relates to the final judgment when the issue is how a man has used or misused his gifts and opportunities. Each servant is given a task or responsibility well within his capabilities. The first two work hard and double the money entrusted to them so that when the master returns he praises them highly and rewards them by giving them further responsibility; so this does not necessarily refer to the final judgment at all. The third servant, having done nothing with his money, tries to make excuses by laying the blame for his inactivity on his master's hard character. It is interesting that the master does not attempt to defend himself—life can appear to be very hard and unjust at times. The last servant should at least have put the money on deposit where it would have gained some interest. His punishment for lack of enterprise is simply that he is deprived of further opportunity.

Matthew has added a final comment (*v* 30) which does not fit the parable, as the punishment has already been administered. The pronouncement of eternal damnation is in keeping with Matthew's interpretation. Note the reiteration of 'the dark' and the familiar 'wailing and grinding of teeth'.

Discussion
For Jesus man belonged to God and the purpose of his existence was to serve God with his whole being. In the parable therefore the rewards and punishment are from God. In what sense do you consider the teaching to be appropriate to ordinary life, leaving God out of the question altogether?

(c) The Last Judgment—Matthew 25:*31–46* This is a fitting climax to the teaching of Jesus as found in Matthew's gospel and ends the fifth discourse. The chief characters in the drama are—The Son of Man, who is the judge and later called 'the King';

the King's father, who is God; the angels and all the nations of the earth. A man's character and conduct are known beforehand and so here is the clear-cut division between those who are on the right hand—the side of honour—and those on the left—the place of rejection. Sheep and goats would be a conventional way of describing two kinds of people as these animals were often herded together during the day but separated at night.

The basis of the decision is how a man has acted in meeting the need of another i.e. the hungry, the thirsty, the stranger, the naked, the sick, the imprisoned. However it is possible to interpret 'the brother of the King' as Jesus' disciple, which is perhaps how Matthew sees the judgment given. Admittedly Jesus declared his spiritual family to be those who both heard the word of God and obeyed it, but to assume that it is only the needs of Jesus' disciples which are to be met is to ignore the universal character of Jesus' mission. In the parable of the Good Samaritan (*p* 150) he clearly indicates that love discovers anyone in need as a neighbour. The whole purpose of the Kingdom's coming is to establish the reign of compassion in men's hearts and lives. For this reason a man is judged by his attitude towards others. Is he for or against the Kingdom? Help given to those so desperately in need is help given to Jesus himself.

The dreadful imagery of hell fire or eternal judgment is a striking feature of Matthew's gospel as is the clear-cut decision between the accepted and rejected. The spiritual truth behind these images is the fact of man's relative free will. Within limitations, human beings have freedom to make moral decisions. We cannot be morally neutral because such a stance leads in the end to negation. We can decide to be on the side of life, love and concern for others, or we can pursue a selfish way which in the end cuts us off from the true experience of living, creative relationships. This is the kind of spiritual death which is perhaps exemplified by the annihilating symbol of fire.

Discussion

1 When caring for the destitute, the homeless, the leper and the dying, Mother Teresa of Calcutta says, 'Every person is Christ for me, and since there is only one Jesus, that person is the only person in the world for me at that moment'. How do you think she and her sisters interpret 'the brother of the King'?

2 Would you agree with Mother Teresa's words? 'The biggest disease to-day is not leprosy or tuberculosis, rather the feeling of being unwanted, uncared for and deserted by everybody. The greatest evil is the lack of love and charity, the terrible indiffer-

ence towards one's neighbour who lives at the roadside assaulted by exploitation, corruption, poverty and disease.'

Work

Go back over the whole section and carefully make a list of the characteristics of Matthew's gospel. What fresh insight has he given into Jesus' teaching? Consider particularly the parables of the Kingdom.

Chapter 21

The Teaching Ministry of Jesus according to Luke

This section deals with the chapters which are, in the main, peculiar to Luke and illustrate his particular purposes and characteristics. For the Chapters not covered by this section, see reference index at the back.

(i) Luke 7:1–8:3;

(a) The Centurion's Servant and the Widow's Son at Nain—Luke 7:1-17; (Matthew 8:5-13) Luke places this story at Capernaum immediately after Jesus' Sermon on the Plain and before the final comment on the relationship between Jesus and John Baptist. The original form of the incident is possibly that reported in Matthew, where the Centurion comes in person to Jesus and the slave or servant is called a 'boy', which implies that he is the Centurion's son. There are close parallels with the healing of the Syro-Phoenician woman's daughter in Mark (7:24–30; cf p 39). In both cases the faith of a parent, expressed in an apt saying to Jesus, is so great that a Gentile child is healed without being seen.

Luke's story is remarkable because the Centurion approaches Jesus through two embassies. Firstly the Jewish elders bring the Centurion's request because they are grateful to him for having built them their synagogue (Egyptian inscriptions show that this did occasionally happen) and secondly his friends report the actual words of the Centurion. He is aware of Jewish sensibilities about entering a pagan's house; and as he is a man of authority who knows what it is to give and receive orders, he recognises in Jesus a spiritual power over the so-called demonic forces responsible for the illness. The climax of the story is Jesus' comparison between the greatness of the Gentile's faith and that which he had found in Israel.

(b) The Widow's Son at Nain—Luke 7:11-17 In Luke's account of Jesus' visit to Nazareth, Jesus refers to Elijah's miraculous healing of a widow's son (1 Kings 17:17–24). There is only

144

one other raising from the dead in the Old Testament; Elisha (2 Kings 4:*17–22, 32–37*) heals the son of a Shunemite woman. (Shunem was only two miles away from Nain.) It is possible therefore that what was originally a healing, as in the case of Jairus' daughter (Mark 5:*21–43*), has become in later tradition an account of a more miraculous raising from the dead.

The story is vividly told. Jesus comes to the city at the moment when the funeral procession is leaving it. He feels intense compassion for the widow as she will now be very poor with no husband or son to support her. He touches the stretcher containing the corpse, a thing no rabbi would do as contact with the dead made a person ceremonially unclean for seven days, and raises the young man with a word of command. In *v* 13, Luke uses his characteristic title for Jesus, the Lord, one which is seldom found in Mark's or Matthew's gospels.

(c) John Baptist and Jesus—Luke 7:*17–35* (Matthew 11:*2–19, cf* Mark 6:*14–29*) It is only in Matthew's and John's gospels that John Baptist recognises Jesus as the Messiah from the beginning (Matthew 3:*13–15*), so it is not clear from the text whether the Baptist's question is the beginning of doubt about Jesus' messiahship or the beginning of faith but, more probably, the former. John in prison has heard of Jesus' activities, especially his preaching on mercy and loving kindness. John believed the Messiah would bring judgment and destruction on sinners (*cf* Luke 3:*1–20, p* 113), but Jesus has maintained his purpose is to heal the sickness of sin (Luke 5:*27–32, cf* Mark 2:*13–17, p* 15). Jesus' reply is in poetic form and recalls the prophecies of Isaiah regarding the Messianic Age (Isaiah 26:*19*; 29:*18f*; 35:*5, 6*; 61:*1*); in effect, 'Yes, I am the Messiah, but not what you had anticipated. Therefore, do not be disturbed at the way my ministry is turning out.' Jesus refuses to declare himself publicly. Men must interpret who he is and what he does according to their own insights.

Jesus then speaks of John to the people. A reed bends with every wind that blows but John is not that kind of person. He is austere and uncompromising, that is why he is in prison and not one of the king's courtiers dressed in fine clothes. John is a prophet in line with the great prophets of old but he is much more than that. Jesus quotes from Malachi 3:*1* (Mark 1:*2–8, p* 6), identifying John with the return of Elijah who would herald the coming of the Messiah. He also takes positive action, hence his name, The Baptist. He is the greatest figure in the old order but he does not belong to the future. He is like Moses who led the children of Israel up to the Promised Land but did not himself enter it. The Kingdom of God is now a present reality with Jesus and his disciples. They belong to the new order. The greatness of John is not contrasted with the greatness of a Christian simply in terms of personal heroism and sacrifice, for John's own example could not be bettered except in the illumination which has come through Jesus. The ordinary people had accepted John's message but the religious leaders had rejected it, therefore setting themselves against God's purpose (*cf* Mark 12:27–33 where Jesus identifies himself with the mission of John).

The passage ends with a parable about children in the market place who will not play at weddings or funerals. John was called a madman because he was too austere. Jesus is criticised because he behaves in a perfectly normal fashion and above all because he befriends the social and religious outcasts of society. However although John and Jesus may have seemed to fail with some sections of the Jewish people, others had responded totally, in itself proof that God was at work in them.

If you look back to Luke 3, you will see how John's message differed from Jesus' as exemplified in the Sermon; so John's figure of the Messiah, noble though it was, was rejected by Jesus. He was not the righteous judge but the suffering servant of God who, through his message of love, had come to save men from themselves.

(d) Jesus is anointed by a Sinful Woman—Luke 7:*36-50* (*cf* Mark 14:*3-9*; Matthew 26:*6-13*) Jesus is probably on a teaching ministry and both Simon the Pharisee and the woman have heard him in the city. Simon is curious about Jesus and invites him to his home but neglects to provide Jesus with water to wash his feet and does not give him the kiss of peace, a greeting of respect. The meal would be held in the house which was left open so that it was possible for the woman to approach Jesus. Again we see the extravagant gestures of love which we noted in Mark's story, but this time the woman washes Jesus' *feet* with her tears, wipes them with her hair, kisses them and then anoints them with myrrh. To Simon the woman is completely untouchable. He is very critical because Jesus does not realise what kind of a woman this is and therefore lets her touch him. However Jesus knows not only what Simon is thinking but much more about the woman than do the rest of the company. He answers Simon's thought by a parable in which the money-lender is God, the first debtor the Woman and the second debtor is Simon himself. The lesson is quite clear. He who has been forgiven most, loves most. This implies that the woman has already responded to Jesus' offer of forgiveness and has come to the house to express her gratitude. Jesus accepts the woman's great love and publicly reinstates her by forgiving her sins, which provokes a similar reaction as did the healing of the

146

paralytic man (Mark 2:*1–12, p* 13). But on this occasion Jesus goes further by praising the woman for her faith (as well as her love) which has brought about her spiritual healing.

In 8:*1–3* Luke mentions the names of several women who supported Jesus and the Twelve financially in their preaching work. Mary of Magdala has been cured either of some illness or perhaps, of an evil way of life. Although Christian tradition has long associated the woman in Simon's house with Mary Magdalene, there is no evidence to support this assumption. Mary Magdalene has also been identified with the unknown woman in Mark 14 and with Mary of Bethany in John 12:*3.* We know from John (19:*25)* that Mary Magdalene stood by the cross, that she was one of the women who visited the tomb (Mark 16:*1)* and that the risen Jesus appeared first to her (Mark 16:*9–10* which is a shortened version of John 20:*11–18).*

Discussion and Work

1 There are some people who claim to 'faith heal at a distance' even to-day. What do you think about this?

2 Look up the Marcan story. Remembering that Luke does not include an anointing at Bethany, decide whether you think Luke's account is a different occasion or a variant of the one found in the other three gospels.

3 The real point of Luke's story is the contrast between Jesus' attitude and the Pharisees. People suffering from all kinds of physical, mental and spiritual maladjustments are made whole in Jesus's presence. Can you think of modern day attitudes comparable to those which are represented by Jesus and the Pharisee?

4 Make a note of the characteristics of Luke's gospel which are illustrated in this chapter and also discuss what special significance certain stories would have for Luke's readers.

5 Be quite clear about John Baptist's function. Add the information gained from this chapter to your dossier about him.

(ii) Luke 9:*51–62*—The Beginning of the Journey up to Jerusalem

(a) The Samaritan Villagers—Luke 9:*51–56* In the introduction (*p* xi) the origin of the Samaritans was briefly outlined. There was much hostility between Jews and Samaritans, especially as the Samaritans resented the very superior attitude which the Jews adopted towards them. They had their own temple on Mount Gerisim, built almost in defiance of the returned Jewish exiles from Babylon who refused to allow the Samaritans to help them recon-

struct the Jerusalem Temple. Their own Greek version of the Jewish Scriptures contained the first five books of the bible. Galilean pilgrims sometimes went up to Jerusalem via Trans-Jordan (*cf* Mark 10:*1–12*) simply to avoid passing through Samaria although the latter was the quickest route (see map *p* 188). It is impossible to be definite about which way Jesus went—indeed, the Marcan and Lucan accounts are not necessarily mutually exclusive. What matters most is to appreciate the significance of this journey to Jesus. We are entering now on the long special section of Luke from 9:*51*—19:*48* which superficially describes the geographical journey but which in reality contains the essence of Jesus' teaching as found in this gospel. The Galilean ministry is now over. Jesus is utterly convinced he must go up to Jerusalem although he knows what probable fate awaits him there. Luke brings out very strongly Jesus' inner conflict (especially in 12:*49,50*) but the whole section opens on a triumphant note with *v* 51 looking forward to the Ascension which symbolises the return of Jesus to his heavenly home.

James and John wish to punish the inhospitable villagers. Their reference to Elijah probably recalls 2 Kings 1:*9,10*. However punishment is not Jesus' way. Maybe the brothers' nickname 'Sons of Thunder' was given them at this time (*cf* Mark 3:*17*).

(b) The Nature of Discipleship—Luke 9:*57–62*; Matthew 8:*19–22* Luke gives three examples of would-be disciples, Matthew only two. Matthew has set this passage in the Capernaum ministry, possibly out of chronological order.

Jesus advises the first man to think deeply about what discipleship involves. In Luke 13:*32* Jesus calls Herod a fox, so in this passage 'fox' could stand for the Edomite foreigner who usurped the throne of David. 'Birds of the air' (*cf* Mark 4:*32*; Luke 13:*19*) is a Jewish phrase for Gentiles and could even refer to the Romans; the Son of Man is Jesus himself, the true Israel, dispossessed even amongst his own people.

The second would-be disciple asks leave first to fulfil one of the most sacred of all Jewish obligations—to give a decent burial to his father. Speaking with an ironic inflexion, Jesus again tests the man's sincerity. To follow Jesus is to become spiritually alive, to reject him is to be spiritually dead e.g. the 'prodigal son' was described as one who 'was dead' (15:*32*).

The third example is an implicit comparison with Elijah's call of Elisha (1 Kings 19:*19–20*); Elisha was permitted to say goodbye to his parents before following Elijah. Jesus makes the man realise that discipleship is not a temporary affair but a permanent commitment, otherwise it is useless.

Discussion

Do you consider that Jesus reacted harshly to these three men? From what we have studied of Jesus' teaching and poetic way of expression, would you consider he meant what he said literally?

(iii) Luke 10:*1-42*

(a) The Mission of the Seventy-two and Jesus' gratitude to the Father—Luke 10: *1-24* (Matthew 9:*37-38*; 10:*7-16*; 11:*21-27*; 13:*16-17*)

Luke has already recorded the sending out of the Twelve Apostles (9:*1-6*) so it is highly unlikely that he should duplicate or make up this further mission charge. It must have been in his source. According to the Jewish number symbolism of both the Hebrew and Greek Old Testament, seventy or seventy-two stands for the nations of the world. Thus Luke would see the sending out of the Twelve Apostles as the mission to the Jews and the sending out of the seventy or seventy-two as the universal mission of the church to the world. It is not impossible that Jesus sent out his disciples on two separate missions. Here there is a specific reference to harvesting; a warning about the dangers of their task and its great urgency. Jesus gives them two procedures to follow, one where the reception is friendly and the other where it is not. There is a sense of crisis over the whole passage as if the Day of Judgment were imminent. The Sodom reference (*v* 12) relates to the story in Genesis 19. In Jewish tradition Sodom became a supreme symbol of evil living, so Jesus' comparison is harsh indeed when he considers the fate of those who reject his message. The gospels tell us nothing of Jesus' ministry in Chorazin or of any mighty deeds done at Bethsaida. Capernaum was of course the centre of Jesus' Galilean ministry. These three cities are condemned for their lack of response and are unfavourably compared with the pagan cities of Tyre and Sidon. In *v* 16 we see the underlying principle of all work undertaken in Jesus' name and authority; the disciples represent Jesus and Jesus represents the Kingdom of God.

The disciples return from a successful mission. They have been able to exorcise (cast out devils) in Jesus' name—this power is a sign of the presence of the Kingdom. Jesus responds to their success in the poetic language of a visionary experience. The defeat of evil has already begun and the disciples must rejoice, not only because the power of God is at work in them but because the inheritance of the Kingdom is secure. In Jewish literature (Exodus 32:32) there are several references to the Book of Life or of the Living, a kind of heavenly register containing the names of those who are destined for life as God's chosen people.

149

Jesus' poetic rhythm is very strong in the thanksgiving which follows (v 21–24). As a result of some great response to his ministry, Jesus speaks to his disciples about his own spiritual experience. From an early age (Luke 2:49) he has been aware of a unique relationship with God, whom he called Abba, the intimate name for Father. At his baptism he had received confirmation of this special relationship and of his task. After Peter's confession he may have told his disciples of his wilderness conflict concerning his messianic role. Now he declares that the Father has revealed himself specifically to and through the Son. Jesus knows God in the deepest and fullest sense and is known by him, thus he is able to pass on this knowledge to others. It is not a matter of theoretical learning or academic qualifications but the spiritual perception which results from a close relationship. Prophets and kings of the old order looked and hoped for the coming of the Kingdom of God. Now it has indeed come with Jesus, so the disciples are doubly blessed because they are seeing and experiencing it as a present reality.

(b) The Lawyer's Question and the Parable of the Good Samaritan—Luke 10:25-37 (Mark 12:28-31; Matthew 22:34-40) In Mark, Jesus himself gives the answer to the question, 'Which is the greatest commandment?' Here it is the lawyer who asks Jesus what must he do to inherit eternal life and in reply to Jesus' question, gives the summary of the Law. Possibly these are two separate occasions because the point of Luke's story is the answer to the lawyer's further question 'Who is my neighbour?'

In Leviticus 19:18, neighbour meant fellow-Israelite, so the lawyer wants a further definition from Jesus but he does not get it straight away. The central point of the parable is simply that if a man has a loving, compassionate outlook anyone in need is his neighbour. Jesus further clarifies his attitude towards keeping the Law. In their concern with ritual purity and observance, the priests and the Levites saw only that contact with blood or the dead would make them ceremonially unclean so they failed to keep the essence of God's commandment. The Samaritan was a despised half-caste, ritually outside Judaism altogether, yet he saw what 'keeping the law' in its truest sense was all about. Oil and wine were thought of as healing agents in Jesus' day and the Samaritan's gift of money was generous. At the end of the story comes the acid test for the lawyer who is instructed 'Go and do as he did'. For a rabbi to be told he must follow a Samaritan's example was bitter indeed, but he had shown himself ignorant of God's will by thinking in legalistic terms of 'who is my neighbour?' For Jesus, it is love that is fundamental.

150

(c) Martha and Mary—Luke 10:38–42 We know from John's gospel that the sisters lived in Bethany with their brother Lazarus (John 11). Jesus is still a long way from Jerusalem so Luke has inserted this story too early in his chronology. Perhaps he included the story here because its theme, that of discipleship, runs throughout the section. We can imagine the situation where Martha is fussing too much about the meal and feeling annoyed that Mary is not helping her. But Mary has a different perspective. She sees in Jesus the Kingdom of God; she wants to be totally his disciple. She is the opposite of the three would-be disciples in Luke 9:57–62.

Discussion

1 This chapter has given us a further insight into the person of Jesus. His joy at the success of his disciples' mission, his strong reaction to those who reject him, although he does not take it upon himself to punish them, his parable about compassionate neighbourliness and his praise for Mary's insight—women have as much right to be interested in theology as men. Do you think Luke has added anything at all to the Marcan picture of Jesus?

2 Can you think of contemporary people who are like the Priest, the Levite and the Good Samaritan?

3 Have you sympathy for Martha? Was Jesus a little harsh to her? Is it fair to think that Mary only stands for those who dream away their lives without coping with the stern realities of practical living?

Work

1 You should compare the story about the Lawyer with that of the Rich Young Ruler in Mark, as both men ask the same question.

2 Also compare the Martha-Mary story with the Marcan Anointing at Bethany. This also deals with the question of perspective.

(iv) Luke 11:1–54

(a) The Lord's Prayer—Luke 11:1–4; Matthew 6:9–13 Luke's is a shorter and slightly different version of the prayer found in Matthew. The origin of the prayer is given when the disciples ask Jesus to teach them how to pray, as John Baptist had given his followers a set form. The prayer of Jesus is based on his own experience of the Fatherhood of God. Men can submit their whole lives with faith and confidence to the Father's loving care and purpose.

(b) The Parable of the Importunate Friend and other sayings concerning prayer—Luke 11:5-13 (cf Matthew 7:7-11) Matthew follows the Lord's prayer with a further emphasis on the need for a forgiving spirit. In Luke however, Jesus tells a parable which illustrates God's willingness to give to those who ask of him (cf Luke 18:1-8). The story is told with humour and would mean more to Jesus' contemporaries than to us because in his day the giving of hospitality, whether by day or night, was a sacred obligation. God cares for us much more than any human friend and in the verses which follow (see p 128) the conclusion is that we can trust the Father with all our needs.

(c) The Beelzebub Controversy—Luke 11:14-23; Mark 3:20-30; Matthew 12:22-37; (Matthew 9:32-34) Luke differs from Mark in that he introduces this story with Jesus performing an actual exorcism and members of the crowd accuse him of black magic, whilst others demand a sign from heaven. Jesus wonders how their own Jewish exorcists would react to such an accusation and strongly asserts that his own authority over evil spirits is a sign that the Kingdom of God is already present in their midst. There can be no neutrality in the conflict between good and evil.

(d) The Parable of the Unclean Spirit and other sayings—Luke 11:24-36; Matthew 12:38-45 Both Matthew and Luke include the parable of the Unclean Spirit as an appendix to debate about exorcisms. In this story Jesus simply accepts popular beliefs about demons and demon-possession, assuming that the desert was the home of evil spirits. Although the form of the story is strange to us, the meaning is perfectly clear and appropriate to our time. It is not enough merely to get rid of an illness or a bad habit; it must be replaced by positive health and wholeness, otherwise the last state is worse than the first. In Jesus' view, if the power of God expels the demon, then God must take possession of the vacant dwelling. In Matthew and Mark this controversy is followed by the arrival of Jesus' mother and brothers, but Luke has included this episode on an earlier occasion (8:19-21). However he seems to be making a similar point in v 27-28 when a woman pays Jesus' mother a pious compliment and receives a somewhat curt reply on the blessedness of those who hear the will of God and keep it.

In v 17 the crowd had demanded a sign from Jesus; (Matthew attributes this demand to the Scribes and Pharisees). Jesus now deals sternly with this desire for some stupendous manifestation, which he sees as a symptom of spiritual malaise. In Mark (8:11-13) the request was met with a flat refusal but in Luke Jesus gives two examples from Israel's past history. The Ninevites (Gentiles) responded to the preaching of Jonah by repenting, seeing in it a sign from God; similarly, the Queen of Sheba reacted to the wisdom of Solomon. God is now speaking through the Son of Man. Jesus himself is the sign and the only sign which will be given, because man's response must not be manipulated by brain-washing techniques. The true sign from heaven is the light of revelation which shines in Jesus (cf Matthew 5:15; Mark 4:21).

Discussion and Work

1 Sometimes it appears from Jesus' teaching that we have only to ask God for something and we will get it, but an indulgent parent is not a true picture of the Fatherhood of God. Could Jesus be expressing a psychological truth that by voicing our desires and needs we come part way to understanding whether they are worthy or not?

2 Look up the temptations of Jesus and link this recurrent demand for a sign with his own rejection of the miracle worker or propagandist image.

(e) Controversy with Pharisees and Lawyers—Luke 11:37-54; Matthew 23:1-36

Jesus is now invited to a meal by a Pharisee who is very critical of Jesus because he did not ceremonially wash before eating. Mark has reported in full (7:1-23; Matthew 15:1-20) Jesus' definition of religious purity as right motivation, not a matter of ritual observance. Here Luke takes the matter further by including six criticisms which Jesus levels against the Pharisees and the Lawyers. The Pharisees were practising Jews and the essence of their life was strict obedience to the Law:

The first fault Jesus finds in them is an obsession with trivialities (cf Matthew 23:23 p 139). The Pharisees were over-scrupulous in their adherence to the Law, yet neglected mercy and love which really mattered to God.

The second criticism concerns spiritual pride. The Pharisees revelled in the honour and deference paid to them.

The third is a charge of hypocrisy (cf Matthew 23:27-28 where the emphasis is slightly changed p 139). The Pharisees were like unmarked graves, exercising a bad influence on those who were unaware of it.

The Lawyers (who usually came from the Pharisaic sect) were concerned with the interpretation of the Law.

Firstly Jesus accuses them of making God's law an intolerable burden on men and doing nothing to help lighten the load.

Secondly the only prophet the Lawyers honour is a dead one who will cause no further trouble. Jesus saw the inspiration of God behind the prophets, so many of whom had been martyred. Of the 94 Old Testament quotations used by Jesus only 24 are from the Law. The rest are from the prophetic books and Psalms.

Thirdly the 'key of knowledge' refers to the revelation of God to his children. The Lawyers have obscured men's understanding of God's will by their preoccupation with details. They have not found the Kingdom themselves and have prevented others from reaching it. Jesus himself reduced the Law to the fundamental principle of Love (Mark 12:*29–31*).

Not unnaturally, the Pharisees and Lawyers were incensed by Jesus' criticisms.

Matthew does not set the dispute in a Pharisee's house and in his version Jesus' denunciation is much harsher, in keeping with the strong anti-Jewish tone of Matthew's gospel. (See separate notes on passage, *p* 138-140.)

Work

1 Make a note about Jesus' teaching on prayer and list the parables included in this chapter.
2 Add to your dossier on the Scribes and the Pharisees these further serious charges against them.

Now that you have read both accounts compare Matthew and Luke's treatment of Jesus' criticisms.

(v) Luke 12:*1-59*

(a) Conclusion of the controversy with the Pharisees and a warning of persecution to the disciples—Luke 12:*1-12*; Matthew 10:*26-33*; (*cf* Mark 4:*22*, 8:*38*, 3:*28-29*, 13:*11*) In Mark 8:*15* Jesus had warned the disciples of the leaven of the Pharisees without specifying what evil influence he had in mind. Here hypocrisy is explicitly mentioned.

The following sayings about darkness and light (*cf* Mark 4:*22*) relate in Luke's story to a time of coming judgment when the folly of Jesus' Pharisaic opponents will be made obvious. The disciples must not be afraid of persecution's physical danger, fearing only God upon whose ultimate decision a man's real fate hangs. But for Jesus the fear of God is all bound up with trust in his love. Sparrows are the cheapest bird on the market but even these are not outside God's universal care. The disciples must be fearless, trusting and also loyal to Jesus because in him the Kingdom of God is revealed (*cf v* 8, 9 with Mark 8:*30*, *v* 10 with Mark 3:*28, 29* and *v* 11 with Mark 13:*11*). Luke has inserted these separate sayings here because they illuminate his main theme about steadfast discipleship, a topic which he expounds further in Acts.

(b) The Parable of the Rich Fool—Luke 12:*13-21* A man asks Jesus, whom he regards as a rabbi, to give judgment over some family dispute. Jesus deals with the matter on a much deeper level. The cause of the trouble is plain greed and self-seeking. Remove the cause and the matter will be resolved. He then tells a story to illustrate his point. A man becomes very rich and decides to retire on the proceeds of his fortune, so that he can spend the rest of his life on pleasure. However he dies and his money is of no more use to him. In fact he faces another kind of judgment because he has been utterly selfish, concentrating on material wealth and forgetful of the things which really matter in the eyes of God (*cf* Matthew 6:*19, 20*).

(c) Freedom from Anxiety—Luke 12:*22-34*; Matthew 6:*25-33* Luke's passage is very similar to Matthew's version. Luke's 'ravens' are Matthew's 'birds' but in both the poetic form is striking. Jesus means that if a man has implicit trust in God he can look at life free from anxiety. He is *not* to be taken literally as if a proper provision for the future is wrong. He is not saying we should be layabouts and leave everything to God. The previous story sets the pattern of thought in Luke.

(d) The Future for the Disciples, Jesus himself and Israel—Luke 12:*35-59* Jesus knows a time of crisis is upon them. Having talked of forthcoming persecution and advised his disciples, he now looks further ahead.

Firstly for the disciples: (v 35–48). They must be watchful (*cf* Matthew 25:*1-13*). Luke includes two different parables which stress the unexpectedness of the end i.e. the Second Coming of the Son of Man (*cf* Matthew 24:*43-44*). One is about a man coming home from a wedding party whose servants stay up all night to be ready for his return and the other about a householder and a burglar.

Peter perhaps is thinking in terms of privilege when he asks whether the rewards of the faithful servants apply only to the twelve or to others. Jesus does not answer directly but points to the additional responsibilities of those who are closest to him. In a third parable a servant is made responsible for other servants in his master's absence. He betrays his master's trust and is punished accordingly but the severity of the punishment depends upon whether the unfaithful servant acts in ignorance or not (*cf* Matthew 25:*14–30*). In Jesus' teaching (*cf* Mark 10:*42–45*) greatness is measured in terms of service, so here Jesus says in effect 'as my disciples you have been given great responsibilities. It is the spirit in which you carry out the set tasks which is all-important. He who would be greatest in the Kingdom must be the servant of all' (*cf* Mark 9:*35*).

Secondly the future for Jesus himself: v 49–53 are in poetic form and give us further insight into the mind of Jesus. His tension and conflict are expressed in strong imagery. He who has such tenderness and love for all men knows that his coming creates strife and division even in the heart of the family. The metaphor recalls John Baptist's prophetic use of fire to denote the coming judgment. Jesus cannot speak peaceful words to his people; the coming of the Kingdom means warfare with deeply entrenched evil. Jesus also knows that he personally will be involved in terrible suffering (*cf* 'baptism', Mark 10:*39*). Matthew places two verses from this passage in a different context (10:*34–36*).

Thirdly the future for Israel: (v 54–59, *cf* Matthew 16:*2–3*, 5:*25–26*.) Jesus comments that his hearers, like good countrymen, know how to interpret weather omens but they lack any spiritual understanding to interpret the signs of the times. His coming has inaugurated a crisis but they are blind to God's sign, which is Jesus himself. The parable (v 58) shows that men would know how to cope with financial bankruptcy but are unaware of their equivalent spiritual state (*cf p* 122).

Discussion and Work

1 Look up the relevant passages and discussion in Mark and Matthew relating to Jesus' teaching about wealth and greatness. Do you think Luke's presentation of the matter adds anything to our understanding of it?

2 In this chapter Luke brings out the heavy feeling of crisis, not only for Jesus himself and his immediate contemporaries, but also for Christians in Luke's own day who faced intense persecution for the sake of their faith. What crises does mankind face today which demand sound moral judgment? Are the contents of this chapter in any way relevant to our own society?

(vi) Luke 13:*1–35*

(a) A Warning of Disaster and the need for repentance—Luke 13:*1–9*

Despite the witness of the Book of Job, it was generally believed in Old Testament thought that misfortune came upon a man because he had sinned against God. Jesus is now told of an atrocity committed by Pilate against a group of Galileans worshipping in the Temple area. The tellers' motives are not clear; perhaps they hoped to rouse Jesus to militant action against Rome or tempt him to indiscreet condemnation of Pilate. Jesus takes the issue on to a different plane. He totally rejects the theory that suffering is always a punishment for sin and mentions another case of sudden death which had nothing to do with guilt. As a man's life can come to an abrupt end at any time, he should repent now and be right with God. In the parable about an unfruitful fig tree (perhaps the origin of Mark 11:*12–14*), he sees Israel as the barren fig tree and his coming as the nation's last chance.

(b) The Crippled Woman—Luke 13:*10–17* (*cf* Mark 3:*1–6* and Luke 14:*1–6*) It would be generally assumed that Satan was responsible for the woman's curvature of the spine. Jesus, teaching in the synagogue on the Sabbath, sees the poor creature and heals her. The President of the Synagogue, not liking to address Jesus directly, criticises him for being a Sabbath-breaker. This poignant story shows the spiritual blindness of the religious leaders! The coming of the Kingdom meant the overthrow of evil in all its forms and Jesus had just demonstrated his power over Satan. Moreover, when the rulers permitted a man to care for his cattle on the Sabbath, why were they such hypocrites as to condemn Jesus' care for a fellow human being who was also an Israelite?

(c) Two Parables of the Kingdom—Luke 13:*18–21*; Matthew 13:*31–33*, (*cf* Mark 4:*30–32*). Luke includes the parable of the mustard seed as found in Mark but adds a further story about a woman baking her bread. Here leaven or yeast (the preaching of the Kingdom) is a good influence, unlike the leaven of the Pharisees (Luke 12:*1*).

(d) The Two Ways—Luke 13:*22–30*; Matthew 7:*13–14*, *cf* 25:*10–12* and 8:*11–12* Luke's setting for Jesus' uncompromising words about the moral choices which face men is different from Matthew's. Luke has also attached further sayings which are found in another context in Matthew. Someone asks Jesus a favourite question in Judaism at that time, presumably because the Jews felt they had an exclusive place in God's plan of salvation and looked forward to the privileged enjoyment of the messianic banquet when the Gentiles (especially the Romans) would be finally condemned. Jesus squashes these nationalistic and religious pretensions. The way of salvation is through a narrow door which does not stay open indefinitely. Inside the house is light and joy with the patriarchs, prophets and men of other nations. Outside are those who have forfeited their right of entry by an evil life. Salvation has nothing to do with race, position or power but depends on repentance and a man's response to all that Jesus represents (*cf v* 30 with Mark 10:*31* and Matthew 19:*30*, 20:*16*).

(e) The Hostility of Herod and the Lament over Jerusalem—Luke 13:*31-35* The unfriendly attitude of the Samaritans (*cf* 9:*51-56*) may have caused Jesus to cross the Jordan into Peraea, governed by Herod Antipas. Jesus had probably left Galilee earlier (*cf* Mark 6:*14*, Luke 9:*7-8*) because he had inside information about Herod's hostility. Joanna, wife of Chuza, Herod's steward, was one of his disciples (Luke 8:*3*). It is impossible to know whether this warning from the Pharisees was friendly or not. Jesus' reply is bitterly ironic. He will finish his work in the area and go when he is ready ('after three days' means 'in a short time') but in any case it is not for 'that fox Herod' to have his blood. Jerusalem has prior claim to be the place where the prophets of God meet their death. For the political implications of 'fox' see Luke 9:*57-62*. In Rabbinic literature the fox was also used to signify a worthless, insignificant man. The Lament over Jerusalem is in poetic form (*cf* Matthew 23: *37-39*). The wording implies that this is not Jesus' first visit to Jerusalem (as Mark's gospel suggests). There are not many recorded deaths of Jewish martyrs in Jerusalem but the capital city probably stood for Israel as a whole. The tender imagery of a mother hen gathering her chicks beneath her wings is also found in the Old Testament (Psalms 17:*8*. 36:*7*). For Jesus it symbolised bringing men into the Kingdom but the Jewish people would not accept his ideas of what the Kingdom stood for. They were obsessed with dreams of a national vindication by God when Jerusalem would not only become the capital city for all men, but the Temple would be regarded as the one and only true shrine of worship. These false concepts could lead only to destruction, as Jesus foresees with great anguish of spirit. (Jerusalem and the temple were destroyed in AD70 during the Jewish uprising against the Romans, see Mark 12, *p* 65.)

In John's gospel the evangelist makes clear that he regards Jesus as the Temple of God i.e. the proper place where God reveals himself to men (John 2:*21*, 4:*21-24*).

The end of *v* 35 contains a quotation from Psalm 118:*26*, which had special association with the Feast of Tabernacles. The crowd greet Jesus with these words on the Triumphal Entry into Jerusalem (Matthew 21:*9*, Mark 11:*9*, *cf* 19:*38*). In Matthew the Lament over Jerusalem follows the entry so that the words imply Jesus' second coming in glory. In Luke the meaning is not so straightforward. Perhaps Jesus was hinting that by the time the Jews did welcome him (as on Palm Sunday) it would be too late. In any case, regardless of that triumph, the religious leaders totally rejected Jesus and his way of peace, bringing eventual downfall upon themselves and their people.

Discussion and Work

This chapter is overlaid with a sense of impending disaster. By now Jesus fully realises his own fate but the Jews do not. You should (1) look up the references in Mark and Matthew and (2) make a list of the qualities which typify the unfruitful Israel. Do these symptoms of moral ill-health appear in our society?

(vii) Luke 14:1-35

(a) At the Table of the Pharisee—Luke 14:1-24 There are four parts to this section. Jesus' first action on this Sabbath is to cure a man suffering from dropsy, another example of the value Jesus puts upon a human being (cf Luke 13:10-17).

Secondly using the well-known rabbinical rules for giving and receiving hospitality, he turns them into a parable of the Kingdom. Note the recurrence in v 11 of one of Jesus' favourite principles.

Thirdly real hospitality arises from the desire to give to those in want, not to those who can repay. Similarly spiritual riches should be shared with those who need them. The example is Jesus himself, 'the friend of publicans and sinners' as opposed to the exclusive habits of the Scribes and Pharisees.

The parable of the Great Feast has become a marriage banquet in Matthew (22:1-10); Luke's presentation is much clearer. According to Matthew the unreceptive subjects kill the king's servants and are punished by the king's army. Obviously the death and revenge are an intrusion making nonsense of the remaining verses.

Luke introduces the parable with a guest's pious exclamation at the actual dinner party Jesus is attending. The messianic banquet was a favourite Jewish symbol for the good time coming with the Kingdom. Jesus is not at all sure of the man's sincerity—hence the story in which the host is God; the banquet is the Kingdom, the supreme blessing God wishes to bestow; the servant is Jesus himself. According to rabbinical sources, the double invitation was in accordance with Jerusalem custom. The guests are the righteous Jews; when the time comes, all offer different excuses which mean the same thing (cf Luke 9:59-62). The servant is sent on two further missions, one to the poor of the city representing the irreligious Jews, the other to those outside the city who could symbolise the Gentiles. Thus the terms of Jesus' ministry are clearly placed within the purpose of God whose bounty extends to all men. The parable refers therefore to those who reject the Kingdom, as presented by Jesus. They remain outside by their own choice, based on a wrong perspective (*cf* 13:*22–30, 34–35*). This is the tragic situation which caused Jesus so much sorrow.

(b) The cost of discipleship—Luke 14:*25-30* Jesus is now accompanied on his way to Jerusalem by great crowds who perhaps have glorious messianic expectations. Jesus warns them of their unrealistic approach. Discipleship is an extremely costly business. Compare *v* 26, 27 with Matthew 10:*37–38*. In several Old Testament passages 'hate' is used in the sense of 'loving less' (e.g. Genesis 29:*31–33*; Deuteronomy 21:*15–17*) so to take Jesus literally is to misunderstand his point. Priorities have to be clearly established even where two loyalties are not in conflict with one another (*cf* Mark 10:*7*). Loyalty to the Kingdom must come first. (Compare *v* 27 with Mark 8:*34*; Luke 9:*23*; Matthew 16:*24*.)

The two parables which follow concern the preparations and calculations a man must make to build a tower and a king to make successful war against another. Discipleship too must be a matter of deeply-felt and thought-out commitment, not impulse, especially as the cost and risks are so great. Luke's saying on salt is an extension of Mark's (9:*50*). Matthew's words 'You are the salt of the earth' (5:*13*) describe the function of the Christian in society.

Discussion and Work
1 As the passages in Luke refer constantly to verses contained in the other two gospels, it is important you check on Matthew and Mark and see how Luke has arranged material in his own way to suit his own purposes.
2 You should add the parables we have read so far to your list.
3 What do you think about the teaching contained in the story of the Great Feast? In what sense could the claims of the Kingdom come first before family life and how far would you agree with this?

(viii) Luke 15:*1-32*—Three Parables

Some commentators describe the section from chapter 15 to 19:*10* as Luke's Gospel of the Outcast. In it Jesus demonstrates his particular concern for those whom the rest of Jewish society despised and rejected.

(a) The Lost Sheep and the Lost Coin—Luke 15:*1-10*; Matthew 18:*12-14* The chapter opens with a sharp criticism of Jesus by the upright Scribes and Pharisees who cannot condone his association with disreputable people (*cf* Mark 2:*15–17*). They consider that a man is known by the company he keeps, but Jesus is equally convinced that God intends him to restore the morally unhealthy to wholeness (see Matthew 18:*12–14* for comment on the Lost Sheep, p 134). Jesus often told twin parables, both making the same point. All people belong to God, whether righteous or sinner; the sinner, like the lost sheep or the lost coin, must be sought for and brought back to his rightful place, to the intense joy of the owner. It was this extraordinary sympathy and compassion which the irreligious sensed in Jesus which brought them into his company, despite the fact that in him was no compromise at all.

(b) The Two Sons—Luke 15:*11–32* *cf* Matthew 21: *28–32* There are two points in this well-known story, the first being the father's consistent love for the younger son, which represents God's love for the sinner. It is this love which ultimately enables the son to repent, change his ways and return in contrition to his home. The second concerns the attitude of the elder son to his brother, which is in sharp contrast to the father's. The elder brother is the righteous Jew, the Scribe or Pharisee, who resents the father's generosity and has in his heart disowned his wayward brother. The father corrects 'this son of yours' to 'your brother'. Loving both his sons, the father goes out to meet both of them.

Jews did not keep pigs so they considered swine-herding as the lowest and most degrading form of labour.

Discussion and Work

1 Read carefully through the story generally known as the Prodigal Son noting all the finer points. Have you any sympathy with the elder brother? Do you think that love is sometimes reckless? Note how the younger son was firm in his resolve that he was no longer worthy to be called a son.
2 Look again at the stories in Matthew and note the different treatment which Luke gives Jesus' parables.

(ix) Luke 16:*1–31*

(a) The Unjust Steward—Luke 16:*1–9* This is a very difficult parable to interpret and we must appreciate that Jesus was probably speaking with fine irony, maybe using a well-known local incident as illustration. In the section as a whole Luke is discussing Jesus' way with sinners in contrast to that of the religious leaders. It has been suggested that this story is probably an appendix to the last one studied insofar as it is a criticism of the Pharisees' policy towards the irreligious, which is as unwise in a worldly sense as it is uncharitable in a religious one. The steward or bailiff used his wits to get himself out of a nasty scrape. He made sure that his master's debtors would be grateful enough to give him a home when he was dismissed for dishonest dealings. When the master found out what had happened, he was amused and admiring of the bailiff's astuteness, even if he had sacked him for his dishonesty. Jesus' comment is in effect 'don't be so spiritually minded that you are of no use in worldly matters.' Verse 9 concerns the right use of money indicating that it can be generously turned to God's service. It may not be part of the parable as it makes a different point. Whereas the parable shows a bad man taking infinite pains to make friends for his own selfish ends, *v* 9 urges a good man to take the same trouble for more noble and unselfish reasons (*cf* Matthew 6:*19–21*; Mark 10:*21*; Luke 12:*32–34*).

(b) Sayings about wealth—Luke 16:*10–13* These sayings reflect the teaching of Jesus as found in the parable of the Talents (Matthew 25:*14–30*) or Luke's Parable of the Pounds (19:*11–27*). Faithful service in little things is rewarded by greater responsibility. The wealth of this world is contrasted with heavenly or spiritual wealth. If the disciple has not been found trustworthy with this world's goods, how can he hope to be trusted with the wealth of the Kingdom? (For comment on *v* 13 see Matthew 6:*24*.)

(c) Pride condemned and some sayings about the old and new way of life—Luke 16:*14–18* The detached saying of verses 14 and 15 does not really fit into its present context because the Pharisees did not particularly love money; this description better fits the Sadducees. Moreover this aristocratic sect did not believe in an after-life so they would be much more likely to ridicule the idea of treasure in heaven. Although the Pharisees were guilty of spiritual pride, the Sadducees were members of the rich and powerful priestly class and therefore it is likely that on this occasion Jesus condemned them for their worldly arrogance and wealth.

Verse 16 has a parallel in Matthew 11:*12–13*. Luke's version is probably to be preferred although these questions of textual differences are difficult to resolve. It has been suggested that two historical periods are being contrasted, the old and the new. The old dispensation of the Law and the prophets reached up to and included John Baptist within its province (*cf* Luke 7:*28*). The new order, the present Kingdom of God, has begun with Jesus and his ministry. When the Kingdom is seen at its true value, then everyone will make the greatest effort to enter it (*cf* Matthew's parables of the Hidden Treasure and Pearl of Great Price 13:*44–46*).

In view of verse 16 we can only take verse 17 as an ironic comment (*cf* Matthew 5:*18*, see *p* 122). The 'dot' or the 'stroke' probably referred to scribal ornamentations of the Hebrew Scriptures; these were not part of the Law itself. Jesus pictures the end of the world coming about before the Scribes will change their scrupulous traditional preoccupation with inessential trifles. He was deeply critical of this habit of mind.

Verse 18 shows that Jesus felt he had the authority to amend the Jewish Law, in this case on the question of marriage and divorce. (For full discussion *cf* Mark 10:*1–12*, *p* 53–55; Matthew 5:*31–32*, *p* 122f.) Jewish law differentiated between men and women; Jesus puts them on an equal footing.

(d) Parable of the Rich Man and Lazarus—Luke 16:

19–31 There are two points to this story. Firstly the selfishness of exclusive worldly riches is condemned (*cf* 12:*13–21*). Secondly there is a life-after-death. We cannot take the parable as a literal description of this existence but it is a further stage in which present inequalities and injustices are ironed out.

The rich man of the story is probably a typical Sadducee who lived out his life in selfish pleasure, believing there was no personal survival after death. This belief makes his attitude to Lazarus, whom he knows, all the more callous. The beggar's existence was immeasurably wretched. When the rich man realises the consequences of his mistaken views, he makes three requests. Ironically enough the first is that Lazarus should alleviate his torment, secondly that his five brothers might be warned of their probable fate by the messenger from Abraham, and thirdly that Lazarus himself might be permitted to return from the dead, which would surely convince his family of the reality of eternity and of the possible consequences of their worldly lives. Abraham's mention of Moses and the prophets is directly related to Jesus' answer to the Saducean question in Mark (12:*24–27, p.* 68f). The religious leaders of course were not convinced when according to early Christian experience, Jesus himself was resurrected. (This lesson is further illustrated by the Raising of Lazarus incident in John 11.)

It is likely that the basis of this parable was a popular tale known both in Egyptian and Jewish circles. We need not therefore suppose that Jesus believed in eternal torment, rather that he used the current Pharisaic idea of rewards and punishments after death to drive home to the Sadducees the moral folly of their hard and utterly selfish way of life. In this respect this passage is an intrinsic part of Luke's Gospel for the Outcast.

Discussion and Work

1 You should add the parables in this chapter to your list of Jesus' teaching about different topics, also the specific references to the

Pharisees and Sadducees, remembering that it is conjecture that the last story was told about a Sadducee.

2 Look up previous discussion about belief in life after death and eternal damnation.

(x) Luke 17:1–37—The Journey to Jerusalem continues

(a) Various sayings to the disciples—Luke 17:1–10

On causing sin: v 1–2 should be compared with Mark 9:42 and Matthew 18:6–7 but when the three passages are put side by side there are obvious differences.

On forgiveness: v 3–4, *cf* Matthew 18:15, 21–22. The way in which Matthew handles the matter of disputes within the Christian fellowship suggests that he is writing at a later date when the problems had become more acute.

On faith: v 5–6, *cf* Mark 11:22 (*p* 63) Matthew 17:20. The context of this saying is different in each of the three gospels although both Matthew and Mark have 'mountain' as opposed to Luke's 'sycamore tree'. Maybe there were originally two sayings on faith in which Jesus used different symbols. Luke links the need for faith with the almost impossible ideal of perpetual forgiveness.

On serving God: v 7–10. This is a parable using contemporary social conditions of master and slave or servant. A human master could expect his servant to do his job both on the land and in the house before he looked after his own needs. For Jesus man belonged to God (*cf* Matthew 25:14–30) and the disciple in particular had voluntarily entered into a total commitment to Jesus. Therefore the emphasis here is not on the master's harsh treatment of his servant (which we and Jesus would condemn anyway) but on the principle of dedicated service to the Kingdom, through which the disciple could demonstrate God's love for all men. Jesus did not ask of his friends more than he was prepared to give himself. He also believed we could safely trust in God's generosity (*cf* Matthew 20:1–16) rather than believing we could earn our reward, as the Pharisees apparently maintained.

(b) The Ten Lepers—Luke 17:11–19 Luke has already recorded (5:12–16) the Marcan story of the healing of the leper (Mark 1:40–45) so the moral here is something different. Passing near the boundary of Galilee and Samaria on his journey to Jerusalem, Jesus heals ten lepers but only the one foreigner, the Samaritan, returns to thank Jesus for his compassionate act. Note the commendation of faith which results in wholeness.

164

(c) The Day of the Son of Man—Luke 17:*20-37* The Pharisees' question about the Kingdom is rather like the request for a sign (11:*16*, cf Mark 8:*11-13*). The Kingdom is here and now in their midst, in the person of Jesus himself, but, like the seed (Mark 4:*26-29*) it will achieve its consummation at some future date. Natural forces of growth are always used by Jesus as symbols of spiritual power.

In *v* 22, Jesus turns again to his disciples. Their longing to experience the Second Coming of the Son of Man will make them susceptible to false Messiahs but they must not be enmeshed; when it comes the true revelation of God is something quite unmistakable, like lightning in the sky. Both Mark (13:*21-23*) and Matthew (24:*26-27*) have similar warnings against false leaders.

Although Jesus believes his cause will be completely vindicated by God, he also knows he has to suffer and be rejected by his own people (*v25* cf Mark 8:*31*, 9:*31*, 10:*33-4*). In Luke, Jesus also foretells suffering and persecution for his disciples as well as himself (12:*11, 12, 49-53*, 13:*33*) so in this passage 'Son of Man' may be used in a corporate sense.

V 26-30 are in poetic form (cf Matthew 24:*37-39*) and deal with the Last Days (i.e. the Parousia) as in Mark 13. But whereas in Mark the end comes after a series of catastrophes, here everything is normal when disaster suddenly strikes. Luke's version, which is probably based on Q, is thought to be original Jesus rather than the composite structure of Mark (see discussion *p* 73f). In Genesis there are two examples of sudden destruction, the flood and the fire which wiped out Sodom. Both Noah and Lot were saved because they anticipated the catastrophe, unlike their complacent and indifferent contemporaries. V 31-32 are similar to Mark 13: *14-16*. Although the reference to Lot's wife has linked these verses to *v* 26-30, they do not really follow as they apply to a situation such as arose in the Jewish war and siege of Jerusalem. In Mark 13 we saw how Jesus' genuine prediction about the Fall of Jerusalem became transformed into part of an Apocalyptic discourse on the end of the world.

V 33 seems out of place here as Luke has included a like saying after Peter's Confession at Caesarea (9:*24*), the place where it is also found in Mark (8:*35*) and Matthew (16:*25*). Matthew also has a duplicate verse after the Mission Charge in 10:*39*. Perhaps Luke reports the saying a second time because he found it in his source (Q) and because he realised that although there were circumstances in which the disciples must save their lives, at other times they must be prepared to die for their faith. The Day of the Son of Man will divide people (*v* 34-37, cf Matthew 24:*40-41* and 24:*28*). Jesus had foreseen this previously (12:*52*).

The question about when the end of the world will come or when God will vindicate the Jewish cause is not strictly answered by Jesus (cf Mark 13:32). He believed they were at that moment experiencing the end of an age. A new order was coming into being; therefore the disciples must be alert, quick to see the signs and act upon what they observe. The vulture's swiftness was a proverbial saying (e.g. Exodus 19:4).

Discussion and Work
1 This is a difficult chapter to study because it seems to be a collection of various sayings which we have found elsewhere. Look up the variants in Matthew and Mark. The whole set-up illustrates the process by which the original sayings of Jesus, remembered for many years before they were written down, were used by the Christian community at different stages of its development.
2 It is foolish to live our lives in anticipation of an imminent end of the world. The early Christians did so and made many mistakes in consequence. But the general principle of alert awareness · which is the opposite of blind, complacent preoccupation with immediate everyday things, is a lesson which is generally applicable. Can you think of examples where this rigorously critical attitude is needed today?

(xi) Luke 18:*1-43*

(a) Two Parables on Prayer—Luke 18:*1-14* Both these parables are distinctive in that a reason for telling them is given at the beginning. The first story told to the disciples is that of the Unjust Judge or Importunate Widow. The point is similar to that of the Friend at Midnight (Luke 11:5-8). If an Unjust Judge can be persuaded against his inclination to deal with a widow, who represents the most defenceless and helpless strata of society, how much more will God deal justly with his servants who suffer injustice at the hands of the wicked. But when Jesus looks for such indomitable faith, he is not sure whether he finds it.

The second parable is addressed to the self-righteous and self-confident Pharisees—people like the elder brother in the Parable of the Prodigal Son (15:*25-32*). The Pharisees managed to maintain a very high standard of conduct, living extremely good, moral lives. Their besetting fault was that they despised others who did not attain the same standards; this made them spiritually conceited and self-satisfied.

In the story two men go to pray at the Temple. The Pharisee, who is completely devoted to keeping the Law, spends his time telling God what a fine fellow he is; he even goes beyond the Law in the matter of fasting and tithes. (On fasting *cf* Mark 2:*18–22*, *p* 16: on tithes, Luke 11:*42*, *p* 153). The second man represents the lowest form of irreligious life in Judaism at that time (*cf* Mark 2: *13–17*, *p* 14); he is a tax collector, very conscious of his own unworthiness and he asks God for forgiveness. This is the one thing in his favour. Being aware of his need, he receives something from God, whereas the Pharisee is quite satisfied with himself and therefore can receive nothing from God. The last clause of verse 14 has become attached to the parable for obvious reasons (*cf* Luke 14:*11*; Matthew 18:*4*, 23:*12*).

(b) For the rest of the chapter, Luke now follows the Marcan record (*p* 55–57)

v 15–17   Blessing the children, *cf* Mark 10:*13–16*
v 18–30   The Rich Young Ruler and the danger of riches, *cf* Mark 10: *17–31*.
v 31–34   Jesus again predicts his death, *cf* Mark 10:*32–34*.

Luke omits the request of James and John because he includes a similar dispute in his account of the Last Supper (22:*24–27*).

In *v* 35 Luke reports the healing of an unnamed blind man as Jesus enters the city of Jericho. Perhaps Luke altered the order of proceedings as reported in Mark (10:*46–52*) because he wished to include the story of Zacchaeus.

Discussion and Work

1 It is good revision to look up the Marcan record again and see for yourselves how closely Luke follows the second gospel.
2 If God is all that Jesus believed him to be, why is it necessary for those who believe in him and trust him to pray? Elsewhere (Matthew 6:*8*) Jesus says, 'Your Father knows what your needs are before you ask him.' Does this contradict the spirit of persistent prayer exemplified in the Importunate Friend and Importunate Widow?
3 Do you agree that spiritual pride is the most deadly of sins?

(xii) Luke 19:*1–48*

(a) Zacchaeus—Luke 19:*1–10* We are still studying Luke's Gospel of the Outcast and it is easy to see why we find this important story here. Jericho would have a notable customs station, situated as it was near the Jordan on the route from Judaea to the lands of East Jordan. Zacchaeus was obviously well-known and heartily disliked so Jesus is strongly criticised for entering his house. However Zacchaeus responds whole-heartedly to the presence of Jesus and spontaneously gives away half his wealth to charity, promising to make full restitution for any former dishonest practice. His attitude can be sharply contrasted with that of the Rich Young Ruler in Mark 10:*17–22*. Jesus' words are similar in tone to those which he spoke at the house of another tax collector, Levi (Mark 2:*14–17*) where the Pharisees doubt his righteousness because he is taking food with sinners. Jesus tells Zacchaeus that he has been restored to his rightful place in the house of the true Israel because the purpose of the Son of Man is 'to seek and save what is lost'. Note the emphasis on 'seek' which is exactly appropriate to Jesus and this tax collector. Look back at the Parables of the Lost Sheep and the Lost Coin (15:*1–10*) with which this whole section began. Here, at its end, Jesus perfectly demonstrates his own effective way with sinners.

(b) The Parable of the Pounds—Luke 19:*11-27*, cf Matthew 25:*14-30* Although superficially this parable appears to be like that found in Matthew, *v* 12, 14, 15 and 27 are additions which change its character. Some scholars attribute these additions to a piece of Jewish history associated with Archelaus (Herod the Great's son, see *p* 186), who built a palace at Jericho. Luke probably found it as an allegory in his source. As it now stands the certain nobleman is Jesus, who went to a far country, which is heaven, to receive his kingship from God. The servants are his disciples on earth who are left to carry out his work. The citizens are the Jews who have rejected him. His return signifies the Last Judgment when men will be rewarded or punished according to their deserts. In Luke's setting this story is told because of the popular enthusiasm that Jesus, as Messiah, will restore the lost fortunes of Israel. Through this parable Jesus categorically states that the king will have to go away before he establishes his kingdom and that his return is not in any sense a political happening but the Final Judgment.

When this additional material has been removed, the story is very like that found in Matthew, except that ten servants are each given an equal but comparatively small amount of money. On the return of the master only three give an account of their transactions; the first two receive ten and five cities respectively in recognition of their faithfulness. When the lazy servant's pound is taken away from him and given to the first man who had made ten, the astonishment of those standing by prompts the final saying in *v* 26.

(c) The Entry into Jerusalem—Luke 19:*28-36*; Matthew 21:*1-11*; Mark 11:*1-11* Luke is here following the Marcan narrative but with some additional material of his own which is given below.

(d) The Pharisees' criticism of Jesus' enthusiastic reception—Luke 19:*37-40*, cf Matthew 21:*14-16* As the pilgrims look across the Kidron Valley to the golden walls of their sacred city, they cry out with a great song of praise and expectation specifically acknowledging Jesus as their Messianic King (cf Mark's version). This outburst of joy causes some Pharisees in the crowd to remonstrate respectfully with Jesus but on this occasion he refuses to damp down his followers' enthusiasm, using a proverbial expression. It was then commonly accepted that material objects responded to great events cf the rending of the veil of the Temple at Jesus' death.

In Matthew the setting is after the Triumphal Entry and cleansing of the Temple when the sick people came to Jesus to be healed and children cry 'Hosanna to the Son of David.' The Scribes and chief priests complain both about the miracles and the children's shouting. Jesus replies by quoting from Psalm 8:2. For various reasons, particularly that the lame and blind were not allowed in the Temple area, the Matthean account is considered to be less authentic than Luke's.

(e) Lament over Jerusalem—Luke 19:*41-44* This is a prophetic oracle in sombre and desolate mood when Jesus weeps over the city and foresees its ultimate destruction. His reaction is in tragic contrast to the expectations of the crowd (cf also Luke 23:*28-31*, p176). By rejecting Jesus himself and the way of peace which he offered, the Jewish nation inevitably turned to open rebellion against Rome which ended in the appalling siege and total despoilation of Jerusalem and its citizens in AD70 by Titus (cf Luke 13:*34, 35*; Matthew 23:*37-39* and Mark 13).

(f) The Cleansing of the Temple—Luke 19:*45-48*; Matthew 21:*12-17*; Mark 11:*15-19* Luke's account of Jesus driving out the traders from the Temple is much briefer than Mark's and he does not make it clear whether Jesus did this on the same day as the Triumphal Entry (as in Matthew) or the next day (as in Mark); for comment cf p 62–63.

Discussion and Work

1 Look up the Marcan reference mentioned in the Zacchaeus story and revise the whole Gospel of the Outcast, noting the important teaching contained in it.

2 The Parable of the Pounds is probably an example of how later tradition has altered original stories told by Jesus. Taken literally, the execution of the king's enemies is a contradiction in terms to Jesus' main theme of forgiveness, but it can be interpreted as Jesus' characteristic recognition that a certain course of action brings inevitable consequences. How do you understand this parable or allegory?
3 Note the Lucan additions to Jesus' entry into Jerusalem and look up the Matthew passages.
4 Link together all the Lucan passages from this section which have given us further insight into Jesus' own mind and heart, in particular into his tensions, courage, resolution, sorrow and compassion.

Chapter 22

The Last Days: The Passion and Resurrection Narratives according to Luke 22-24 and Matthew 26-28. (With references to Mark 14-16)

(When studying this section it would be helpful if you were constantly able to refer to the *three* gospels side by side. For the sake of revision we shall take Mark as the basis and note the variations in the other gospels.)

(i) Luke 22:*1-71*; Matthew 26:*1-75*; Mark 14:*1-72*

(a) The Sanhedrin conspire to arrest Jesus—Luke 22: *1-2*; Matthew 26:*1-5*; Mark 14:*1-2* Luke follows Mark, but Matthew has a slightly fuller account in which Jesus prophesies his coming death and the High Priest is named as Caiaphas. Note also the familiar formula to end a great discourse.

(b) The anointing at Bethany—Matthew 26:*6-13*; Mark 14:*3-9* Luke omits the anointing in the house of Simon the Leper. He has an alternative story in Luke 7 (see *p* 146). Matthew's story is taken from Mark and is shorter.

(c) Judas' treachery—Luke 22:*3-6*; Matthew 26: *14-16*; Mark 14:*10-11* Luke attributes Judas' action to the work of Satan (*cf* John 13:27) and underlines the significance of his betrayal in enabling the authorities to arrest Jesus privately. Matthew gives us the price paid by the authorities for the information.

(d) Preparation for the Passover—Luke 22:*7-13*; Matthew 26:*17-19*; Mark 14:*12-16* Luke includes the names of the two disciples who went into the city. In Matthew Jesus again indicates that he knows what is going to happen to him.

(e) The Last Supper—Luke 22:*14-38*; Matthew 26: *20-30*; Mark 14:*17-26* Luke's account differs in several important details. The matter is further complicated by uncertainty about the actual text. Using one ancient Greek text and a group of ancient Latin manuscripts, the New English Bible and Revised Standard

Version omit the second half of *v* 19 (thus ending with 'This is my body') and the whole of *v* 20. Modern scholars generally agree that the shorter text is what Luke wrote and that the longer version was added later to bring the Lucan account into line with early Christian tradition based on Paul's account in 1 Corinthians 11:*23–25*, where the wording is almost identical with *v* 19b–20. We do not know whether Luke re-wrote the Marcan narrative of the Last Supper for his own theological purposes or whether he found the present account in his own Judaean source. In view of his careful treatment of Mark the latter view is probably preferable.

In Luke, Jesus first declares how he has longed to eat the Passover with his friends before he dies. We have noted in Mark the careful preparations he took to avoid an early arrest. This solemn religious occasion was an essential climax to Jesus' fellowship with his disciples when he summed up the significance of his whole ministry. (John makes this point very clear in his gospel by the inclusion of final discourses.)

Secondly in *v* 16 Jesus explains the intensity of his feelings by telling his friends he will not eat another Passover with them until the whole point of the festival finds its fulfilment in the coming of the Kingdom.

Thirdly Jesus takes the cup before the bread. If the shorter version is authentic the emphasis is on the future coming of the Kingdom of which this meal is a foretaste, the Passover being thought of as a prophecy of the messianic banquet. At the time Luke was writing, Christian rites and services were still in a fluid state. He reports in Acts (2:*42, 46*) that to break bread together was common Christian practice. By sharing in the same loaf, which Jesus describes as his body, the disciples symbolise their fellowship with each other and with their Master.

Fourthly Jesus announces the presence of the traitor after the meal, not before it, as in Mark. Luke's account, which is shorter than Mark's, includes the disciples' enquiring amongst themselves which of them could possibly commit such a crime.

Lastly Luke incorporates at this point a final discourse. Presumably both Luke and John are right in believing that Jesus had specific things to say to his disciples on this last occasion together. It was also customary to include a discourse at the Passover meal in answer to the question 'What is meant by this service?' (*cf* Exodus 12:*26*). V 24–30 concern greatness in the Kingdom of God. In Mark (10:*42–45; cf* Matthew 20:*25–28*) James and John ask Jesus for the chief places in his Kingdom. Luke omits this request in Chapter 18 where he is following Mark, which suggests that he had already found a similar incident in his Passion narrative. In John's gospel we read of Jesus washing the disciples' feet (13:*4–5, 12–14*) which seems to illustrate the parabolic saying in Luke 22:27. The promise to the Twelve in *v* 28–30 is paralleled in Matthew 19:28.

In the setting of the last meal together, the whole passage as Luke has described it, is poignant and moving. The way of the world is sharply contrasted with the way of the Kingdom. The disciples are told that leadership involves service as their master Jesus himself is the servant of all. However, their faithfulness to Jesus during his ministry and beyond will not go unrewarded; the disciples will share in the riches of the Kingdom and also in its responsibilities, symbolised by the picture of thrones and judgment (*cf* 19: *11–27*).

V 31–34 contain the prophecy of Peter's denial of Jesus, which occurs later in Mark (10:*26–31*). Peter, the acknowledged leader of the Twelve, will be severely tested by the forthcoming events. (Note how this trial is attributed to Satanic influences.) But Jesus has interceded for them all and especially for Peter. Peter will fail but his faith will be restored and he will be able to strengthen the others.

In *v* 35–38 Jesus looks back on the success of their earlier ministry (Luke 10); now all is changed. He is going to his death and he explicitly identifies himself with the Suffering Servant of the Lord (Isaiah 53:*12*). In stark contrast to his earlier instructions, he now suggests with bitter irony that the disciples buy a sword. They do not understand and take him literally. If the Master is going to make a fight of it they have two swords already. Jesus sees the impossibility of further comment and breaks off the conversation. 'Enough' refers to ending the talk, not that two swords are sufficient.

Matthew follows Mark in his account of the Last Supper but there are several additions. Judas is mentioned by name in *v* 25; 'and eat' is included in *v* 26, perhaps to make the passage fit into the early church's worship, which might also explain 'Drink of it, all of you' (*v* 27) and the description of the blood of the covenant being poured out 'for the forgiveness of sins'. Matthew may also have been referring to Jeremiah's prophecy concerning the new covenant to be established by God (Jeremiah 31:*31–34*). 'I will forgive their iniquity, and their sin will I remember no more'. In *v* 29, Jesus refers to the Kingdom as 'My Father's'.

(f) On the way to Gethsemane — Luke 22:*39*; Matthew 26:*31–35*; Mark 14:*26–31* Unlike Luke, Matthew follows Mark quite accurately.

(g) The Garden of Gethsemane — Luke 22:*40–46*; Matthew 26:*36–46*; Mark 14:*32–42* Luke's account is shorter. He omits the special reference to Peter, James and John as all the disciples appear to have accompanied Jesus to the Mount of Olives (which Luke does not mention by name). Jesus only prays once but such is his anguish of spirit that his sweat is said to be like great drops of blood. Luke also adds an angel's visit to give Jesus strength to face his terrible ordeal and attributes the disciples' sleep to being worn out by grief (for Luke's interest in angels see p 109).

Matthew has a very similar version to Mark's except that he gives Jesus' words in the second prayer.

(h) The Arrest — Luke 22:47-53; Matthew 26:47-56; Mark 14:43-52 Luke omits that Judas actually kissed Jesus as in his version Jesus forestalls his betrayer's action by a stern rebuke. The disciples offer to fight for their master and when one of them strikes the servant of the High Priest, Jesus stops them and heals the man's ear. Luke does not say that the disciples ran away, but he uses darkness as a strong image for the powers of evil.

Matthew also records that Jesus spoke to Judas. His words may mean 'What are you here for?' V 52-54 are peculiar to Matthew. Jesus refuses the way of violence (cf John 18:36 where he says to Pilate that his kingly authority comes from other than this world). However it is hard to reconcile Jesus' claim that he has twelve legions of angels at his disposal if he wished, with his words in Gethsemane. Nor can we credit that Jesus acted as he did simply to fulfil the scriptures (see p 94). The reference would be Isaiah 53:5, which presumably Matthew also has in mind for v 56.

(i) The trial before the Sanhedrin — Matthew 26:57-68; Mark 14:53-65; Luke 22:63-71 As can be seen from the references, Luke's order is again different from Mark. With dramatic intensity Peter's denial comes before the trial scene; the soldiers also indulge in brutal mockery. This may be because Luke has merged the two meetings of the Sanhedrin into one, held legally in the early morning. There is no mention of the false charge that Jesus claimed to destroy the Temple; instead he is asked if he is the Messiah. Jesus has no reason to suppose they will believe him but using the Daniel concept of the Son of Man's coming glory (cf Mark) he says enough to satisfy his interrogators even though he makes it clear that their interpretation of messiahship is different from his own.

Matthew mentioned Caiaphas by name and the High Priest puts Jesus on oath to answer the direct question about his messianic role. Jesus replies 'The words are yours', but goes on to use the same Daniel imagery as that recorded in Mark. The Council decree that he is guilty of blasphemy and should die.

174

(j) Peter's denials — Luke 22:54–62; Matthew 26:58, 69–75; Mark 14:54, 66–72 Luke omits Peter's protesting oaths but the poignant scene is heightened by 'The Lord turned and looked straight at Peter', who has also been on trial but has failed to acknowledge what he is.

Matthew follows the Marcan order of events.

Discussion and Work

1 You must now study carefully not only Mark's gospel but the notes on it in the text book. From a comparison with Luke you will see how certain characteristics in both gospels are highlighted.
2 Note the precautions taken by Jesus against premature arrest: He entrusted the preparations for the Passover to his favourite disciples;
The room was selected by a secret sign;
He told his friends to keep watch in the garden outskirts and in the grounds.
3 If you had only the shortened version of Luke's account of the Last Supper, what different interpretation might you have put on it?
Although Luke always presents Jesus as 'The Lord' note how he highlights Jesus' ironic turn of speech, his bitter disillusionment with his own people and his capacity for intense suffering.
4 Look carefully at Matthew 26:52–54 recalling previous discussions about his use of 'proof-texts' then observe the characteristic way in which he ends the passage.

(ii) Luke 23:1–56; Matthew 27:1–66; Mark 15:1–47

(a) The Trial before Pilate — Luke 23:1–5, 13–25; Matthew 27:1–2, 11–31; Mark 15:1–20 Luke's account of the proceedings is significant as he lists three specific Jewish charges levelled against Jesus. According to their lights, the religious guardians of their ancient faith perhaps had some justification for accusing Jesus of being a bad influence among the people. He had disregarded the scribal tradition about sabbath observance and showed his contempt for their interpretation of God's will. If universally accepted, his radical approach to many problems would have completely changed the Judaism of his day. However there was no truth in saying he had opposed the payment of tribute to Caesar or that he had courted kingship in a political sense.

Luke has inserted *a trial before Herod* before Jesus' final condemnation (*v* 6–12). It is possible to accept the authenticity of this account even though it is not mentioned in the other gospels, as Luke had private information about Herod's court (*cf* Luke 8:*1–3; p* 158). As this gospel apparently waters down Pilate's guilt in Jesus' death (*cf v* 14–16, 20, 22), some scholars attribute this passage to Luke's own pen. When Pilate realises Jesus is a Galilean he sends him to Herod Antipas, who had come to Jerusalem for the Passover as a token gesture to the Jews. Herod is curious to meet Jesus but is disappointed by his silence and apparent inability to perform any wonders. Contemptuously he sends Jesus back to Pilate and from that time onwards the two men become friends. Having included an account of mockery by Herod and his men, Luke omits the Roman soldiers' mockery recorded later by Mark (15:*16–20*). Only in Luke (see above) does Pilate make three protestations of Jesus' guiltlessness (*v* 14–16, 20, 22) and offer flogging as a substitute for crucifixion.

Matthew has interesting additions to the Marcan narrative: Firstly *the death of Judas, v* 3–10. No reason is given for Judas' remorse, nor does Matthew indicate how Judas' private conversation with the chief priests later become known to Christian circles. 'Blood-money' would defile the temple precincts, therefore it was used to buy a piece of land known as the Potter's Field. This story gives one of two explanations as to why a strangers' cemetery outside Jerusalem was called 'Blood Acre'. Acts 1:*18–19*, which has a different account of Judas' death, offers the second explanation for the name 'Akeldama' (the field of blood or 'Blood Acre', N.E.B.). In *v* 9 Matthew has given a wrong reference for his scriptural passage which is from Zechariah 11:*12–13*, not Jeremiah.

Secondly the introduction of Pilate's wife (*v* 19), whose dreams made her warn her husband to have nothing to do with Jesus. This led to Pilate's hand-washing before the crowd and declaration of innocence regarding Jesus' death. The people's sombre response is to accept responsibility for Jesus' execution (*v* 24–25).

(b) The crucifixion, death and burial of Jesus — Luke 23: *26–56*; Matthew 27:*32–61*; Mark 15:*21–47*

Luke alone mentions that Simon of Cyrene walked behind Jesus carrying the cross-bar, thus symbolising a true disciple (9:*23*). The usual crowd follows the condemned man but among them are a group of weeping women who raise a lamentation over Jesus. Recovering a little strength because the cross-bar has been lifted from his shoulders, Jesus is able to turn to the women and address them in compassionate but prophetic terms, 'Daughters of Jerusalem' (*cf* Song of Songs 1:*5*). If only they realised the terrible fate which awaited them in the forthcoming destruction of Jerusalem, they would weep for themselves and their children rather than Jesus. Barrenness was considered a curse for a Jewish woman (*cf* Luke 1:25, *p*101) but in the coming holocaust the childless woman will be better off because she will not have to endure the agony of seeing her children suffer. The suffering will be so intense that people will pray for a convulsion of nature (the words are taken from Hosea 10:8) to end it all. Verse 31 appears to be a proverbial saying which could be applied in a religious, political or universal sense, 'they' being either the Jewish leaders, the Romans, or mankind in general. The meaning seems to be 'if this is the fate of the young, vigorous, creative and innocent man, what will happen to the old, corrupt, decaying and useless person, or nation, or institutional religion?' But as Jesus was often enigmatic and ironic in his comments it is impossible to be precise about his allusions.

Luke has also several very important additions to the crucifixion scene, notably Jesus' words from the cross. Out of the depth of his understanding of men Jesus utters the prayer to his Father for his persecutors' forgiveness. Thus Luke brings to a climax Jesus' love for the sinner, the theme which runs throughout his whole gospel. The words of Jesus are all the more poignant as only Luke records that the soldiers in mockery offer him their sour wine and by implication further taunt the crucified man with the inscription 'This is the King of the Jews.'

The two criminals were crucified one on each side of Jesus. Significantly one reacts with abrasive jeering to the presence of the so-called Messiah — 'Save yourself and us.' The other, like the prodigal son and the publican in the Temple, recognises his own unworthiness and by comparison the injustice of Jesus' punishment. Amazingly he reaches out to Jesus as if his realisation of his own sinfulness had brought with it some hope of reconciliation. He is not let down. He receives the promise of fellowship with Jesus in Paradise.

Luke has omitted the trial charge that Jesus threatened to destroy the Temple so the mocking reference to this is left out at the crucifixion. Nor does he give Jesus' cry of dereliction and the subsequent mention of Elijah. Instead he records an eclipse of the sun (*cf* 'darkness' symbolism in 22:53) and the last cry of Jesus which could have been taken from Psalm 31:5. Luke's explanation for the darkness which covered the land is not physically possible at the time of the full Paschal moon; it was far more likely to have been caused by a sandstorm (see Mark notes). Jesus dies, submitting himself in total trust to the Father's tender care. So also, Luke reports in Acts, (7:59) did Stephen, the first Christian martyr, commit himself to Jesus. The centurion declares Jesus' innocence and the crowd go home lamenting the happening.

According to Luke, Joseph of Arimathea, a man of outstanding character and integrity, had dissociated himself from the Sanhedrin's decision to do away with Jesus. Luke agrees with John (19:41) in saying that the body of Jesus was lain in a new tomb.

On the whole Matthew faithfully follows the Marcan narrative but there are some alterations and additions. He does not mention Simon of Cyrene's two sons, presumably because in his day this detail was no longer of any interest to his readers. Jesus is reported as tasting the drugged wine but refusing to drink it. When he mentions gall Matthew probably has Psalm 69:21 in mind. The title on the cross bears Jesus' name and the soldiers not only dice for his clothes but keep watch. The bystanders preface their taunts by 'If you are the Son of God' and later 'he said he was the Son of God' — a reference to Jesus' trial. V 39 and 43 seem to echo Psalm 22:7 and 8 respectively and Jesus' cry of desolation (Psalm 22:1) is given in Hebrew rather than Aramaic. Matthew's phrase 'breathed his last' (Greek 'yielded up his spirit') suggests that Jesus had some control over the timing of his death. His loud cry showed that he did not die from physical exhaustion.

Matthew adds that at Jesus' death there was a severe earth tremor which caused rocks and tombs to split open. Perhaps his account that strange visions of departed saints were experienced in Jerusalem is a misplaced story connected with Jesus' resurrection. On the other hand the early Christians believed that Jesus went and preached to the dead spirits (1 Peter 3:19) and that he secured victory over death not only for himself but for others who believed in him. The centurion and others keeping watch were moved to awe by all that had happened.

Matthew names three of the devoted women who had been present at the crucifixion, Mary of Magdala (cf Luke 8:1–3), Mary, the mother of James and Joseph and the mother of the sons of Zebedee, whom Mark presumably calls Salome (Mark 15:40). As he tells us that Joseph of Arimathea was rich and a disciple of Jesus, it is possible to get quite a composite picture of this remarkable man from the gospel tradition. Matthew adds the further point that the new tomb in which Jesus was lain was Joseph's own.

(c) The guard at the tomb — Matthew 27:62-66 This section, which is found only in Matthew, raises difficulties and many scholars believe that even though Matthew found it in his source, it originates in a Christian refutation of the Jewish claim that the disciples had stolen the body. The chief problem lies in the improbability of a deputation from the Sanhedrin visiting Pilate, a pagan, on the Sabbath. In any case, why should they consider the remote possibility that Jesus might rise from the dead when even his own disciples had not understood this at all? Alternatively it is perfectly credible that the authorities should wish to take every precaution against any possible action by Jesus' supporters. After all he had admitted to being the Messiah and had talked openly at his trial about being vindicated by God. The two deceptions mentioned by the delegation are first a belief that Jesus was the Messiah and second that he had risen from the dead. According to this tradition the tomb was sealed and made secure with a Roman guard mounted over it to foil any subversive plot by the Galilean's following.

Discussion and Work

1 Look over these long and important chapters very carefully, particularly noting the Lucan additions and alterations to the Marcan story which suggest that he had his own independent source of information. As well as his marked pro-Roman approach there is his strong presentation of Jesus as the friend of the outcast and sinner.

2 Various reasons have been put forward for Judas' remorse e.g. that he did not intend Jesus to die but wanted to force his hand in declaring his intentions. Look again at the discussion on Judas' possible motives for betraying Jesus and try to assess his suicide.

3 Do you think it likely that Pilate dramatically washed his hands in front of the crowd? Look up Deuteronomy 21:1-7. Do you think this may have influenced Matthew's presentation of the story?

4 In what ways does Luke's story of the penitent criminal strengthen the Christian's conviction of life after death?

5 Note Matthew 27:19, 24-25, 62-66 and 28:11-15, all to do with Pilate. It has been suggested that Matthew gathered his material from a Palestinian source.

(iii) The Resurrection Narratives — Luke 24:1-53; Matthew 28:1-20; Mark 16:1-8

(a) The empty tomb — Luke 24:1-12; Matthew 28:1-8; Mark 16:1-8 Luke, emphasising their angelic presence (Acts 1:10), has two men in dazzling garments in place of Mark's young man in a white robe. The words spoken 'Why search among the dead for one who lives?' and the reminder that whilst in Galilee Jesus predicted his suffering, death and resurrection are also alterations of the Marcan text. Luke does not record a meeting between the risen Jesus and his disciples in Galilee, as is promised in Mark, but he reports that the women returned to the eleven and told them of the angels' words but were not believed. Some manuscripts add another verse (12) 'Peter, however, got up and ran to the tomb and, peering in, saw the wrappings and nothing more; and he went home amazed at what had happened.' V 24 seems to be referring back to this visit so it is not at all clear why it should have been omitted from other important manuscripts.

Matthew heightens the drama of the situation by saying that there was a great earthquake, an angel rolled back the stone from the tomb and sat down upon it. At this fearsome sight the guards were prostrate with terror. The women were not carrying spices (as in Mark) and the special reference to Peter is omitted.

For the sake of clarity, we shall now consider Matthew's and Luke's gospels separately, as they diverge at this point and there are no comparable Marcan passages.

(b) The resurrection appearances according to Matthew To the women v 9–10 — as they hurry back to tell the disciples of what they have seen. They actually touch Jesus' feet and receive from him the same message as that given by the angel. Some scholars think this story is a variant of John 20:*11–18* or else a repetition of the angelic incident given above.

To the guards v 11–15 — This is a sequel to Matthew 27:*62–66*. The soldiers have witnessed the resurrection but they do not tell others about it because they have been bribed by the Jewish Council to spread the false story that whilst they slept the disciples stole the body. Thus Matthew answers the current accusation of his day that the body of Jesus disappeared through the action of his followers. But the startling fact remains that for the Jews as well as for the Christians there was an empty tomb which had to be explained.

To the eleven disciples in Galilee v 16–20 — Jesus meets them on a mountain, apparently by pre-arrangement. There he reinstates them after their failure and sends them out into the world to teach his way, promising to be with them always. For Matthew the significance of the mountain (perhaps where he visualises Jesus' preaching his Sermon on the Mount) is the Old Testament association with Mount Sinai and Moses. But here is one greater than Moses, as is indicated by the worshipful attitude of the disciples and the claim to universal lordship made by Jesus himself. His new law will supersede and fulfil the old one. Doubts have been expressed as to whether Jesus actually commanded his disciples to baptise in the name of the Father, Son and Holy Spirit, especially as in Acts (2:*38*, 8:*16*, 10:*48*) the first converts were baptised into 'the name of the Lord Jesus Christ'. The phrase 'in the name' really meant 'into the possession of' i.e. into the new creation of Jesus the Christ or into the Kingdom as envisaged by him. It is probable that the baptism into the Trinity was the common practice in the community of Matthew's own day which had developed at a later stage.

Although Matthew's gospel was written for Jewish Christians, it is significant that it both begins with the story of the Gentile Wise Men and ends with Jesus' commission to spread the gospel to all the nations of the earth.

(c) The resurrection appearances according to Luke To two disciples on the road to Emmaus *v* 13–35 — In this wonderfully vivid story Luke draws together several important points about early Christian belief. On the first day of the week, later to be called Sunday, Cleopas and someone else, possibly his wife, are sadly walking from Jerusalem to Emmaus. They are joined by a stranger whom they do not recognise as the Lord. They talk to the stranger about Jesus, describing him as the man whom they had hoped would liberate Israel, and about the incomprehensible events of that day. The stranger charges them with lack of understanding, especially regarding the prophecies of a Suffering Servant Messiah (Isaiah 52:*13*–53:*12*). Beginning with Moses he illuminates the scriptures for them in relation to himself. Matthew's gospel has shown how essential to the early Christians was this link with the Old Testament. Jesus was the fulfilment of what had gone before. His death and resurrection were all part of God's saving design for mankind.

When the travellers reach the village the two disciples press the stranger to stay overnight with them. As the stranger breaks the bread and hands it to them at the meal, their eyes are opened and they recognise him. The familiar action and words penetrate their incredulity and they realise that the resurrection has in very truth taken place. So for Luke in the fellowship of the young church the presence of the risen Lord was experienced (*cf* Acts 2:*43*–*47*) in the common meal and the united act of praise and thanksgiving.

The disciples hurried back to Jerusalem and found the Eleven already convinced of Jesus' resurrection as he had appeared to Simon Peter (*cf* 1 Corinthians 15:*5*).

To the disciples in Jerusalem *v* 36–49 — While they are talking together Jesus appears among them. They cannot believe their eyes but he demonstrates his reality by eating a piece of fish in front of them. That Jesus' resurrection body was tangible was part of the Apostolic witness according to Luke (*cf* Acts 10:*41*). As in the previous story, the significant phrase lies in 'then he opened their minds' to understand, in this case the scriptures. Luke intends to draw out the different kinds of 'seeing' and of 'understanding' which were essential parts of discipleship and of belief in the resurrection itself. In this he is very like the author of John's gospel.

The disciples are then given a missionary charge to proclaim in Jesus' name the forgiveness of sins to all nations, beginning from Jerusalem. They will be empowered to carry out this work by the Father's promised gift which will come to them in Jerusalem itself. Thus Luke prepares the way for his story of Pentecost in the second volume of his great work (Acts).

The Leavetaking *v* 50–53 — According to Acts (1:3) forty days passed between the Resurrection and Ascension. The gospel narrative seems to be an abridged version of that found in Acts (1:*1–11*) although if we had not got Acts we could assume that Jesus left them at Bethany after blessing them when he had given them their final instructions. The concept of an ascension is difficult for twentieth century minds to accept for we know so much more about outer space than those first century Christians. Interestingly enough, the best manuscripts omit that Jesus was carried up into heaven. Luke is simply saying that on a distinctly memorable occasion the physical Jesus left his friends for good. From now on they are to be aware of his spiritual presence in their midst in a different yet more compelling way. The disciples are to spend the next ten days (according to the time schedule of Acts) in the Temple praising God, but when the gift of the Spirit comes they are all together in an Upper Room (Acts 2:*1–4*).

Discussion and Work

1 In our first discussion of the arguments for and against a belief in the resurrection we did not take into consideration the Lucan and Matthean narratives. Now that you have studied them which resurrection story do you consider to be most significant for Christian belief?

2 Look carefully at the evidence of the kind of young Christian communities which Luke and Matthew represented and wrote for. In what respects do you think their hopes and ideals differed from the Christian church of today?

3 Both Matthew and Luke report that 'some doubted' the evidence before their eyes of the resurrection. What theological idea do you think they are trying to represent by this piece of honesty?

4 Now that you have read all the three gospels with their different viewpoints and interpretations, what picture of Jesus of Nazareth have you formed in your own mind? What kind of a man do you consider him to have been?

APPENDIX A

Notes on the Jewish Law

(a) The heart of the Law is the Ten Commandments given to Moses on Mount Sinai, and the Book of the Covenant, an expansion of the commandments (Exodus 20:*1-23:33*). To this kernel of sacred instructions were added many others constituting the book of Leviticus and part of Exodus. All were traditionally attributed to Moses but could not possibly have come from him. Many of them deal with matters relating to a settled community life not the wilderness-wandering period which he knew.

The Law is roughly divided into two kinds of regulations (*cf* Mark 12:*28-34 p* 69), those concerned with ritual and those concerning morals. It is not a division between religious and social requirements because Israel recognised the demands of an ethical God and worshipped him according to a strict morality as well as specific rites.

The term the TORAH covers the first five books of the Old Testament. It stands for the Law in the fullest sense as these books contain the will of God for his people.

(b) There was also the Oral Tradition called the MISHNA, which had been built up over centuries of study of the sacred scriptures. The lawyers, who were called Scribes/Rabbis in Jesus' day, endeavoured to interpret the ancient regulations according to their own times and argued amongst themselves about the meaning of certain texts (eg. Mark 10:*1-12, p* 53). Jesus consistently downgraded this Oral Tradition (eg. Mark 7:*1-23, p* 38).

(c) Eventually the Oral tradition came to be written down. The TALMUD is the name given to the vast encyclopaedic work containing the Mishna itself and further controversial interpretation and elaboration.

Religious institutions in New Testament times

(a) **The Home** The home and family have always been the centre of the Jewish faith. When the Passover meal is eaten in the home the father presides and the youngest son asks the meaning of the rite. In Jesus' day the Passover was observed in Jerusalem by those who could make the pilgrimage there and families procured Passover lambs slain in the Temple (Deuteronomy 16:6). The rite of circumcision was also performed in the home eight days after the birth of a Jewish boy. This was the mark of belonging to a Covenanted people.

(b) The Synagogue (*cf p* 9) Although the Law prescribed sacrifices in the Jewish Temple in Jerusalem, the synagogue was the local centre of worship and teaching. Even in Jerusalem itself there were many synagogues.

(c) The Temple (*cf p* 62) The system of sacrifices, prescribed by the Law, was concentrated in one place (Deuteronomy 12:5–7). The Temple of Jesus' day, built by Herod the Great, had been begun about 20–19BC but not completed until about AD64 (see plan). The Temple was the centre of the Jewish priestly ministry, the priests alone carrying out the sacrifices, although Jewish men were regularly present in the Court of Israel to witness the daily sacrifices. Praise and prayer were also offered at morning and evening incense.

The Sanhedrin, the highest Jewish religious and official court, met in Temple area and was presided over by the High Priest.

(d) Special days and festivals
   (i)   the Sabbath;
   (ii)   the Autumnal New Year celebration;
   (iii) the Day of Atonement (a day of fasting in September/October);
   (iv) The Feast of the Passover and Unleavened Bread (Spring);
   (v)   the Feast of Weeks or Pentecost, fifty days later;
   (vi) the Feast of Booths or Tabernacles, on 15th day of 7th month, for eight days, which originally celebrated the grape harvest.

APPENDIX B

Family Tree of Herod the Great

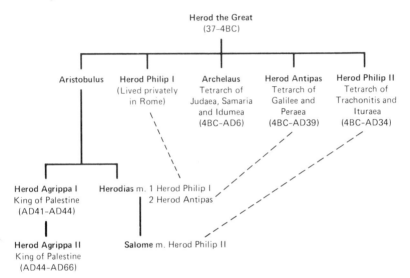

Herod the Great was the son of Antipater, an Idumean. The Romans first made him governor of Galilee and then later King of the Jews. He was unswervingly loyal to Rome throughout his reign and endeavoured to repair the disorder of the previous twelve years, making the political life of Palestine stable. He protected the country from invasion and took strong measures to suppress internal confusion. He genuinely believed the future of the Jews was bound up with the Roman Empire.

For obvious reasons Herod was not popular among the Jews. His reign represented the control of Rome which was deeply resented. He had destroyed the royal house of the Hasmoneans, widely regarded as the rightful kings of Palestine. Although he rebuilt the great Temple in Jerusalem, he regarded himself as a great king in the eyes of the Roman world and so was a benefactor to Greek cities, building temples and market places with money raised by taxing Jews! To his credit, the country became much more prosperous during his reign and new cities emerged, the chief among them being Caesarea on the coast (built between 22–10BC) which later became the seat of the Roman Procurator. The high priests of his reign were his nominees and therefore politically subservient to him.

Herod had ten wives and numerous children, all of whom filled his palace with slander and plots. They were divided into two factions, an Idumean (or Edomite) and a Jewish one, as he had married Mariamne, a Hebrew of the royal house of the Hasmoneans. His last years were made terrible by the intrigues of his household. He was an extremely cruel man and put to death not only Mariamne but three of his sons for suspected plotting against him. His suspicious nature helped to create the treacherous web in which he was entangled.

On the death of Herod his kingdom was divided among his three sons: *Archelaus* received Judaea, Samaria and Idumea but was deposed in AD6. (The Romans then made Judaea and Samaria into a province under the governorship of a procurator. Pontius Pilate was the sixth Roman Procurator, appointed in AD25–26.) *Antipas* received Galilee and Peraea. He married first a daughter of Aretas, King of Arabia. Later he persuaded Herodias, the wife of Herod Philip I, to leave her husband and marry him. Aretas made war on Antipas and defeated him. The Jews believed this defeat was Antipas' punishment for the murder of John Baptist. Herodias later persuaded her husband to go to Rome to obtain the title of King but he was opposed by Herod Agrippa and banished in AD39. *Herod Philip II* received Ituraea and Trachonitis and was responsible for rebuilding the cities of Caesarea Philippi and Bethsaida. He married Salome the daughter of Herod Philip I and Herodias. He died in AD34.

In AD41 a grandson of Herod the Great, *Herod Agrippa I* was made king of all Palestine (*cf* Acts 12). He died in AD44 and was succeeded by his son *Herod Agrippa II* (Acts 25). As Herod Agrippa II was only seventeen years old on his father's death, the Romans placed Palestine under a Roman Procurator. This arrangement continued from AD44 until the outbreak of the Jewish war in AD66.

APPENDIX C

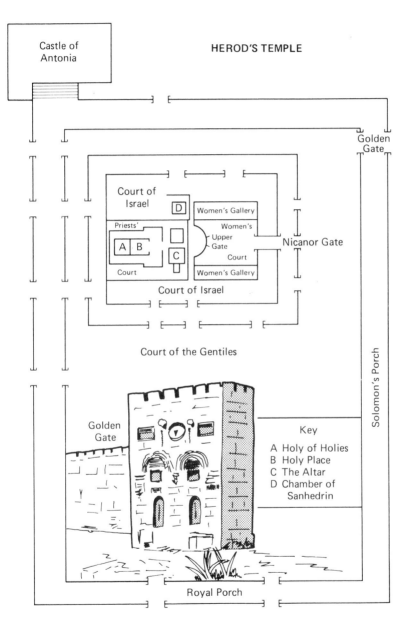

Castle of Antonia

HEROD'S TEMPLE

Golden Gate

Court of Israel

Priests'

A | B

Court

D

C

Court of Israel

Women's Gallery

Women's

Upper Gate

Court

Women's Gallery

Nicanor Gate

Court of the Gentiles

Golden Gate

Solomon's Porch

Key

A Holy of Holies
B Holy Place
C The Altar
D Chamber of Sanhedrin

Royal Porch

APPENDIX D

Palestine in the time of Jesus

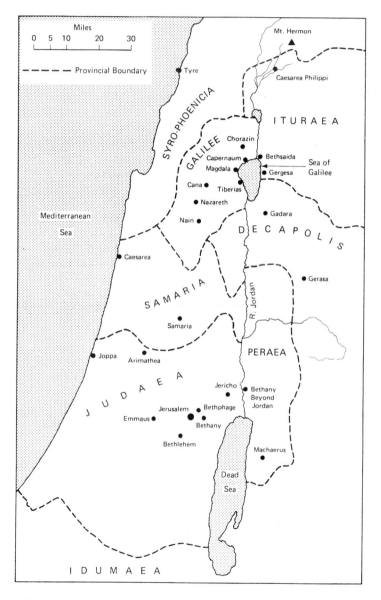

APPENDIX E

Scriptural passages in Matthew not listed in Contents

8:    *1–4*   *cf* Mark 1:*40–45*, *p* 11.

      5–13   *cf* Luke 7:*1–10*, *p* 144.

     14–17   *cf* Mark 1:*29–34*, *p* 11. (Matthew refers to Isaiah 53:*4*, which he thought of as being fulfilled by Jesus' healing work).

  18,23–27   *cf* Mark 4:*35–41*, *p* 26. (Note how Matthew tones down the disciples' bluntness.)

     19–22   *cf* Luke 9:*57–62*, *p* 148. (This seems out of chronological order as Luke's dating is more appropriate to Jesus' comment in *v* 20.)

     28–34   *cf* Mark 5:*1–20*, *p* 29. (Matthew has two mad-men instead of one and Jesus directly commands the evil spirits to enter the swine—an example of Matthew's heightening of the miraculous.)

9:    *1–8*   *cf* Mark 2:*1–12*, *p* 13.

     9–13   *cf* Mark 2:*13–17*, *p* 14. (Note Matthew's quotation from Hosea 6:*6* in *v* 13.)

    14–17   *cf* Mark 2:*18–22*, *p* 16. (In Matthew John Baptist's disciples ask the questions.)

    18–26   *cf* Mark 5:*21–43*, *p* 36.

    27–31   *cf* Mark 8:*22–26*, *p* 44. (In Matthew it is two blind men who are healed *cf* also Matthew 20:*29–34*, with Mark 10:*46–52*.)

    32–34   *cf* Mark 3:*22–30*, *p* 20. (*cf* also Matthew 12: *22–37*; Matthew 9 is possibly a duplicate account.)

    35–38   is linked to a comparable account in Mark 6:*7–13*, *p* 33, but *v* 35 reads like a duplicate of Matthew 4:*23*, *cf* Mark 1:*39*, *p* 11, and *v* 36, *cf* Mark 6:*34*, *p* 35, whereas *v* 37–38, *cf* Luke 10:*1–2*, *p* 149.

189

10: *1,5–16* *cf* Mark 6:*7–13*, *p* 33. (Matthew gives the names of the disciples here in *v* 2–4, *cf* Mark 3:*13–19*. He also adds to Mark's account an instruction that the Mission is solely for the Jews and a prohibition against shoes and staff; *cf* also Luke 10:*1–12*, *p* 149. Matthew has perhaps conflated various instructions given by Jesus to his disciples. V 16 contains a proverb found only in Matthew.)

2–4 *cf* Mark 3:*7–19*, *p* 20.

17–33 (This section appears out of place in the Galilean ministry. It is perhaps a collection of Jesus' sayings, brought together for the benefit of the early Christian community, *cf* Mark 13:*9–13*, *p* 74, and Luke 12:*11–12*, *p* 155, Luke 21:*12–17,19*, *p* 195.

Note how in *v* 23 Jesus could not have predicted to the Twelve the return of the Son of Man before all the Israelite towns have been visited on that particular missionary tour.)

For *v* 24–25, *cf* Luke 6:*40*, *p* 128 and for *v* 26–33, *cf* Luke 12:*2–9*, *p* 154, also *cf* Mark 4:*22*, *p* 25.

34–36 *cf* Luke 12:*51–53*, *p* 156.

37–39 *cf* Luke 14:*26–27*, *p* 160. (The saying in *v* 39 appears six times in the gospels, *cf* also Luke 17:*33*, Matthew 16:*25*; Mark 8:*35*; Luke 9:*24* and John 12:*25*.)

40–42 *cf* Mark 9:*37, 41*, *cf p* 51 (V 41 seems peculiar to Matthew).

11: *1* (Note the familiar formula with which Matthew ends his great discourses.)

2–19 *cf* Luke 7:*17–35*, *p* 145 (for *v* 12–13, *cf* Luke 16:*16*, *p* 162, Matthew refers to Malachi 4:*5* in *v* 14 and Malachi 3:*1* in *v* 10 which equals Luke 7:*27*.)

20–30 *cf* Luke 10:*13–16, 21–24*, *p* 149–150. (*v* 28–30 are peculiar to Matthew and seem to echo Ecclesiasticus 24:*19–22*, 51:*23–27*. In Judaism the Wisdom of God came to be thought of in personal terms *cf*. Proverbs 1:*20–33* and 8:*1–36*.

In Christian circles Jesus later became identified with God's Wisdom or Word, as in John's gospel (1:*14*). It is debatable however whether in this passage, whose authenticity does not seem in doubt in view of the strong Aramaic poetic rhythm, Jesus was speaking of himself as anything other than the representative of the Kingdom. The 'yoke' therefore is that of the Kingdom, which means accepting the rule of God in your life, following the example of Jesus in loving service to other men. The yoke of the Kingdom is easy and light compared to that of the Law.)

12:    1–8   *cf* Mark 2:*23–28, p* 17. (Matthew omits 'the Sabbath was made for man' and gives instead *v* 5–7 which may originally have had a different narrative context. For the Temple priests there was exemption from the Sabbath law, otherwise they could not carry out their sacrificial ritual. So Jesus here says that something more important has come than the Temple and its ritual and that is the Kingdom. The claims of the Kingdom have priority over all else. V 7 is a reference to Hosea 6:*6 cf.* Matthew 9:*13.*)

   9–14   *cf.* Mark 3:*1–6, p* 19. (For *v* 11–12 *cf.* Luke 14:*1–6, p* 159. It is possible that these verses and *v* 5–7 above all came from the same narrative setting.)

  15–21   *cf* Mark 3:*7–12, p* 20. (In *v* 17 Matthew inserts a fulfilment of prophecy from the first of the Servant Songs, Isaiah 42:*1–4* and he interprets Jesus' command for silence as indicative of his own personal humility.)

  22–37   *cf* Mark 3:*22–30, p* 20. (Matthew introduces his account with a healing of the blind and dumb demoniac which makes the people wonder whether Jesus is the Son of David *cf* Matthew 9:*32–34.*)

  38–42   *cf* Mark 8:*11–21, p* 42, and Luke 11:*29–32, p* 152. (See also Matthew 16:*1–4.*)

  43–45   *cf* Luke 11:*24–26, p* 152.

  46–50   *cf* Mark 3:*20–21, 31–35, p* 20–22.

14:   1–12   *cf* Mark 6:*14–29, p* 34.

  13–21   *cf* Mark 6:*30–44, p* 35.

  22–36   *cf* Mark 6:*45–56, p* 36. (Note the additional mention of Peter.)

15:   1–20   *cf* Mark 7:*1–23, p* 38. (Matthew omits Mark's details but mentions Peter by name.)

	21–28	*cf* Mark 7:*24–30*, *p* 39. (Matthew calls the woman a Canaanite which is a much more contemptuous term and Jesus is reported as being rather harsher in his treatment of her.)
	29–39	*cf* Mark 7:*31–37*; 8:*1–10*, *p* 41.
16:	1–4	*cf* Mark 8:*11–13*.
	5–12	*cf* Mark 8:*14–21*, *p* 42.
	13–20	*cf* Mark 8:*17–30*, *p* 44. (Matthew has numerous additions in *v* 17–19, a very important section for Roman Catholic doctrine because upon it rests the supremacy of Peter, traditionally the first Bishop of Rome, and through him that of the Popes of Christendom. The majority of Protestant scholars doubt whether these verses are genuine to Jesus because the idea of one apostle being primate over others is not found elsewhere in his teaching *cf.* the request of James and John. Also the word 'church' occurs only here and in 18:*17*, *p* 134 where it obviously refers to the Christian community of Matthew's day rather than Jesus' own time. It is probable therefore that this saying reflects a later period in church history. See Acts and Paul's letters also for the position of Peter in the Apostolic church.)
	21–28	*cf* Mark 8:*31*–9:*1*, *p* 45.
17:	1–13	*cf* Mark 9:*2–13*, *p* 48.
	14–21	*cf* Mark 9:*14–29*, *p* 50. *v* 20 *cf* Luke 17:*5–6* *p* 164.
	22–23	*cf* Mark 9:*30–32*, *p* 50.
19:	1–12	*cf* Mark 10:*1–12*, *p* 53. (See also Matthew 5:*27–28, 31–32*, *p* 122, the addition in *v* 9 supports Matthew 5:*32*. In Jewish Law, fornication made subsequent marriage null and void.)
	13–15	*cf* Mark 10:*13–16*, *p* 55. (Matthew omits Jesus' indignation.)
	16–30	*cf* Mark 10:*17–31*, *p* 55. (Matthew has rephrased the question and answer avoiding any implication that Jesus might not be good. In *v* 28 he endorses his theme that the twelve apostles were to be the new Israel in the new world which was to come. His imagery is appropriate to Jewish Christian Apocalyptic writing.)

21: *1–11* *cf* Mark 11:*1–11*, *p* 60 (Matthew also adds 'Son of David' to the shout of the crowd.)

12–17 *cf* Mark 11:*15–19*, *p* 61–63 (Matthew makes the Cleansing of the Temple the final act in the Triumphant Entry. He also adds *v* 14–16, *cf* Luke 19:*37–40*, *p* 169.)

18–22 *cf* Mark 11:*12–14*, *20–24*, *p* 61. (Matthew's account is simpler as the fig tree withers away immediately after Jesus has cursed it. Matthew's story is apparently meant to demonstrate the power of faith.)

23–27 *cf* Mark 11:*27–33*, *p* 63.

33–46 *cf* Mark 12:*1–12*, *p* 65. (In Matthew, Jesus' hearers themselves answer the question in *v* 40 and in *v* 43 the 'nation that yields the proper fruit' is the Christian church.)

22: *15–22* *cf* Mark 12:*13–17*, *p* 66.

23–33 *cf* Mark 12:*18–27*, *p* 68.

34–40 *cf* Mark 12:*28–34*, *p* 69 (In Matthew the questioner seems to be a hostile Pharisee.)

41–46 *cf* Mark 12:*35–37*, *p* 70. (Matthew has rephrased the Marcan account.)

24: *1–51* *cf* Mark 13:*1–32*, *p* 72f. (Matthew uses Mark's chapter as the basis for his apocalypse but for *v* 26–28 *cf* Luke 17:*23–24*, *37*, *p* 165. V 27 implies that the manifestation of the Son of Man will be visible throughout the entire world. For *v* 43–51 *cf* Luke 12:*39–48*, *p* 155.)

Scriptural passages in Luke not listed in Contents.

5: *12–16* *cf* Mark 1:*40–45*, *p* 11 (Luke has only changed the order of events.)

17–26 *cf* Mark 2:*1–12*, *p* 13.

27–32 *cf* Mark 2:*13–17*, *p* 14 (Luke has marginally altered the words of Jesus to 'to call sinners to repentance', a favourite theme in this gospel.)

33–39 *cf* Mark 2:*18–22*, *p* 16 (Luke has watered down the succinctness of Jesus' saying. Jesus was far too practical a person to suggest that one took a patch from a new garment to mend an old one!)

6: *1–5* *cf* Mark 2:*23–28*, *p* 70 (Luke omits 'the Sabbath was made for man' as does Matthew.)

193

	6–11	cf Mark 3:*1–6*, p 19 (Luke omits the detail that Jesus was angry.)
	12–19	cf Mark 3:*7–19*, p 20 (Thaddaeus has become Judas or Jude in Luke. In v 17–19 he sets the scene for the Sermon on the Plain.)
8:	4–8, 11–15	cf Mark 4:*1–9, 13–20*, p 24 (In v 8 Luke says the good seed produced a hundredfold as against the Marcan suggestion that this also was subject to a variable degree of yield. It is an interesting exercise to analyse how Luke has slightly modified Mark's account.)
	9–10	cf Mark 4:*10–12*, p 24.
	16–18	cf Mark 4:*21–25*, p 25.
	19–21	cf Mark 3:*20–21, 31–35*, p 22.
	22–25	cf Mark 4:*35–41*, p 26. (Luke tones down the disciples' appeal to Jesus, as does Matthew. Because these gospels were written so much later the Apostles had become much more venerated in the Christian community.)
	26–39	cf Mark 5:*1–20*, p 29.
	40–56	cf Mark 5:*21–43*, p 31. (Luke has one or two slight modifications to the story. He omits any slight criticism of the medical profession, he makes the disciples more polite to Jesus in v 45 and he does not give the Aramaic words spoken by Jesus to Jairus' daughter. He also implies by the words 'her spirit returned' that the girl was truly dead.)
9:	1–6	cf Mark 6:*7–13, 30*, p 33. (Luke omits that the disciples went out in pairs and the anointing of the sick. Like Matthew, he records that the disciples were forbidden to take a staff.)
	7–9	cf Mark 6:*14–29*, p 34. (Luke only briefly mentions the death of John Baptist and in his version Herod does not believe that Jesus is John Baptist risen from the dead, cf Luke 3:*18–20*.)
	10–17	cf Mark 6:*31–44*, p 35. (Luke identifies the place where the crowd were fed as Bethsaida and says that Jesus preached to them about the Kingdom of God.)
	18–21	cf Mark 8:*27–30*, p 44. (Luke's order is interesting. Before putting the vital question to his disciples as to his true identity, Jesus prays.)

22–27	*cf* Mark 8:*31*–9:*1, p* 45. (Luke omits Peter's protest and Jesus' reply.)
28–36	*cf* Mark 9:*2–13, p* 48. (Luke is less precise about the timing of this event—'about eight days' after the previous conversation. He is more careful in his description of Jesus' transfiguration, omitting this somewhat ambiguous word, and says that Jesus was at prayer when his face and clothing changed. Only he records the subject of the conversation between Jesus, Moses and Elijah. The vision comes to Peter and his companions after they had awoken from a deep sleep and Luke's language suggests that Peter spoke up impulsively about the three shelters as the reality about Moses and Elijah began to fade. This is the fifth time that Luke draws attention to Jesus at prayer, a subject of considerable importance to him *cf* 1:*22*, 5:*16*, 6:*12*, 9:*18*.)
37–43	*cf* Mark 9:*14–29, p* 50. (Luke omits any mention of the father's inadequate faith and the disciples' enquiry as to the cause of their failure to heal the boy.)
44–45	*cf* Mark 9:*30–32, p* 50. (Luke's version is abbreviated. It almost seems that he attributes the disciples' lack of understanding to the action of God.)
46–50	*cf* Mark 9:*33–50, p* 51.

20:	*1–8*	*cf* Mark 11:*27–33, p* 63.
	9–19	*cf* Mark 12:*1–12, p* 65. (*v* 18 is an addition to the Marcan narrative. There is perhaps a contrast between those who find the stone a stumbling block *cf* Isaiah 8:*14*, Romans 9:*32–33* and those who base their lives upon its sure foundation, Isaiah 28:*16*, 1 Peter 2:*6–7.)*
	20–26	*cf* Mark 12:*13–17, p* 66.
	27–40	*cf* Mark 12:*18–27, p* 68.
	41–44	*cf* Mark 12:*35–37, p* 70.
	45–47	*cf* Mark 12:*38–40, p* 70.

21:	*1–4*	*cf* Mark 12:*41–44, p* 70.
	5–38	*cf* Mark 13:*1–32, p* 72f. (Luke uses Mark as his basis but because he is writing at a later date he has made some alterations e.g. compare Mark 13:*11* with Luke 21:*14, 15*, also

Luke 12:*11f*. For *v* 18 *cf* Matthew 10:*30*. In *v* 20–24 he specifically mentions the fall of Jerusalem, the Jews being led captive away and the time of foreign oppression. He omits Mark's parable about the absent householder but underlines the great need for watchfulness in order to be able to stand in the presence of the Son of Man when he comes again.

Luke ends this section by saying that Jesus spent the night on the Mount of Olives whereas Mark records that he went back to Bethany each evening.)

Bibliography: for further reading

Pelican Gospel Commentaries and the *Cambridge Bible Commentaries* are useful for a modern translation of the text and verse by verse commentary with chapters on date and authorship.

Peake's Commentary. Useful for all aspects of New Testament studies if index is consulted.

S.C.M. '*A Source Book of the Bible for Teachers*'. Excellent for background references.

The Living World of the New Testament, Kee & Young.
A New Testament History, Floyd V. Filson. These provide interesting historical background material.

Introducing the New Testament, A.M. Hunter.
Introduction to the Theology of the New Testament, Alan Richardson.

Jesus, Master and Lord, H.E.W. Turner.
The Work and Words of Jesus, A.M. Hunter, for a comprehensive picture.

The Parables of the Kingdom, C.H. Dodd.
Interpreting the Parables, A.M. Hunter.

Interpreting the Miracles, R.H. Fuller.
The Miracle Stories of the Gospels, Alan Richardson.

Jesus as they saw him, William Barclay, for a detailed account of Jesus' titles.

The Sayings of Jesus and *The Teaching of Jesus*, T.W. Manson are two essential books on the teaching of Jesus in the synoptic tradition.

Re-dating the New Testament, J.A.T. Robinson. A fresh and controversial look at some old problems.

Index

199